Much Ado About Mutton

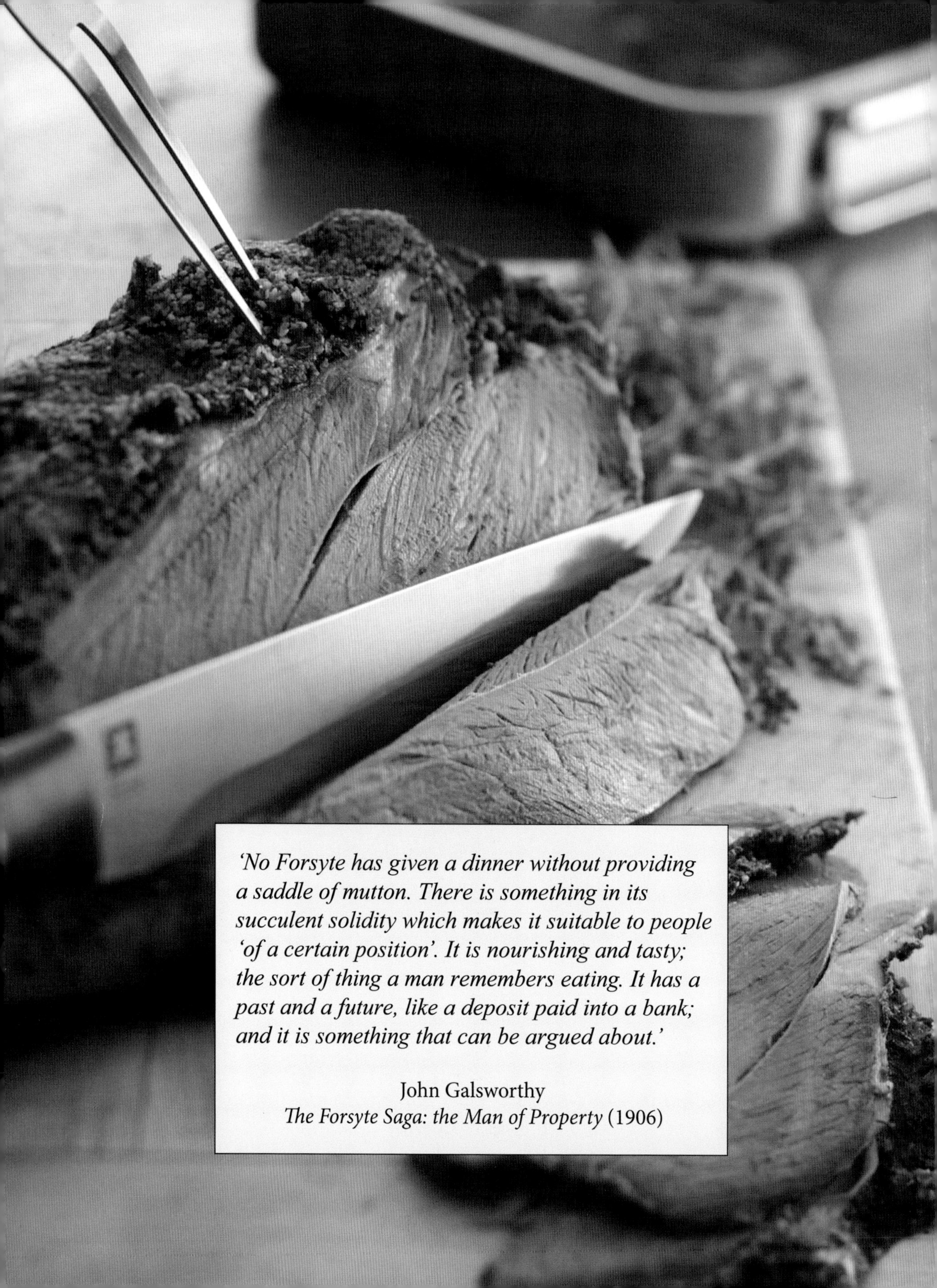

'No Forsyte has given a dinner without providing a saddle of mutton. There is something in its succulent solidity which makes it suitable to people 'of a certain position'. It is nourishing and tasty; the sort of thing a man remembers eating. It has a past and a future, like a deposit paid into a bank; and it is something that can be argued about.'

John Galsworthy
The Forsyte Saga: the Man of Property (1906)

Much Ado About Mutton

Bob Kennard

Merlin Unwin Books

First published by Merlin Unwin Books, 2014

Merlin Unwin Books Ltd
Palmers' House, 7 Corve Street,
Ludlow, Shropshire, SY8 1DB
www.merlinunwin.co.uk

A CIP record of this book is available from the British Library.

Printed and bound by 10/10 Printing International Ltd

ISBN 978-1-906122-61-4

This book is dedicated to my wife Carolyn

Contents

Foreword ix
Introduction x

PART 1

MUTTON THEN AND NOW 1

What is Mutton? 1
Types of Sheep Meat 2
Types of Mutton 3
Why Does Mutton Taste Different? 5
Mutton as a Super-meat? 12
Whatever Happened to Mutton? 15
Wether Mutton Disappears 16
Lambs Reared in a Year 17
Wartime Effect 18
Modern Lifestyles 19
Mutton in British Culture 20
Origin of the Name Mutton 20
Sheep and Plants 20
Sheep and Mutton in Names & Places 22
Mutton in Literature 23
Mutton in the Bible and Islam 24
Mutton in Nursery Rhymes 25
Mutton as Slang 26

PART 2

MANAGING MUTTON 29

What Have Sheep Ever Done For Us? 29
Nothing left but the Baa 30
Mutton Fat 32
Tallow in Soap Manufacture 33
Mutton Candles 34
Sheep Origins 36
The Bronze Age 36
Roman Occupation 37
The Vikings 37
Middle Ages 37
Land Enclosures 39
The Highland Clearances 42
Consequences of the Enclosures 44
Sheep Numbers 45
Demand and Supply for Sheep Meat 46
Mutton and the New World 48
New Zealand 49
South Africa 52
Australia 54
USA 56
Sheep and the Landscape 58
Sheep on the Hills and Mountains 58
Hefts and Hirsels 59
Hills, Ticks, Sheep, People and Grouse 62
Sheep on the Downs 62
Sheep on Lowland Arable Farms 62
Shepherding 65
Counting Sheep 73
Names of Sheep 75
Shepherd's Equipment 77
Crook 77
Shepherd's Smock 78
Shepherd's Gaiters 80
The Sheepdog 81
The Shepherd's Year 84
Autumn Sorting of Ewes 84
Flushing 85
Tupping 85
Summer and Autumn Dipping 86
Feeding 87
Winter Warmth 87
Lambing 88
Tailing, Castrating and Weaning 91
Washing 91

Shearing 91
Good Breeding 96
Robert Bakewell & John Ellman 97
Breeds Today 101
Mountain 101
Hill 102
Downland 102
Lowland 102
Longwool 103
Primitive & Parkland 103
Halfbreds & Mule 103
Breed Numbers 104
Mixing the Breeds 105
The Mountains 105
The Hills 106
The Lowlands 106
Changes in Modern Sheep Farming 110
Wool 110
Silage 110
Chemical Fertiliser 112
Modern Breeds 112
Sustainability of Mutton Production 114
Fertility of the soil 114
Use of 'Permanent pastures' 115
Land Use 116
Maintaining the View 116
Wool Production 117
Future of the Family Sheep Farm 117
New Zealand's Drovers 126
Australian Droving 127
American Droving 128
The Arrival of the Railways 128
The End of the Drovers' Road 131
When To Market? 132
Abattoirs 133

PART 3

MUTTON IN THE KITCHEN

Choosing your Mutton 135
Which Breed? 137
Opinions on Age 140
Some Effects of Feed 141
Salt Marsh Mutton 142
The Ideal Mutton Carcass 143
Historic Advice on Buying Mutton 143
Reviving "Bad" Mutton 144
How to Revive a Dead Sheep 144
Mutton Ham 145
Shetland Vivda Mutton 147
Reestit Mutton 148
Braxy Ham 150
Cooking Mutton Through the Ages 151
Mutton in the Antipodean Diet 154
Mutton for the Modern Cook 157
What's Available? 157
What to Look For 158
Seasonality 159
What to Buy? 159
Mutton Cuts 159
Mutton Butchery 160

MUTTON RECIPES 165–182

DIRECTORY OF SUPPLIERS 183–194

Scotland 184
Northern England 186
Midlands 188
Wales 189
South-West England 190
South-East England 192
London 193

UK SHEEP BREEDS 195–203

National Mutton Organisations 204
Glossary of Sheep Terms 205–209
References 210–211

INDEX 212–213

Acknowledgements and Credits 214

Llandovery butcher with a leg of mutton 1890

Blueface Leicester and Welsh Mule ewes

Foreword by HRH Prince of Wales

CLARENCE HOUSE

The disappearance of mutton from our dining room tables, after hundreds of years as one of the nation's favourite foods, has long been one of my concerns and it was therefore one of the reasons why in 2004 I launched my Mutton Renaissance campaign. It is therefore very timely that the first comprehensive book on the fascinating story of mutton should appear now, ten years after Mutton Renaissance first set out to reawaken interest in this underrated quality product.

It is vital to the continued life and soul of the upland communities of Britain that sheep farming remains financially viable, so having a flourishing market for good quality mutton is an essential element in ensuring that. Mutton, once the best of British food, has all but disappeared in the last thirty or forty years, whereas once it was more common than beef. Good-quality mutton needs to be rediscovered, not only for its superb flavour, but also for its health benefits and for the income it generates for our threatened farming communities.

Too often we hear the cry, 'I used to enjoy mutton but where can I buy it today?' In fact, as this book demonstrates, quality mutton *is* easily available if you know where to look, and what to look for. *Much Ado About Mutton* not only tells the fascinating story of mutton's historical popularity and the reasons for its decline but, importantly, it reveals mutton's bright future and shows how easy it is for us to enjoy once again this often overlooked staple of British cookery.

Introduction

Mutton production has been entwined with our landscape, our history, our wealth and our wellbeing since prehistoric times. For many hundreds of years, mutton was the main form of sheep meat eaten in these islands. Yet over the past 40 years, it virtually disappeared from our shops and menus - and we were in real danger of losing one of our iconic foods, as much part of our culture and heritage as roast beef. Happily, the current revival of interest in mutton is putting it back in the spotlight, celebrating the versatility as well as the long tradition of this fabulous-tasting meat.

The story of sheep and mutton is very much part of the story of the United Kingdom, and indeed of our Empire. Mutton fed our people through the upheavals of the Industrial Revolution, its fat lit our homes, it was served at the last lunch on *The Titanic* in 1912, and was a birthday meal on Captain Scott's last expedition. Our uplands today are only enjoyed by walkers because of the sheep that have grazed them for hundreds of years. Mutton may even have had a part to play in saving us from invasion by the forces of Napoleon, as a dish of mutton was a favourite of the Duke of Wellington. It is difficult today to appreciate just how ubiquitous mutton once was. As the authoritative Mrs Beeton exclaimed in 1861 'Mutton is undoubtedly the meat most generally used in families.'

There was of course good and not so good mutton. The tragedy is that in losing mutton as a part of our national cuisine, we almost lost the opportunity to experience the best, and at its best, mutton is superlative amongst meats.

New research shows the important nutritional benefits mutton has to offer. Grass-fed mutton can also play a lead in the transition to sustainable lower carbon farming.

Out of fashion since WWII, a revival in demand for the fabulous taste of mutton is now well overdue. Some are already championing the meat – such as the Prince of Wales' enterprise 'Mutton Renaissance', as well as a small group of enthusiastic farmers, butchers and chefs.

Apart from the influence of mutton on the heritage of these islands, people are once again beginning to appreciate the unique taste of this culinary icon, which we nearly lost. The complexity and depth of flavour is like no other. In a world of bland-tasting meat, mutton is king.

This book sets mutton in its true context of British history, farming, landscape, culture and cuisine. I hope it will encourage more of us to enjoy the unique flavour and taste of history which is British Mutton.

Bob Kennard, Llanfihangel Rhydithon. May 2014

www.muchadoaboutmutton.com

Part One
MUTTON THEN & NOW

What is Mutton?

Mutton is simply the meat from older sheep – just as beef is mature veal, so mutton is mature lamb. There is no legal definition of mutton. Today, it is generally taken as being sheep over two years old. Even in the 1930s 'lambs' were reared during the summer ready for market, and any sheep meat sold after Christmas was referred to as 'mutton'. In some parts of the world (especially the Indian subcontinent), mutton also includes goat meat, although for the purposes of this book, mutton refers to sheep meat.

The popularity of mutton has waxed and waned over the millennia in this country, and availability of it has often dictated the choice on dinner tables across the social classes. As the demands for meat, wool, milk and even manure have risen and fallen, so have the fortunes of the sheep industry. The revolution in productivity which has overtaken the farming industry over the past two centuries has also contributed to the type of sheep meat

Above: Welsh Mountain ewes in mid-Wales

we eat. Whilst once it was the ubiquitous mutton which was in demand, farming now produces lambs ready for eating in a reliable and efficient fashion at a much younger age, and so mutton is a rarity. We can see how widespread mutton was in the well-known Victorian ditty sometimes known as 'Vicarage Mutton':

'Hot on Sunday
Cold on Monday
Hashed on Tuesday
Minced on Wednesday
Curried Thursday
Broth on Friday
Cottage pie Saturday'

> *'Mutton's mutton,' said the Baronet, 'and a devilish good thing. What SHIP was it, Horrocks, and when did you kill?'*
> *'One of the black-faced Scotch, Sir Pitt: we killed on Thursday.*
> *'Who took any?'*
> *'Steel, of Mudbury, took the saddle and two legs, Sir Pitt; but he says the last was too young and confounded woolly, Sir Pitt.'*
>
> William Makepeace Thackeray
> (1811-1863) *Vanity Fair*

Types of Sheep Meat

The names of different types of sheep are extensive (see the section on Names of Sheep), and definitions often vary with time and region within the UK, but the four main names to remember when it comes to sheep meat are 'lamb', 'hogget', 'wether' and 'ewe'.

LAMB

When is a lamb not a lamb? When it's a hogget. In farming terms, a lamb born this year will continue to be called a lamb until Christmas, when to farmers it becomes a hogget. Hoggets are the source of butchers' lambs until the new crop of 'Spring lambs' becomes available, traditionally from around Easter. Hoggets are just older lambs which didn't finish on the summer's grass, so are fed over the following winter. Hogget meat is not mutton, it is just a word for slightly older lamb, and in shops it will still be called lamb, and is normally under a year old.

YEARLING SHEEP

This is an animal one to two years old, which includes castrated males (wethers) as well as young females (ewes) which were not able to produce lambs. By the time the animal is over a year old, the more complex flavours of mutton have started to develop, and this process increases until the animal is about four years old. The change in flavour is the start of the processes, driven by age, which steadily alters the comparatively bland meat of lamb into the deeper, more complex flavours of true mutton. A yearling sheep is therefore a halfway house between lamb and mutton.

TYPES OF MUTTON

In mutton's heyday in the 19th century, there were considered to be different classes and qualities of mutton, and each type had its supporters and champions. Broadly, the two traditional types of mutton were divided by age and breed – 'wether' and 'ewe'.

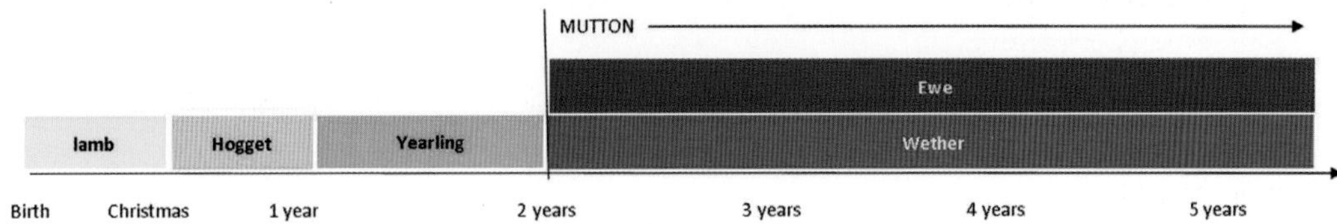

WETHER MUTTON

After a yearling, the next age for sheep is generally known as a wether (an Anglo-Saxon word), regardless of it being a male or female. This is an animal which has not bred, but which has been grown for its wool crop. Traditional three or four-year-old wether mutton came mainly from flocks of wether sheep which were used to graze the high mountain areas where the conditions were too harsh for the older breeding ewes. Wether mutton is rather darker than lamb, and has an exceptionally fine flavour. To improve its tenderness, joints required traditional natural maturing, or hanging, for some days. The best Welsh mountain wether mutton, according to John Roberts in 1913, were those finished on grass, as *'corn feeding has often the effect of producing too much internal fat.'* Roberts believed that *'well fattened wethers produce most excellent mutton, the joints being fine, sweet and also economical.'* The classic three and four-year-old wether mutton was, even by the 1930s becoming rarer as farming practices changed and it became increasingly difficult for farmers to make money out of a three or four-year-old animal. Indeed, by 1930, there were said to be fewer than half the number of wethers there had been in 1875. Wethers would produce an annual crop of wool, which could be produced profitably only when the price of wool was sufficiently high to cover the cost of shearing, and an extra margin for profit. The final blow to wether mutton was the dramatic collapse of the wool price in 1966-7 when synthetic fibres became readily available. Indeed wether mutton has now virtually disappeared altogether from the market as it is simply uneconomic to produce. In today's market, lambs must be 'finished' for the butcher in under a year, as without a profitable wool crop, it is not worth the farmer feeding it any longer.

> *'I could not conjure up one melancholy fancy upon a mutton chop and a glass of champagne.'*
>
> Jerome K. Jerome
> (1859-1927)
> *Idle Thoughts of an Idle Fellow*

A last birthday dinner of mutton for Captain Robert Scott (seated at head of table) before setting off to the South Pole, 6 June 1911

EWE MUTTON

Almost all of today's production of mutton meat in the UK is from ewes – older breeding female animals which are no longer suitable for that purpose, normally after they have had three or four crops of lambs. In mutton's Victorian heyday, ewe mutton was considered by many experts as the best, as the older animals had fully developed the real complexity and depth of the classic mutton flavour.

A writer in the 1930s remarked that *'The meat from ewes varies largely according to the age at which they are killed. The meat of young ewes that have had, say, one crop of lambs, while somewhat darker in the flesh than that of yearling sheep, is of good eating quality when well finished. The flesh of older ewes tends to become rather dark, and joints require more hanging. However, flavour is deeper.'*

It is the exceptional flavour of mature mutton which is its main attraction.

It is difficult to imagine today just how ubiquitous mutton was for hundreds of years, in the UK and abroad well into the 20th century. Not only were grilled mutton chops with mashed, fried and baked potatoes served to the First Class passengers at the last lunch served on board the Titanic, but several carcasses of mutton were taken by Captain Scott's tragic last expedition to the South Pole. As Scott recorded in his diary for Tuesday 6th June 1911 *'It is my birthday, a fact I might easily have forgotten, but my kind people did not. After my walk I discovered that great preparations were in progress for a special dinner, and when the hour for that meal arrived we sat down to a sumptuous spread with our sledge banners hung about us. Clissold's especially excellent seal soup, roast mutton and red currant jelly, fruit salad, asparagus and chocolate – such was our menu. For drink we had cider cup, a mystery not yet fathomed, some sherry and a liqueur.'*

Earlier, in 1840, farmer Mr Clark Hillyard wrote *'Mutton is more easy to sell at a fair, remunerating price, than beef; it is the meat which people can feed on daily for the longest time without being tired; it is the meat best suited to all the middle classes of the community, and to most of the lower – and therefore being the food of the chief part of the population of the country, must ever be in good demand ...'*

As we shall see, apart from age, the other characteristic of mutton which the Victorians hotly debated was breed.

Why Does Mutton Taste Different?

The reason why good quality mutton was so popular was its flavour. But what produces flavour in meat?

There are, according to research by the UK's Meat Research Institute (now part of Bristol University), two main factors which give meat its taste.

Firstly, **the age of the animal**. The older the animal, the greater the flavour. So, as farming has intensified, it has been producing animals for meat at younger and younger ages. As a result, the flavour of meat has diminished over the last 50 years. This applies to all species, including red meat and particularly pork and chicken. The flavour of lamb is less intense and complex than that of the mutton, in the same way as veal is less flavoursome than beef. Beef cattle are a couple of years old at least, compared with a veal calf of a few months, and the difference in the flavour and even the texture of the two meats is very apparent. Chicken is often said to be pretty tasteless, and this is hardly surprising. Most

Author Bob Kennard (centre) with his butchers and mutton carcasses

'My manner of living is plain and I do not mean to be put out of it. A glass of wine and a bit of mutton are always ready.'

George Washington (1732-1799)

chickens are now slaughtered as early as 42 or even 35 days old, compared with the many weeks it took to produce a mature chicken, before intensive broiler chickens became available in the 1960s. The flavour of an older bird is significantly more intense. As virtually all butchers' lambs are now slaughtered at under a year, compared with the greatly favoured four to five-year-old mutton of 100 years ago, it should be no surprise that some Victorians considered lamb inferior to mutton, complaining that it lacked the depth of flavour.

The second factor the researchers found produces tasty meat is the **traditional practice of 'hanging'**, or naturally maturing meat. This is something which butchers through the ages have understood and practised. It will work for all species, but is more generally associated with beef, sheep and game. Pork is rarely matured for more than a few days, and regulations have virtually put a stop to the hanging of chicken, although it does make all the difference to the flavour, if done properly. To achieve the natural maturing of chicken, they are left intact but plucked, with their guts in, for a week or so after slaughter, and stored in a cold room. In this state they are known as NYD – variously explained as New

Mrs. Near-the-Bone: I want a sheep's head, and leave the eyes in. I want it to see me through the week.

A traditional butcher's display, Eastman's Butchers in Luton, Bedfordshire

York Dressed or Not Yet Dressed. Pheasants are still often processed in the same way.

To traditionally 'hang' red meat, whole or split carcasses are kept cool (today in a refrigerated cold-room) for around three weeks in the case of beef, or about two weeks for mutton. Even lambs can benefit from hanging for a week. This period of storage enables the naturally occurring enzymes within the meat to tenderise it and develop the flavour.

The traditional hanging of red meat carcasses was still a common sight in the High Street until the 1960s with spectacular displays of poultry and meat both outside and inside butchers' shops. Even up to the 1930s, cookery books were clear about the advantages of hanging meat *'English meat should be well hung before it is cooked, therefore it is advisable to order in time for the butcher to hang the meat'*. Mutton in particular benefitted greatly from hanging, as readers of *Enquire Within Upon Everything* in 1858 found out: *'If you wish mutton tender it must be hung as long as it will keep; then a good eight-tooth (i.e. four year old mutton) is as good eating as venison.'* The 'hanging as long as it will keep' approach to maturing mutton appears popular, as it is repeated in other 19th century cooking guides. One limitation to this principle is the amount of fat on the carcass. Without at least a thin covering, carcasses don't keep so well for long when hanging.

'My wife and I to church this morning, and so home to dinner to a boiled leg of mutton all alone.'

Diary of Samuel Pepys
6th January 1661

A fine piece of butchered mature mutton

The traditional practice of hanging whole carcasses to naturally mature meat almost died out with the advance of the supermarkets, as it involves storing the meat for weeks before sale, which both ties up capital and adds storage costs. Added to this is a loss of moisture and therefore weight, during the maturing process. All these factors are extra costs involved in selling the best quality meat.

Whilst the impact on texture which hanging brings is not so important when using younger animals, the results can be dramatic in terms of flavour. For lamb there is now scientific backing to this tradition. Hanging lamb carcasses for 10 days was found to produce a 'major and positive' improvement of both texture and flavour in a trial in 2004[1].

Happily, most specialist mutton producers today are aware of the importance of flavour and texture, and the vast majority make use of the traditional and natural maturing technique of hanging.

It is generally agreed that in fact there are two further pointers to mutton's exceptional flavour. Firstly **the breed of sheep is important.**

Many Victorians thought that superior flavour was to be enjoyed from the mountain breeds of Scotland, northern and western England, and Wales; or breeds of chalk downs such as Southdown and the 'primitive' breeds of the Scottish islands, Isle of Man and Portland. One reason for these preferences is the distribution of fat. Many of the breeds of sheep suitable for wool production also have the unfortunate habit of laying down plenty of fat on their backs when older, which makes the mutton unattractive – even to

1 Meat Eating Quality – A Whole Chain Approach; Factors Affecting Lamb Eating Quality. Final Report to SEERAD 24 November 2004.

Below: Upland herb pasture in Wales – difficult to farm but perfect for mutton grazing

Mountain ewe, grazing. The wild herbs and grasses influence the flavour and texture of the mutton

a Victorian palate. The right amount of fat in the right places can add hugely to the flavour of red meat. The secret is to have a modest covering over the outside of the carcass, and some within or between the muscles (known as intra-muscular fat, or 'marbling'). As the meat cooks, so this marbled fat melts within the meat, imparting flavour and juiciness to the cooked product. One of the major differences between breeds of sheep and cattle is these natural deposits of fat. Those breeds which have a balance of adequate fat but not too much within and on the outside of the meat, together with large blocks of muscle (lean meat), normally make the best eating.

The final contributing factor to the flavour of mutton is **feed**. Supporters of mountain mutton will say it is the herbs and wild plants found in their wild native habitats which greatly enhance their flavour. The Southdown was another favourite mutton breed, and Rudyard Kipling put this partly down to feed, as he wrote in one of his stories *'Press your face down and smell to the turf,' Mr Dudeney tells the children. 'That's Southdown thyme which makes Southdown mutton beyond compare, and, my mother told me, 'twill cure anything except broken necks, or hearts. I forget which.'*

John Lawrence in 1809 agreed with many others that the best mutton was to be had from the mountain and downland breeds, but thought that both breed and feed were important factors in flavour. *'The quality of the mutton varies much in the different breeds. In the large, long-haired sheep it is coarse-grained, but disposed to be fat. In the smaller, and short woolled breed, the flesh is closest grained and highest flavoured; but the quality of the flesh is probably most affected by that of the food upon which the flocks are fed. That which range over the mountainous districts of Wales and Scotland, or the chalk downs of England, and feed upon the wild herbage, possess a flavour very superior to those kept in rich pastures and on marsh land. The Welsh mutton is particularly small and lean, but of the finest flavour, and the south-down mutton is also excellent.'*

Farmer Clark Hillyard, writing in 1840, agreed with Lawrence that the local environment was an important factor in developing flavour. *'It must be admitted that the Southdown mutton, from age, is the finest flavoured meat, without being too fat in the primest part, the back; but Southdown mutton, fed in Northamptonshire, will not have the same fine flavour as that fed on the South Downs.'* He put that down to exercise: *'... the animal* [on the Downs] *is kept in great exercise while procuring its food, and is much longer getting fat; thus its flesh becomes fasted upon ... and not so frothy as the flesh quickly put on.'*

Research is now beginning to prove the Mountain Mutton lobby and Mr Kipling correct. Recent research[2] has confirmed other findings in showing that the richer diversity of plants found in natural pasture (known as permanent pasture) results in three impacts on the composition of lamb meat. Firstly, higher levels of Vitamin E; secondly, lower levels of skatole (a product of lamb digestion which adversely affects meat taste, particularly when grilled); and thirdly, higher levels of a number of nutritionally healthy fatty acids (notably n-3 polyunsaturated fatty acids and conjugated linoleic acid).

Whilst some scientists believe only negative flavours are produced from feed – such as fishmeal in pork and chicken – a large body of evidence is in favour of the traditional species-rich pastures producing a more enjoyable flavour in blind tests.[3] Indeed, many people who enjoy red meat, and mutton in particular, are convinced that the mountain and downland vegetation does have a positive effect on flavour. Certainly many Victorians heartily agreed that the best-tasting mutton was created by the plants found in these upland flora.

As the popularity of mutton grows, more people are appreciating what a great depth of flavour it has – very different to lamb. That is not to say that lamb is an inferior meat to mutton. It is just that mutton is a surprisingly different type of meat, and it is important that we have the choice. We use sauces liberally to add flavour to meats, when mutton has its own wonderfully deep and complex flavour if we handle it correctly and let it speak for itself.

Taste is a very complicated subject, and much remains to be understood about it. In the end, of course, it comes down to personal taste. Meanwhile, there is great pleasure and interest to be had from trying mutton from different breeds, different environments, and different periods of hanging, to see for yourself what differences these factors make to your enjoyment of the flavour.

Left: Ewes enjoying the sunshine at Knighton market, Powys

Opposite: Blueface Leicester and Welsh Mule ewes

2 Eating biodiversity: an investigation of the links between quality food production and biodiversity protection (PI Professor Henry Buller) University of Exeter 2008.

3 Effects of feeds on flavor of red meat: a review S.L. Melton J ANIM SCI 1990, 68:4421-4435

'Mutton is undoubtedly the meat most generally used in families. And, both by connoisseurs and medical men, it stands out first in favour, whether its fine flavour, digestible qualifications, or general wholesomeness be considered.'

Mrs Isabella Beeton (1861)

Mutton as a Super-meat?

Mutton has some pleasant surprises for us when it comes to its nutritional value. Until recently, reliable data has been hard to come by. There is no official nutritional data on mutton in the UK, and such EU data as there is, is limited both in its scope and reliability.

However, some little-publicised but respected Australian research[4] carried out in 2007 has thrown up some fascinating and important results, particularly in terms of the makeup of the fat in mutton. Animal fat is made up of a number of constituents, including various essential fatty acids (EFAs), of which Omega-3 and Omega-6 are perhaps best known to us. The Australian research has shown that when compared to a wide range of other meats (pork, beef, veal, chicken and lamb), mutton contains a higher level of Omega-3 fatty acids than all the other meats tested. Only fish was shown to have higher levels, particularly oily fish. Omega-3 levels in mutton were 40% higher than in lamb, 60% higher than beef, six times that in chicken, and 11 times that found in pork.

So what is a 3 or a 6 between us when we are choosing our Sunday Roast? In 1979 Hugh MacDonald Sinclair, an eccentric but far-sighted and pioneering nutritionist, carried out what was considered by many at the time as being an outrageous experiment. He joined an expedition to Greenland and for 100 days put himself on an Inuit diet, consisting solely of seal meat, fish (including molluscs and crustaceans), and water. Surely animal fats are bad for us in excess, and are the cause of coronary and other disease by clogging up our arteries? In fact, Sinclair found quite the reverse. His blood was affected by this Inuit diet by reducing its ability to clot, with bleeding times rising from a typical 3 minutes to over 50 minutes. It was also known that the Inuit suffer from nosebleeds. So, rather than clog-up his blood, the Inuit diet had in fact freed it up.

'But Mutton! Thou most nourishing of Meat!
Whose single joint may constitute a treat,
When made a Pudding you excel the rest
As much as that of other food is best.'

William King, poet, (1663-1712)

So why did Sinclair not fall over from a heart attack on the Inuit diet? It is now believed that humans evolved on a diet (when pursuing their main occupation of hunting and gathering) with a ratio of Omega-6 to Omega-3 EFAs of approximately 1:1. Indeed, that is roughly the ratio found in the Inuit diet and is increasingly considered by nutritionists to be the healthiest ratio for us. Amongst the Inuit and the nomadic herdsmen of Africa (such as the Maasai), whose diet traditionally consists of meat and blood, 'Western' ailments such as heart disease are almost unheard of. Initially, it was thought that these people were able to tolerate very high levels of animal fat because of their genetic makeup. In fact, it was found that when the Maasai started moving to the towns of East Africa, and changed their diet, they too developed the familiar heart and circulatory ailments of the Western world.

4 *Nutritional Composition of Red Meat* by P. G. Williams, University of Wollongong, 2007

Mountain ewes: thriving in difficult terrain

As a result of these observations, researchers came to the conclusion that it was something in the Western diet, not the levels of fat alone, which was causing the medical problems, and the evidence overwhelmingly pointed to the Omega 6 : Omega 3 ratio, which for us in the west has strayed very far from the 1:1 relationship of our ancestors. Indeed, for people on a typical Western diet, the ratio of EFAs is today around a staggering 16:1. In some US diets, rich in fast-food, the Omega 6 to Omega 3 ratio can even reach 50:1. It is now increasingly accepted that it is not the eating of animal fat which is the major problem, but the makeup of the fat in our diet, and in particular the Omega 6 : Omega 3 ratio.

The 2007 Australian research shows that mutton, of all meats compared in the trials (again excluding fish) is closest to the ideal 1:1, having a ratio of 2:1, compared to chicken at 8:1, and pork at 7:1.

The Australians went on to compare a range of other nutritional aspects of the meats in their analysis. Their report concluded that in a comparison with meat from other grazing animals (beef, lamb and veal), mutton was *'particularly nutrient dense, and the richest source of thiamin, vitamins B6 and B12, phosphorus, iron and copper'*. Whilst the levels of some minerals, especially phosphorus and copper may be due in part to particular local soils, higher levels of vitamins such as B12 are significant.

So, is there any evidence to explain the different and more balanced ratio of Omega-3 to Omega-6 fatty acid found in mutton? It seems it's down to species, diet and age. Work at Bristol University[5] has shown that sheep have higher Omega-3 levels than cattle. It is thought that this is due to the shorter grass that sheep eat and a faster passage through

5 Personal communication, Professor Jeff Wood, Professor Emeritus, University Bristol

the rumen (stomach), leading to less breakdown of the fatty acids in the rumen. As a result, more of the Omega-3 fatty acids in grass are retained for absorption into the animal. There is now also firm evidence that meat from grass-fed animals is generally higher in Omega-3 than from animals which have been fed a diet containing added grain and other 'concentrate' feeds. Recent work in the US, which compared grass-fed beef with grain-fed[6] concluded that while the overall concentration of total saturated fatty acids (SFAs) is similar between meat from grass-fed and grain-fed cattle, there is a difference in the composition of the fat. Grass-finished beef tends toward a higher proportion of cholesterol-neutral stearic fatty acid, and less of the cholesterol-elevating fatty acids – in other words, the Omega 6 to 3 ratio is closer to 1:1. In addition, several other studies suggest that animals fed on grass-based diets have raised levels of Vitamins A and E, as well as cancer-fighting antioxidants when compared to grain-fed alternatives[7].

This increasing body of research explains why grazing animals fed predominantly on grass produce a more balanced Omega 6 to Omega 3 ratio. This starts to make more sense when we think of mankind's original diet of wild grazing animals which would have been naturally grass-fed. But it doesn't fully explain why the Omega 6 : Omega 3 ratio in mutton is better than lamb. In Australia, the great majority of both lamb and mutton is produced from grass, with little feeding of grain. The fact that the beef fatty acid ratio came a close second to mutton suggests that age of the animal probably has some influence. The older the animal, the better the ratio. So, beef is better than veal and mutton better than lamb. This age-related benefit seems also to apply to other nutrients, and there is now some scientific evidence that the age of the animal has some bearing on fatty acid ratios.[8] The Australian nutrient comparison also concludes that *'for all these vitamins* [included in the research], *older animals tend to have higher concentrations, so the levels in beef are generally higher than those in veal, and mutton has more than lamb'*.

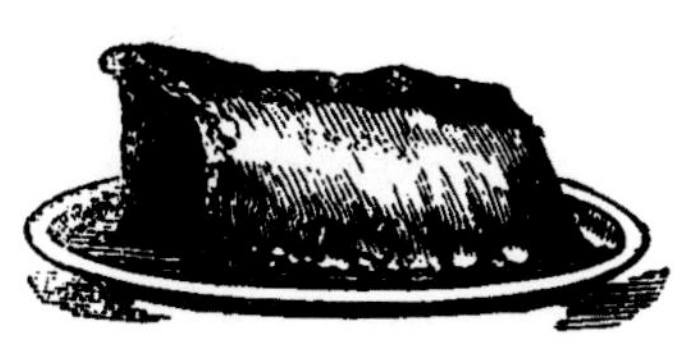

Loin of mutton from Mrs Beeton's 1861 cookbook

The UK's Food Standards Agency was asked to look at the Australian report and concluded[9] that the work was robust and that mutton can be considered as being a good source of some key nutrients (iron, zinc, B6 and B12 for example).

As we understand this subject more, the nutritional benefits of meat and dairy products from grass-fed animals are becoming clearer, and it now seems probable that age adds to these benefits. Quality mutton from a grass-fed system really does offer more than just superb flavour.

6 'A review of fatty acid profiles and antioxidant content in grass-fed and grain-fed beef'. Cynthia A Daley, Amber Abbot, Patrick S Doyle, Glenn A Nader and Stephanie Larson. Nutrition Journal 2010, 9:10 doi:10.1186/1475-2891-9-1

7 ibid

8 'Age and nutrition influence the concentrations of three branched chain fatty acids in sheep fat from Australian abattoirs.' P.J. Watkins, G. rose, L. Salvatore, D. Allen, D. Tucman, R.D. Warner, F.R. Dunshea, D.W. Pethick. 2010

9 FSA private communication

Whatever Happened to Mutton?

Changing farming practices, changing palates and faster life-styles have resulted in the severe decline of mutton over the past 60 years. Most sheep meat now sold to the general consumer is under one year old, and lamb has replaced mutton on British menus. Today just 14% of sheep meat eaten in the UK is sold as traditional mutton. The rest of the UK's mutton production is sold within the ethnic communities in Britain, France and Germany, or is used in the food processing industry. Only relatively recently has quality mutton been available again, and sold as such, mostly in the form of ewe mutton.

Wool caught on a twig

So, why did mutton almost disappear from our shops and restaurants?

Over the millennia, sheep have been kept in Britain to supply a number of products, from milk to wool to meat and even dung and fat (or tallow as it is known). As we will see later, demand for these products ebbs and flows in popularity, and the farmer has had to change his system to take account of this. Indeed, the usefulness of the sheep for its many purposes was recognised as early as the 13th century *'Of the sheep is cast away nothing, His horns for nothes – to ashes goeth his bones, To Lordes great profit goeth his entire dung, His tallow also serveth plastres, more than one, For harp strings his ropes serve everyone, Of whose head boiled whole and all There cometh a jelly, and ointment full royal. For aches of the bones and also for bruises It is remedy that doeth ease quickly Causing mens stark points to recure, It doeth sinews again restore to life. Black sheeps wool, with fresh oil of olive, The men at arms, with charms, they prove it good. And at straight need, they can well staunch blood.'*

During the peak of mutton popularity at the end of the 19th century, sheep meat was produced in three ways. Some lambs would be fattened for market at lower altitude over the summer and early autumn; wethers from the hills would have been slaughtered for wether mutton at about three years old after a couple of wool crops had been taken; and older ewes which were not used for breeding were sent to the butchers as ewe mutton.

Natural wool yarn

Hebridean Blackface sheep on an island off Lewis

WETHER MUTTON DISAPPEARS

When wool was king, from the 12th to 18th centuries, young sheep were kept for several years to produce an annual crop of wool, before being eaten as wether mutton. To the farmer, the second major benefit of this system was the fertilising effect of the sheeps' dung. Indeed, both the wool and dung were often of more value than the meat, added to which younger animals tend to have higher yields of wool than older ones. There was little incentive to cash in your young sheep for sale as meat until you had maximised other, more lucrative incomes from the animal.

It was therefore a major financial blow to producing mutton from wethers when the wool price declined to uneconomic levels in the 1960s, as cheap, oil-based artificial fabrics hit the market. The last year in which the Ministry of Agriculture recorded the price of mutton was 1966.

At the height of wether mutton popularity (in 1864) wool in today's values would be worth around £5.75/kg, compared with 2013 values of around £1.30/kg. One farmer remembered a saying of her father's from the 1950s, which was that a good wool crop would pay the rent on the farm. For today's farmers, the price received for a fleece barely covers the cost of shearing, let alone makes a profit.

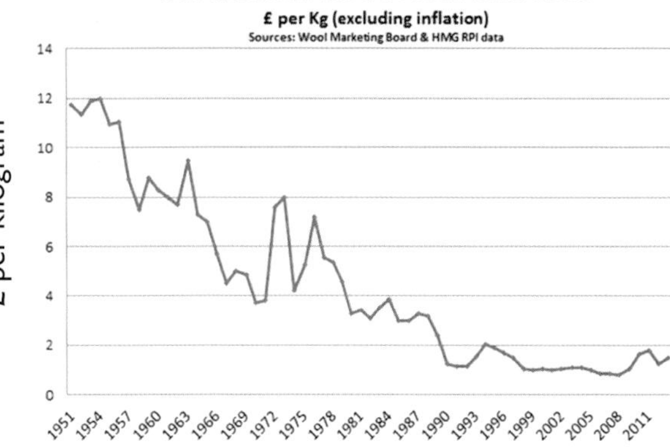

The graph *(left)* shows the decline in real value of the annual wool price since 1951, excluding the effect of inflation. All the prices are in 2013-equivalent values. The wool price in real terms has remained below £2/kg for the past 20 years. It is hardly surprising that with the income from wool reduced so drastically, wether mutton is simply not commercially viable today.

Wether mutton has not completely disappeared from the British farming scene, however. In a few particular circumstances it continues, even today. One such place is the Isle of Lewis, part of the Outer Hebrides off the west coast of Scotland. Here Sandy and Ali Granville are part of a production system which remains as it has been for hundreds of years. The animals are produced by an informal co-operative of crofters from the village of Tolsta Chaolais on the west coast of Lewis. Sandy describes the system: *'Hebridean Black-face wedders* [wethers] *are weaned at four months and then, save for being sheared twice, lead an independent life, until they are slaughtered at about two and a half years old. Many of them are kept on offshore islands and see nobody but passing sailors for months at a time. These animals have had no feeding save what they forage for themselves on the heather hills. By the time they are two years old these big strong animals move across their hills like herds of deer. We believe in minimising stress to the animals by minimising handling and transportation. The mutton is slaughtered on the Island in the early autumn. It is then hung, cut, vacuum packed and boxed and delivered throughout mainland UK in time for Christmas.'* This is therefore a low-cost, low-input/low-output system of farming, where the animals effectively look after themselves. The lack of major outlay compensates for the very modest wool income, and thus the final meat value of the wether ensures a continuing sustainable system.

LAMBS REARED WITHIN A YEAR

The old system of profitable wether mutton production meant there was no great pressure to fatten lambs for the butcher within a year. In many places this was just as well, because both climate and available feed made quick fattening difficult, if not impossible. The trend to produce butchers' lambs within a year, rather than 3-4 year wether mutton, was only completed when farmers had access to imported feeds and improved systems of preserving grass and other forage crops in the second half of the 20th century.

There had always been a large difference between good and bad quality mutton (over 2 years). Poor-quality mutton was only tolerated by the public because it was cheap, and was all that the majority of the population could afford – and many could not even afford that. When it was possible to produce lambs economically, demand for them increased. The bad news for British sheep farmers was that many of these cheaper lambs were coming from the vast expanses of the New World, with their more equitable climates, able to produce grass all year round.

H. Rider Haggard, writing in 1899, thought that preference for lamb over mutton was weather-driven. *'The reason of the fall* [in the lamb price] *is the coldness of the weather ; at least the butchers declare that in an inclement summer like the present the public has no fancy for light meat such as lamb, but prefers to buy beef and mutton.'*

Despite these short-term preferences, even before the First World War, there was an obvious shift from mutton to lamb demand and production. Yet at the time some breeders were still debating the merits of wool compared to meat production, as agricultural expert W.J. Malden commented in 1920: *'Great weight of wool of finest quality, with a carcase of higher class mutton – that is with a great preponderance of lean meat of choicest quality, and with but little fat when matured – is the natural aim of all* [sheep] *breeders.'*

By the late 1930s, the demand for lamb in preference to mutton was increasing, and wool prices were starting to falter. As a review of British Agriculture by Viscount Astor and Benjamin Seebohm Rowntree in 1938 observed *'The length of life of the sheep before it passes into consumption is much shorter, and is being reduced for two reasons. Firstly, lamb is becoming more popular than mutton. 1924 lamb imports equalled mutton, now they are nearly three times as great. Secondly, owing to the fall in the wool price, wool is now treated as a by-product of mutton rather than as a valuable commodity.'* The transformation from wether mutton to lamb had begun.

WARTIME EFFECT

In 1939, Britain remained the world's largest market for mutton, but things were changing rapidly. The market was becoming far more demanding and choosy – a situation which was suddenly halted in September of that year, when war broke out, and only really recovered in the 1970s.

A World War II government publication, advocating eating mutton, beef and rabbit

Meat scientist R. Hirzel wrote in a journal in early 1939 *'Never before in the history of the English meat-eating public has there been such fastidious demand for meat as at the present day, a demand which has made it increasingly difficult for the producer, with the livestock at his command, to put before the consuming public exactly the article which they desire. The chief alterations in public taste have been the growing demand for smaller, lighter, and less fat joints. In bygone years, heavy super-fatted animals were readily sold, but with smaller families, altered economic conditions and a higher standard of living, the public taste now, in lieu of the large fat joint, demands the lighter, leaner article.'* Hirzel went on to predict and explain changed demands for meat in the 21st century: *'Changes in economic conditions have sharply influenced the taste for fat, that is, the improvement of machinery and mechanisation of labour has cut down the amount of hard work done by the labourer per unit of production. With the result that he now needs less calories to supply his day's energy expenditure than he formerly did; and turns first and foremost against fatty meats.'*

> *'Mutton is to lamb what a millionaire uncle is to his poverty-stricken nephew.'*
>
> Pierre des Essarts, French Actor (1740-1793)

With the coming of war, simply keeping the population fed was a major achievement. The niceties of a desire for smaller leaner joints of meat were irrelevant when the U-Boat blockade threatened to cut all outside food supplies. In such desperate straits, people had to accept what was available, and poor quality, fatty mutton was

> *'At the inn where we stopped he was exceedingly dissatisfied with some roast mutton we had for dinner. ... He scolded the waiter, saying, 'It is as bad as bad can be: it is ill-fed, ill-killed, ill-kept, and ill-drest.'.'*
>
> James Boswell (1740-1795), *The Life of Dr Johnson*

often the only meat available. An official booklet entitled 'Communal Feeding in Wartime' dating from 1940, lists recipes for a range of dishes. The only meat ingredients listed are mutton, beef and rabbit. In such a dire situation, one can imagine that the main criterion was quantity, not quality of meat. The communal memory of that poor quality, fatty mutton has taken a long time to fade.

Despite the realities of wartime food supply, in 1944, R. George Stapleton lamented the loss of wether mutton, and blamed its demise mainly on the butchers *'Well-hung wether mutton is undoubtedly a real delicacy. It has probably gone out of fashion for the chief reason that the butchers have made no effort to maintain the supply and to keep it before the public .... the careful hanging of whole carcases (which is essential) entails the use of more space and gives more trouble in the matter of care and supervision than the butcher considers it worth his while.'*

Even after the war, shortages of food, and rationing continued. Meat was rationed until 1954. By 1949, sheep expert Allan Fraser was writing that *'Since 1939 the British public has been forced to a less fastidious outlook upon meat. Meat fat – owing to the scarcity of fat from other sources – has acquired a new value and importance, though these changes are forced on an unwilling public by war and the aftermath of war. There is every likelihood that the trends in mutton production discussed by Hirzel in 1939 will again become evident when the worst effects of world food scarcity have been overcome.'*

Folk memories are long. Since the war until very recently, mutton had simply gone out of fashion.

MODERN LIFESTYLES

Modern lifestyles are the final reason for the decline in popularity of mutton. To enjoy it at its best, mutton needs careful handling – from the quality of the animal, through correct hanging and butchering, to long, slow cooking – requirements not always compatible with supermarket retailing and busy lifestyles of today.

However, as the current revival of mutton gains ground, and with the use of slow-cookers, more people are discovering that the effort is well worthwhile. This increased demand has also stimulated the increase in the number of outlets selling the meat, as well as spurring chefs into developing a modern approach to cooking mutton.

Mutton in British Culture

ORIGIN OF THE NAME 'MUTTON'

The origin of names for domesticated animals and the meat we obtain from them is a glimpse into the history of a conquered people. Almost exclusively, the English names of all our domestic animals are of Anglo-Saxon origin, whereas the meats from those animals are from Norman French. This reflects the relationship between Anglo-Saxons and Normans – Saxon peasants and Norman lords. The Anglo-Saxon peasant looked after animals, but Normans ate the meat!

So, 'ox', 'steer' and 'cow' are Saxon, but 'beef' is Norman; 'calf' is Saxon, but 'veal' is Norman; 'sheep' is Saxon (from Old English word scēap), but 'mutton' is Norman; this is also true of 'deer' (originally meaning any animal apart from human beings) and 'venison', 'swine' and 'pork', 'fowl' and 'pullet'. The main exception to this pattern is 'bacon', which was the only meat which peasants generally came across, as most would keep a domestic pig (a word of mysterious origin first used in Medieval Middle English) to fatten and cure into bacon and ham for the long winter. This practice of keeping the family pig persisted into living memory in many rural areas.

> *'Capital mutton – capital everything.'*
>
> William Makepeace Thackeray (1811-1863)
> *Vanity Fair*

In Anglo-Saxon times, one ate 'sheep', which was also the animal. The word sheep is first used in Middle English. The word mutton developed from the Norman French 'moton', which meant sheep meat and derived from the medieval Latin 'multo', which in turn was probably from a Celtic language of Gaul. Several modern Celtic languages show signs of the original Latin word, such as the Welsh 'mollt', and the Cornish 'mols'. Mutton referred to all sheep meat until around 1620 when the word 'lamb' meaning meat first appears.

Thus, the ultimate victory of Welsh Mutton – not only is Welsh Mountain mutton one of the best types, but it is even from the place where the word was invented.

SHEEP AND PLANTS

The long association of sheep and man is reflected in the names of a number of wild plants in Britain. Most plants probably gained their common names from their attractiveness to grazing sheep, or being in the areas where sheep grazed.

A number of sheep-named wild plants are to be found on thin, acid soils, where often sheep would be one of the few agricultural options for the land. This may be the reason for the association of some of them with sheep names. Shepherd's Knappery or Shepherd's Knot are local names for the slender-leaved and yellow-flowered tormentil (*Potentilla tormentilla*); Sheep's-bit or Sheep's Scabious (*Jasione montana*) is not a member of the scabious family, and has a rather disagreeable smell when bruised – difficult to imagine

Left to right: Shepherd's Weatherglass or Scarlet Pimpernel; Sheep's Bells or Harebell; Sheeps' Scabious or Sheep's Bit.

why it may have been attractive to sheep, although being common on poor acid soils, it may be the best option around in such environments. The name is said to indicate the way in which the plant is cropped or 'bit' by sheep.

Sheep's Sorrel (*Rumex acetosella*) is another plant found on areas with thin acid soils, and although sheep eat it, it has little nutritional benefit as in large amounts its constituent oxalates can prove toxic. Locally common on bare sandy heaths or gravels is Shepherd's Cress (*Teesdalia nudicaulis*), an ephemeral spring flower with small, fleshy leaves.

The Shepherd's Purse (*Capsella bursa-pastoris*), is so named because of the resemblance of its triangular seed shape to a medieval leather purse. In 1657 William Coles wrote *'It is called Shepeard purse or Scrip* [wallet] *from the likeness the seed hath with that kind of leatherearne bag, wherein Shepherds carry their Victualls into the field.'* In Ireland the plant is known as 'Clappedepouch', thought to date from the time when at crossroads lepers could be seen begging with a clapper or bell on a long stick.

Sheep's Fescue (*Festuca ovina*) is a common grass particularly of dry areas, where it offers a good quality sheep fodder. There are several fescue grasses, the name deriving from Latin festuca meaning straw, stalk or rod.

Other plants found in pastures grazed by sheep are Sheep's Bells otherwise known as Harebells (*Campanula rotundifolia*); Milkwort, known in parts of the West Country as Shepherd's Thyme, and the locally common Scarlet Pimpernel (*Anagallis arvensis*), which closes its flowers in damp or dull weather and is known as the Shepherd's Weatherglass.

Shepherd's Rod (*Dipsacus pilosus*), otherwise known as the Small Teasel, by contrast to most sheep-related wild plants, is found in damper, richer-soiled areas, along the edges of woods, hedge-banks and sides of streams.

Shepherd's Needle (*Scandix pecten-veneris*) a common plant of the arable areas of England, originates from Eurasia, and is a member of the parsley family. Its alternative names include 'Old Wives' Darning Needle', 'Hedgehogs', and 'Lady's Comb'.

SHEEP AND MUTTON IN OUR NAMES AND PLACES

Sheep farming and mutton in particular have historically been so intimately part of our culture that echoes of this are still around today. Even in our surnames, sheep references are common – Shepherd, Lamb and Mutton.

Our town and village names are littered with sheep references. Some are obvious, such as Sheppey which is of Anglo-Saxon origin, meaning 'island with the sheep'. Other remnants of Anglo-Saxon can be found in the several Shiptons and Shipleys around England. W.G. Hoskins calculated that 21 of 40 English counties had place names which involved sheep, and all of these communities were of Saxon origin. Other sheep-based place names are less obvious. Wetherby for example is a Viking name meaning sheep town – *wether*,[10] In Scotland traces can be found of the Old Norse word fær, 'sheep' in names such as Fair Isle and Fara; Lama Ness, which includes the Old Norse for lamb, and Sorquoy, from Old Norse sauðr, 'sheep'. On Fair Isle, sheep and wool in particular gave rise to a cottage industry known across the world for its production of Fair Isle sweaters, sadly now only produced by a few skilled islanders. At the other end of the country, Dartmoor, long associated with sheep production, is littered with easily recognisable place names associated with sheep farming – Dip Through Gate, Flock O'Sheep, The Grey Wether, Leg O'Mutton Corner, The Ram's Parlour, The Sheep Path and Sheepfold Corner. Part of the British film industry is to be found at their studios at the 'farmstead of the shepherds' or Shepperton as it now is.

According to the Ordnance Survey, there are Mutton street names throughout the UK, with intriguing variations such as Mutton Dingle (Wales), Mutton Scalp Road (Yorkshire), Muttonhole Road (Scotland), and the rather intriguing Muttonshire Hill in Nottinghamshire. In Sussex, in the heart of Southdown country is the appropriately named Southdown Mutton Hall Hill.

10 See chapter on Names of Sheep page 75

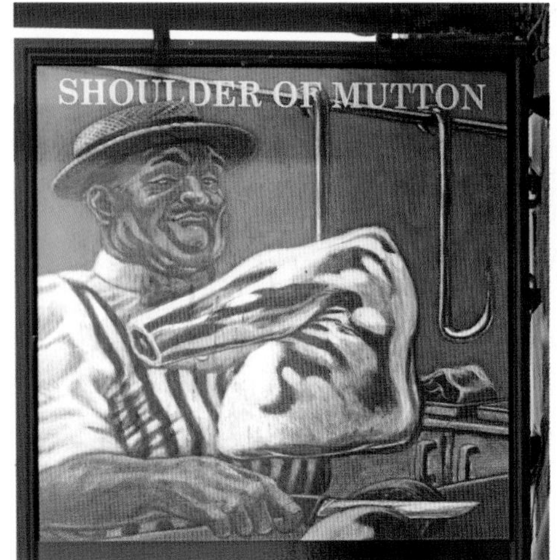

Shoulder of Mutton pub sign at Wantage, Berks

Mutton Dingle, a lane at New Radnor, Powys

The Fleece House (formerly Inn) at Knighton, Powys

Even in the heart of our communities, the *Shoulder of Mutton* is still a popular pub name, being listed at number 71 in the most popular pub names in Britain in 2011[11]. 63 establishments were so named, and perhaps reflecting more modern tastes, 91 were called *The Lamb.* The cooked shoulder of mutton was a favoured dish offered at inns for weary travellers. One pub, at Yapton near Arundel in West Sussex, which had been called the *Shoulder of Mutton* since 1694, added 'and Cucumbers' to its title in 1832. This unique name derived from the publican offering stage coach passengers a dish of shoulder of mutton with the local speciality cucumber sauce. Sadly, the pub closed its doors in 2008 after over 300 years of hospitality to travellers, as a result of falling food sales, and only four parking spaces. It has now been converted into two houses. It is believed that at some inns, the name *Shoulder of Mutton* also indicated that the landlord was a butcher.

Surprisingly, the last pub to carry the previously widespread name *Leg of Mutton* was in Kirby-in-Ashfield in Nottinghamshire, and it closed in 1958. Cooked legs of mutton were central to many celebrations in the 'local', such as the completion of an apprenticeship.

The wool trade is also still remembered in our locals in names such as *The Fleece* and *The Woolpack.*

MUTTON IN LITERATURE

So much was mutton part of the British way of life and culture that our written and spoken language are infused with references to it. Charles Dickens mentions meals of mutton 92 times in 27 of his works. Jane Austen talks of mutton in five of her novels; Sir Walter Scott in sixteen of his books; Lewis Carroll mentioned mutton in six works; Sir Arthur Conan Doyle in sixteen books; Rudyard Kipling in eleven of his works; and so on. British recipe books include mutton dishes from at least 1545.

> *'Mutton yesterday, mutton today, and blimey, if it don't look like mutton again tomorrer.'*
>
> J.R.R. Tolkien
> *The Hobbit* 1937

Mutton in Shakespeare

Mutton occurs thirteen times within eight works:

As You Like It (1)	Twelfth Night (1)
Love's Labour's Lost (1)	Henry IV, Part II (2)
Merchant of Venice (1)	Measure for Measure (1)
Taming of the Shrew (1)	Two Gentlemen of Verona (2)

In Elizabethan English, mutton is also used both as reference to prostitutes and as a common term of abuse – not an entirely positive image for mutton. The word lamb appears in 59 lines of Shakespeare plays, perhaps reflecting the varying nuances of the word.

11 *Daily Mail*

MUTTON IN THE BIBLE AND ISLAM

'This is Mr. Barley's breakfast for to-morrow, served out to be cooked. Two mutton chops, three potatoes, some split peas, a little flour, two ounces of butter, a pinch of salt, and all this black pepper. It's stewed up together, and taken hot, and it's a nice thing for the gout, I should think!'

Charles Dickens (1812-1870)
Great Expectations

Whilst the eating of mutton was familiar to both the Jews and the writers of the King James Bible, there is no use of the word mutton in any major version of the Bible.

'Sheep' occurs in the King James Bible 175 times, and 'lamb' 189 times, although of course the use of both words has a far more symbolic use within the Bible than simply the animals. The sacrificial lamb and the shepherd Christ and his sheep are common biblical themes. Indeed, the name Rachel means ewe or lamb in Hebrew.

According to Bible scholars, the original Greek and Hebrew words for sheep meat did not differentiate between the ages of the animals. However, the reason that 'mutton' does not appear is that there are no references to everyday meals in the Bible, apart from mentions of bread and wine, 'Loaves and the Fishes' and the Last Supper, as well as food in dreams and visions. So, whilst 'sheep' and 'lambs' are mentioned, these are all references to the animals. Sacrificial lambs are mentioned a number of times. The lambs used for such purposes had to be a specific type of animal, a one-year-old male without blemish.

Such was the association between sheep and religion that some scholars believe that a custom practised until the 19th century of marking a cross on the shoulder of a sheep carcass denoted the 'priest's portion'.

Due to the common origins of the Abrahamic religions, the sacrificial slaughter of sheep is familiar to Judaism, Christianity and Islam. The Islamic festival of Eid al-Adha, or 'Festival of Sacrifice' remains an important Islamic occasion, where sheep or other domesticated animals are sacrificed. The Islamic equivalent of baptism is Aqeeqah, which takes place seven days after the birth of a child. Two sheep in the case of a boy or one for a girl, are killed and eaten by family, friends and the poor.

Model sheep from village art competition, Clun valley, Shropshire

MUTTON IN NURSERY RHYMES

Children's nursery rhymes often have political or other deeper messages. Nevertheless, many well-known rhymes, have contemporary mutton references, such as:

A Man, a Stool, a Leg of Mutton and a Dog

Two legs sat upon three legs,
With one leg in his lap;
In comes four legs
And runs away with one leg;
Up jumps two legs,
Catches up three legs,
Throws it after four legs,
And makes him drop one leg.

Little Bo-Peep has lost her Sheep
(attributed to G.K. Chesterton)

Little Bo-Peep has lost her Sheep
But hopes that mutton will soon be cheap
When so many cooks are nothing loth
For the task of spoiling the mutton-broth.
And the lords of the Meat Trust, she has been told,
Have cornered mutton and "got it cold"
Through experts, each guaranteed as fit
For the duty of making a hash of it,
In mutton cutlets and mutton pies
She endeavours in vain to recognise
The face of a single personal pet . . .
. . . But Woollen Goods Will Be Cheaper Yet
In shirts and shapes of every size
For pulling the wool over mortal eyes;
And Bradford mills are a lovely sight
Rows and rows of them, brisk and bright . . .
. . . But somehow or other they never recall
The days she walked on the mountain wall
Where the Shepherd Kings of an elder sky
Hoary as hills on the hills trailed by
And something went with her march along
Of David's valour and Virgil's song
When her voice was a clarion calling a clan
And her crook was a sceptre, the sceptre of man,
To gather her flock where the eagles fly
Or lay down her life when the wolf went by.
Little Bo-Peep is paid in full
Stuffed with mutton and choked in wool
But little Bo-Peep has lost her Sheep
And cannot do anything else but weep.

MUTTON AS SLANG

Mutton Dressed as Lamb

First recorded in literature in James Joyce's *Ulysses* (1922) the phrase was in general use from the 1860s. Prior to that was the phrase 'Old ewe dressed lamb-fashion', first recorded in 1777, and meaning an old woman dressing like a young one. According to Brewers Dictionary of Phrase and Fable, *'the allusion may not simply be to a butcher's tempting display of meat, but to 'mutton' in its slang sense of 'prostitute' and to 'lamb' in its colloquial sense of 'young innocent', 'virgin''.*

In the 16th century, *'mutton'* was the collective euphemism for sexually promiscuous women, or *'food for lust'* (Oxford English Dictionary).

Mutton-head

Slang for a dull or stupid person, originates in the USA from around 1800.

Mutton-fist

A large red coarse hand, or a person having such a hand. A leg of mutton fist featured in a Music Hall song 'O It's a Great Big Shame' performed by Gus Elen, a cockney artist from the 1890s:

I've lost my pal, 'e's the best in all the tahn
But don't you fink 'im dead becos 'e ain't
But since 'es wed 'e as 'ad ter knuckle dahn
Its enufter vex the temper of a saint
'E's a brewer's dray-man, wiva leg of mutton fist
An as strong as a bullick or an 'orse
Yet in 'er 'ands e's like a little kid
Oh I wish as I could get im a divorce.

'He came back again with the boiled mutton, and I was so excited by the appetising smell of it that I forgot the noise of the beast that had troubled me.'

H.G. Wells (1866-1946)
The Island of Doctor Moreau

Mutton Chop

This referred to side whiskers, shaped like a mutton cutlet, particularly fashionable in the 19th century, and revived in the 1970s.

Laced Mutton

Laced mutton is old slang for a prostitute. Even Shakespeare used the phrase in *Two Gentlemen of Verona* when Speed says: *'Ay sir; I, a lost mutton, gave your letter to her, a laced mutton; and she, a laced mutton, gave me, a lost mutton, nothing for my labour'.* From a similar root is the phrase 'Mutton monger': a pimp.

Mutton chops

Bellwether

This phrase was originally an experienced sheep given a bell to lead a flock; now mainly used figuratively for a person acting as a lead and guide.

> *'Sonny, true love is the greatest thing, in the world – except for a nice MLT – mutton, lettuce and tomato sandwich, where the mutton is lean and the tomato is ripe.'*
>
> William Goldman (1931-)

Cockney Rhyming Slang

Many of the early rhymes have now gone out of use; for example, the cockney rhyming slang 'Billy Button' for 'mutton'. 'Mutt 'n' Jeff' or 'mutton' was used for 'deaf' from the 1960s. It is also a slang term for the 'good cop/bad cop' method of police interrogation or any other pair of people or items which are contrasting in size or nature. Mutt and Jeff were cartoon characters created by Bud Fisher in 1907. 'Leg of mutton' is London Cockney rhyming slang for 'button'.

The Mutton Lancers

The Cockney Alphabet

There are many versions of the Cockney alphabet, of which this is one: **A for Horses**; **B for Mutton** and so on.

'Mutton Lancers'

This was used to refer to the Royal West Surrey Regiment (Queens) – from the image of a sheep on their cap badges.

Mutton leg sleeve

The leg-of-mutton sleeve has a bell-shaped outline, just like a leg of mutton. This type of sleeve was first seen in 1824, but made a comeback in the 1890s, when they became very large, but had died out by about 1906.

Mutton leg sleeve

Give Someone the Cold Shoulder

With an unwanted visitor, if you offered them cold shoulder of mutton instead of hot meat, it was a hint that they were not to call again. Some dispute this interpretation. The earliest written example of the phrase is by Sir Walter Scott in 1816.

Mutton Cloth

Mutton cloth (calico) has long been used to cover carcasses, particularly sheep, to protect them from contamination, and to prevent the carcasses from leaving a fatty deposit when being handled. Originally, mutton cloth was made from calico, which is an unbleached, and often not fully processed, cotton plain-woven

Mutton cloth

textile. The fabric is less coarse and thicker than canvas or denim, but owing to its unfinished and undyed appearance, it was and still is very cheap, and therefore could be used for the purpose of protecting meat. It can also be known as muslin. The name calico is derived from the name of the city of Calicut, Kerala, India. It is used a lot in soft furnishing.

Traditional spiced leg of mutton

Part Two
MANAGING MUTTON

What Have Sheep Ever Done For Us?

In understanding the extraordinary story of mutton, it is important to have some knowledge of sheep farming, and how the fortunes of both sheep and mutton have risen and fallen with the great social and economic changes over the centuries.

For several hundred years, sheep were the mainstay of the UK's economy. It made the church and some landed gentry extremely rich, and our specialised sheep breeds were exported all over the world. Wealth from the sheep industry was responsible for arguably the most exquisite architecture conceived in this country, in the form of 'wool churches'. Yet it also resulted in human suffering on a vast scale. As a result of the Enclosures and Highland Clearances, entire communities were forced to move to enable more sheep to graze. Long before we were the 'Workshop of the World' and a 'Nation of Shopkeepers', we were known as a 'Nation of Sheep Farmers and Cloth Manufacturers'.

Long before DNA was ever dreamt of, British farmers' skills with animal breeding meant that we had more breeds of sheep in Britain than in any other country in the world – one for every environmental niche and end product. Over the centuries, we have kept sheep to provide us with meat, wool, parchment, fat, milk and manure. They have clothed us and fed us with butter and cheese, and supplied us with what was for many hundreds of years one of the most ubiquitous of meats – mutton. The demand for these various products has literally re-shaped sheep several times in our history, and continues to do so. So deeply engrained in our culture are sheep that, as we have seen, our language is full of references to them – from being 'fleeced', to 'pulling the wool over our eyes', and 'you might as well be hung for a sheep as a lamb' (from when sheep stealing was a capital offence), to nursery rhymes such as Baa Baa Black sheep. We really were a nation of sheep-keepers.

NOTHING LEFT BUT THE BAA

To the early sheep farmers, meat was a by-product, and the last thing they wanted to do was to kill and eat their animals. There are many products that live sheep gave their keepers. Blood from the living sheep was used as a food (including black pudding) as it still is in a number of pastoralist nomadic societies; milk was drunk fresh or made into cheese, butter or yoghurt for the winter; wool was used to produce felt, fabric for clothing and housing, and grease; and the fertilising benefits of dung were realised in Neolithic times, as was the use of dried dung for fuel.

From archaeological evidence, the original purpose for domestication of sheep was as a source of milk, with wool as a valuable by-product. Sheep milk is a very much more efficient converter of food energy than meat. Even the Romans recognised the food value of sheep's milk, with the writer Varro recording that ewe's milk was the most nourishing of all domestic animals. The rearing of sheep for meat was a much later development. By the turn of the 19th century large-scale milking had declined significantly as it was realised that milking was to the detriment of the lamb crop, and the need to produce more meat was becoming apparent. As a Scottish observer noted in 1807 *'Some of the most judicious storemasters [tenants] have totally given up the practice of milking the ewes after weaning; and others milk for a shorter space of time than formerly; and they now allow the lambs to suck longer, which considerably increases their bone, and is thought not so pernicious to the ewes as the milking.'* The practice continued in Wales, where sheep's cheese was 'highly esteemed'. And of course, milking sheep continues to this day. The major difference now is that milking flocks are bred and managed specifically to produce milk. Historically, as we have seen, milk was simply one of a number of sheep by-products.

> *Charles Augustus Fortescue*
> *He sought, when it was in his power,*
> *For information twice an hour,*
> *And as for finding Mutton-Fat*
> *Unappetising, far from that!*
> *He often, at his Father's Board,*
> *Would beg them, of his own accord,*
> *To give him, if they did not mind,*
> *The Greasiest Morsels they could find...*
>
> Hilaire Belloc (1870-1953)

A slaughtered sheep yielded many useful products, apart from the meat. Fat was used as a food, as well as for the manufacture of candles and soap; bone was cut to make many

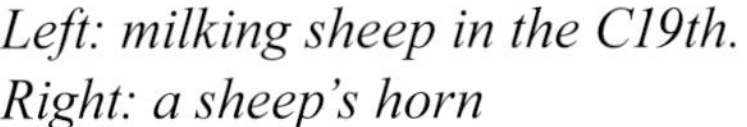

Left: milking sheep in the C19th.
Right: a sheep's horn

different implements and musical instruments, as well as boiled up to make glue; skin was used as whole fleeces to keep warm, as well as producing leather, parchment (original paper sizes such as quarto and octavo were based on the size of sheep skins), drums, bagpipe bags and coracle boats; horn was fashioned into implements, lantern windows and musical instruments; finally the innards of the sheep, apart from the edible offal, yielded raw materials for cords, whips, bowstrings and violin and harpstrings from intestines, and containers from intestines and the stomach.

The many uses of sheep were illustrated in a poem by Leonard Mascall written in 1591:

Praise of Sheep

These cattle [sheep] among the rest,
Is counted for man one of the best,
No harmful beast, nor hurt at all,
His fleece of wool doth cloath us all,
Which keeps us all from extreme cold,
His flesh doth feed both young and old,
His tallow makes the candles white,
To burn and serve us day and night:
His skin doth pleasure divers ways,
To write [parchment], to wear, at all assaies;
His guts, thereof we make [spinning] wheel-strings;
They use his bones for other things;
His horns some shepherds will not lose,
Because therewith they patch their shoes;
His dung is chief, I understand,
To help and dung the Plowman's land;
Therefore the sheep among the rest,
He is for man a worthy beast.

Sheep cheeses

'...and who can be trusted to hold a child the right way up, and not make himself objectionable whenever there is lukewarm mutton for dinner.'

Jerome K. Jerome *(1859-1927)*
Idle Thoughts of an Idle Fellow

An agricultural handbook of 1950 describes the uses of the various parts of the sheep, apart from the main carcass – the so called fifth quarter. The skin was made into Chamois leather, and '*inedible fat or tallow is used in the manufacture of lower grade soaps, glycerine and commercial greases. The intestines are used for the sausage casings, surgical stitches and strings for musical instruments and tennis racquets. The thyroid, pituitary, thymus and prostate glands collected in the large abattoirs are valuable in the preparation of pharmaceutical products.*' Some of these uses continue today, although production of pet food now plays a significant part which was not the case in post-war 1950.

MUTTON FAT

Throughout the history of man's husbandry of sheep, mutton fat was also a very important product. Indeed, for periods in the 18th and 19th centuries, mutton fat was worth twice as much as meat, which encouraged the production of fat animals.

The tallow was produced on the farm when mutton animals were slaughtered. The deposits of fat were cut off the carcass, with any pieces of meat or sinews removed. They were then cut into small pieces and put in earthenware jars, which were placed in a pot with warm water, and placed on the fire. As the pieces melted, the whole contents of the jar were stirred. The fibrous parts of the fat rose to the surface and were removed, and once cool were often fed to the farm dogs. The liquid fat was then poured into a dish with a little cold water where it solidified into a cake – also called tallow. These were then sold or used in the kitchen for cooking, soap and candles.

Mixed with lanolin from the sheep's wool, mutton fat even made a very effective form of skincare for chapped hands, and damaged skin generally.

> *'Another would set a sum – 'If a pound of mutton-candles cost sevenpence-halfpenny, how much must Dobbin cost?' and a roar would follow from all the circle of young knaves, usher and all, who rightly considered that the selling of goods by retail is a shameful and infamous practice, meriting the contempt and scorn of all real gentlemen.'*
>
> William Makepeace Thackeray (1811-1863)
> *Vanity Fair*

Dorothy Hartley noted mutton fat's use in cooking as late as 1954: *'If you use mutton fat for cake-making (and it makes farmhouse gingerbread, apple cake and the homelier kinds of cake very well), beat it to a cream with the lemon juice, or a spoonful of cider, till it whips like snow.'*

In 1861 Mrs Beeton made reference to its importance in antiquity: *'From Scriptural authority we learn many interesting facts as regards the sheep: the first, that mutton fat was considered the most delicious portion of any meat, and the tail and adjacent part the most exquisite morsel in the whole body; consequently, such were regarded as especially fit for the offer of sacrifice.'*

Tallow was used to protect vital parts of ships, such as the steel cables used in sailing ships which were protected by smearing the fat along the cable. It was then wrapped in cloth, and another layer of tallow was added. This protected the cables against the rigours of sea salt and the worst of maritime weather. Another naval example of the use of tallow is Boot Topping. The upper hull of the boat, just below the surface of the water, would be cleaned and then painted with tallow to protect it when at sea.

Mutton tallow played a vital part in early steam-driven piston engines. Most lubricants are washed away by the combination of steam and hot water, but not, it seems, tallow, which was relatively tenacious in such an environment. Thanks to this, tallow and compounds containing it were used in engines for steam ships and railway engines until the 1950s. Such was the demand for this use of tallow during WWII, that supplies were exhausted, and alternatives had to be sought, such as rapeseed oil.

The use of tallow to lubricate rifles sparked the Indian Mutiny of 1857. The Indian Army had introduced a new rifle, the Pattern 1853 Enfield. When loading it, the Sepoys (Indian soldiers) had to bite open the cartridge, which was packed in grease to enable it to slide into the gun barrel. Despite testing these greased cartridges for two years, with no complaints, rumours persisted that the tallow used was not from mutton, but from pigs and cows. This was unacceptable to Muslims and Hindus, who could not eat anything from pigs or cattle. A request to the army that the grease composition should be changed was met with the order that the Sepoys should be issued with clean cartridges and allowed to grease them with whatever they wished. Moreover, any tallow supplied would be that from goats or sheep. This did not halt the rumours, and became the spark which lead to the raising of wider grievances. By this stage, the Indian Mutiny and its bloody consequences was inevitable.

'Home from my office to my Lord's lodgings where my wife had got ready a very fine dinner – viz. a dish of marrow bones; a leg of mutton; a loin of veal; a dish of fowl, three pullets, and two dozen of larks all in a dish; a great tart, a neat's tongue, a dish of anchovies; a dish of prawns and cheese.'

Diary of Samuel Pepys
26th January 1660

TALLOW IN SOAP MANUFACTURE

The word sapo, Latin for soap, first appears in the writer Pliny the Elder's (23 AD – 79 AD) *Historia Naturalis*, in which he describes the manufacture of soap from tallow and ash. However, he only mentions it as a pomade for hair, especially amongst the Gauls and Germans, where the men, he writes rather disapprovingly, were more likely to use it than their women folk. Originally soap was made by boiling wood ash with lime to produce caustic potash. This was then boiled with the tallow to give a soft soap. Adding salt produced a hard soap.

During the 19th Century, vegetable oils and fats began to replace tallow, as they produced a cleaner, softer, whiter soap. Animal fat is rarely used today in soap manufacture.

MUTTON CANDLES

For many hundreds of years, mutton fat, in the form of tallow, lit our humbler homes. The most expensive lighting before oil and electricity was beeswax candles, but for most people, tallow candles were their only source of artificial light, however gloomily they shone. This hierarchy in candle-making dates back to the Middle Ages, when candle-makers, or Chandlers, formed two guilds – one for beeswax candle-makers and one for tallow. The best form of tallow was mutton fat, as it generally gave a better light, and with less smell and smoke than other forms of animal fat.

> *'...a rush light, a little twinkling uncomfortable spark, which one is every moment afraid will vanish in smoke, and which the least wind will extinguish.'*
>
> *Anna Melvil, a novel* by various authors (1792)

Rush lights have been made and used since the time of ancient Egyptians, at least 3,000 BC. The beauty was that they were cheap and the raw materials were always to hand – wild rushes and animal fat.

Such was the only form of lighting, apart from open fires, for the poorest people in the UK until at least the 1850s. One can imagine what relying on such a poor light was like during the long dark hours of winter, with smoke from the fire and rush lights, and the dim, intermittent light. Light sources for the poorest people often had to be made at home, as the cost of buying ready-made candles was beyond the means of most people until the late 19th century.

The 'rush' element of the light was the common or soft rush (*Juncus effuses*). Women and children would harvest them from marshy ground in late summer, when the plants would be at their maximum size. The rushes were then soaked in water to enable them to be peeled. They were then bleached and dried in the sun. Gertrude Jekyll, the garden designer, recorded a conversation with a 90-year-old neighbour in Sussex around 1900. The old lady described how she prepared the rushes for use as candles: *'You peels away the rind from the peth [central pith], leaving only a little strip of rind. And when the rushes is dry you dips 'em through the grease [melted mutton fat], keeping 'em well under. And my mother she always laid hers to dry in a bit of hollow bark. Mutton fat's the best; it dries hardest.'* Mutton or whatever other fat was available, was skimmed off the top of cooking pots as they cooked, and was stored until enough was ready to use for candles. Often households would only have bacon fat from the family pig which would have been killed in the autumn and salted to supply meat over the winter. This made the flame of the rush light splutter more, and gave a poorer light than mutton fat.

Hand-dipped mutton tallow candles

The fat was put into a cast-iron 'grease pan', and melted over the fire. The dried and peeled rushes were laid in the melted fat, and then removed to a cool place for the fat to harden. Some would then repeat the process to produce a sturdier rush light, less prone to breaking.

When needed, the rushes were placed in iron holders, which gripped them near the burning end, allowing them to burn steadily. About an inch and a half (4 cm) of rush would protrude above the jaw of the holder. As it burned, the rush would have to be regularly moved up. Parents would often tell their children to 'mend the light' or 'mend the rush', which was the signal for the child to move the rush along another inch and a half. A 15 inch (38cm) rush light would burn for about 30 minutes. There were ways of automatically 'switching off' a rush light. Two pins crossing in the rush would do the trick, or alternatively laying the rush light on an oak chest would allow the cottager to undress and get into bed before the light was extinguished when it met the oak. Some old oak furniture can still be found with burn marks from rush lights used in this way. If you were feeling very extravagant, and needed extra light, you could adjust the rush in the holder, and light both ends at the same time, halving its burning time, thus 'burning the candle at both ends'.

Common or soft rush (Juncus effuses)

Rush light holders

For the more well-to-do, candles were either bought or made at home. Mutton fat was melted in a pot over a fire and the wick (hemp, linen or cotton) was dipped in and out. The more dips it had, the thicker the candle. A later development was to pour hot tallow into moulds to make the candles.

From the 18th century, candle manufacturers started to look for new raw materials to produce candles, such as whale oil (spermaceti) and coconut oil. Later still, the use of the process used in soap making and known as saponification, meant that items such as skin fat, bone fat, fish oil and industrial waste greases could now be turned into hard white candles. By the late 19th century the mutton fat rush lights and candles had made way for much cheaper and cleaner alternatives.

This was not quite the end of the use of rush lights, for the practice was revived during the Second World War in some rural areas.

Tallow candle

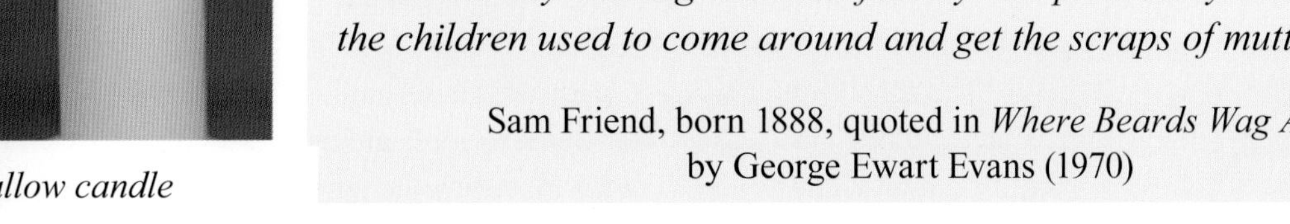

'I remember when I was about five they used to have a candle-factory in the alleyway in Fore Hamlet in Ipswich. They used to boil the mutton fat and then the candles were dipped into the mutton fat. Well, on a Saturday evening when the factory was practically being closed, the children used to come around and get the scraps of mutton.'

Sam Friend, born 1888, quoted in *Where Beards Wag All* by George Ewart Evans (1970)

Sheep Origins

Sheep are reared and eaten in most parts of the world, and sheep meat is the only red meat which is universally eaten by mankind, with no recorded taboos, such as with beef (Hindus) and pork (Muslims and Jews).

The earliest written record of sheep is about 5,500 years ago. They are mentioned in writings from Babylon, Egypt, the Indus and China, all at least 1,300 BC. The Bible describes sheep-keeping around 1,500 BC. The first glossary of sheep terms was found on a Neo-Babylonian tablet of the sixth century BC, where sheep were described grazing on roofs, as they do today in Scandinavia. Specific words were listed on the tablet to describe dried mutton, cooked mutton and roasted mutton.

Soay sheep: ancient survivors

Sheep are not indigenous to the UK. They were brought to these islands during the Neolithic period, but for 6,000 years at least, British farmers have reared domesticated sheep, *Ovis aries* (hence the generic term 'ovine' to describe sheep). Wild Mediterranean mouflon and the horned urial sheep of Central Asia were domesticated, and migrated with people across northern Europe. They appear to have arrived in Britain around 4,000 BC.

We can have an idea of what the original sheep which were brought into this country by the Neolithic settlers looked like from a chance survivor of the very earliest domesticated sheep in Britain. The Soay is a primitive breed of domestic sheep descended from a feral population on the small island of Soay (Norse for 'Sheep Island'), which is part of St Kilda, some 40 miles off the western coast of Scotland. The Soay remains physically similar to its ancient ancestors. It is much smaller than modern domesticated sheep but hardier, and very agile and shy. Colours of its wool vary between solid black and blonde with a lighter brown-white underbelly and rump. A few have white markings on the face. A fascinating insight into our ancestors' activities is the fact that Soay wool can be plucked, and does not need to be cut – an obvious advantage in the days before metal blades.

Soay have another characteristic which has been bred out of modern sheep – they tend not be herded. Attempts to move Soay either with people or sheepdogs, usually result in a scattering of the group, rather than a flocking together. Improved versions of the Soay can be seen in its modern cousins – the Shetland breed.

THE BRONZE AGE

In the remains of a Bronze Age farm at Jarlshof on Shetland is a shippon (farm building), where archaeologists think sheep dung was accumulated in the earliest known example of manure used as a fertiliser for crops in the UK.

Sheep cannot bite through long grass when grazing, nor can they browse bushes and small trees, which means that grassland pastures must be well managed. Immigrants to the UK in the Bronze Age brought with them a new breed of cattle (*Bos longifrons*), which was grazed, together with pigs, in concentrated areas around villages. This prevented re-growth of forest, and over hundreds of years areas of grassland developed, which were then suitable for sheep, and allowed for an increase in numbers. The local environment and terrain determined which domesticated animals were kept in each area.

A tradition developed amongst the Celts of burying meat in human graves, in order to feed the dead on their journey to the next world. When the Romans overran Maiden Castle in Dorset in about 47 AD, the victims of the assault were buried with joints of mutton placed beside them, reflecting the preponderance at the time of sheep in that area of southern England.

ROMAN OCCUPATION

During the Roman period, the invaders brought their own sheep with them, which were larger, white-faced, hornless and had finer wool than the native British animals. As a result, sheep grew in importance and numbers, and regions such as Salisbury Plain became important sheep farming areas, primarily for wool production. English wool had started to develop a reputation for quality on the Continent and woollen cloth became a significant export product from Roman Britain. A woollen mill, supposedly situated at Winchester, is mentioned in a Roman document. It is also possible that wool processing went on in the larger Roman estates around the sheep farming areas.

THE VIKINGS

The next major wave of invasion by the Vikings around 900 brought with it a new type of sheep to Britain. In the northern parts of the country these new horned, black-faced sheep developed into the Blackface, Swaledale and Herdwick breeds of northern Britain.

MIDDLE AGES

Evidence from the Domesday Book shows that in 1086 milk was the most important product of sheep, with wool and manure as by-products. It may seem extraordinary to us, but meat was financially less important. The Domesday Book also showed that sheep were the most common domesticated species, outnumbering all other animals put together. By the early Middle Ages, ewes milk was still a major reason for keeping sheep, and sheep's cheese and butter were widely known and enjoyed. Little wonder, as sheep's milk has five times the fat and twice the protein of cows' milk.

However, this focus on sheep's milk was about to change, as it is for wool that the mediaeval period is so well-known, and it is wool which became so utterly vital to the English economy from the 12th to the 18th centuries, being known in 1656 as '*the flower and strength and revenue and blood of England*'. Indeed, from the 14th century to this day, the Speaker of the House of Lords has sat on a woolsack. In front of the Woolsack in the House of Lords' Chamber is a larger cushion known as the Judges' Woolsack. Senior judges sit here during the State Opening of Parliament, reflecting mediaeval Parliaments, when judges attended to offer legal advice.

During the reign of King Stephen, in the 12th century, the Cistercian order of monks arrived from France. They established 50 monasteries, most with agricultural estates whose specific purpose was the production of sheep to export wool. Fifteen of these estates were in Yorkshire, where it has been estimated that by 1315, monastic sheep totalled 250,000, or half the sheep in the county. Fountains Abbey alone owned one million acres. Indeed, it is estimated that at one stage 21% of the wool production of Britain came from Yorkshire. Other Church properties benefitted greatly from the wool trade. By the 1220s, one third of Leicester Abbey's income was from sheep and wool. Indeed, such was the value of wool in the 14th century that the production from one sheep could be sold for half the value of the live sheep, and of course, wool was an annual crop.

The large monastic and private estates kept vast sheep flocks. As many lambs as possible were kept within the flock for a number of years, and not slaughtered. After their first year, younger animals produce a heavier wool crop than the older breeding ewes. Such was the value of sheep at this time that many were housed in winter, at a time when hunger amongst people was often a fact of life. Even poor villeins kept some sheep at the end of their house. Often sheep were housed from Martinmas (St Martins's Day on 11th November) until Easter, either in houses, or in moveable folds of wooden hurdles, thatched at the sides and tops. During these months they were fed on coarse hay or pea-haulm (stalks and leaves), mixed with wheat or oat straw. For the rest of the year they browsed on the fallow (uncropped) land, in woodland pastures, or on the sheep commons (which were known as the 'Waste of the Manor'). The practice of housing sheep declined after the medieval period, and was only revived to similar levels in the 20th century.

'Very merry at, before, and after dinner, and the more for that my dinner was great, and most neatly dressed by our own only maid. We had a fricasee of rabbits and chickens, a leg of mutton boiled, three carps in a dish, a great dish of a side of lamb, a dish of roasted pigeons, a dish of four lobsters, three tarts, a lamprey pie (a most rare pie), a dish of anchovies, good wine of several sorts, and all things mighty noble and to my great content.'

Diary of Samuel Pepys
4 April 1662

Following the upheavals of the Black Death from 1348 and 1349, and the consequent shortage of labour, the social order of rural areas changed from serfs with a fixed strip of land, to short-term tenant farmers, and free labourers. This also became the first period (apart from the Roman) when farming was carried out for profit rather than subsistence. Also, with the labour shortage, there was a shift from arable farming to less labour intensive livestock production, especially sheep. As trade developed, so did the export market for wool, and with it an increase in sheep flocks.

Maintaining the fertility of field crops was an important function of sheep. Flocks would

English illuminated manuscript from the 13th century

be penned on arable fields, within the open-field system of farming, with the dung from the animals fertilising the next crops. In fact, in Medieval England sheep dung was third in value to milk and wool, and greater than meat. Animals often wandered the country feeding on the local vegetation – in the summer being taken up into the hills, and winter to the lowlands. Whilst the sheep were supposed to keep within the allotted 75 yard-wide tracks, conflicts were frequent between the shepherds and the peasants onto whose land the flocks frequently strayed.

LAND ENCLOSURES

By 1500 there were three sheep to every person in England. With wool so profitable in the 'golden age' of the 14th to 16th centuries, a process was begun of enclosing the previously open fields with hedges, to keep animals confined. This process, known as the Enclosures, accelerated into the 18th and 19th centuries, when statutes were passed regularly by Parliament for the enclosure of particular areas. Across Britain, vast swathes of open land were fenced off from the local peasantry, causing huge suffering in the rural population. Until then they had made a living from the feudal landholding system which had remained largely unchanged since Norman times.

However, by the time of the Dissolution of the Monasteries (from 1534), demand for mutton for the growing towns and cities was starting to increase. This gave an impetus to produce sheep for both wool and now meat.

The practices of enclosing land with fences and hedges and more actively encouraging the growing of grass had a huge impact on the productivity of the sheep. With the enclosures came what we would call today 'land management'. One 16th century writer Thomas Tusser, a supporter of enclosures, compares 'champion' (open) counties, like Norfolk and Cambridgeshire, with 'enclosed' counties, like Essex and Suffolk and says that the latter have:

'More plenty of mutton and biefe,
Come, butter, and cheese of the best,
More wealth anywhere, to be briefe
More people, more handsome and prest. . . .

The effect of the push for increased production following the enclosures is illustrated by Gervase Markham, another 16th century writer on matters agricultural. He is one of the first to discuss individual sheep breeds, based on the quality of their wool. He considered the best animals were from the Welsh Border counties of Herefordshire, Shropshire and Worcestershire, centring on the town of Leominster. Even as late as 1808 in a guide to Leominster, the author eulogises over the local wool around the town. *'The Leominster wool has, time immemorial, been deemed superior to any other in the country.'* The Welsh border country is scattered with some of the finest examples of English 'wool churches'. Amongst the most spectacular is St Laurence's in Ludlow, which Simon Jenkins in his *England's Thousand Best Churches* describes as the 'Cathedral of the Marches'. Medieval wool churches can also be found in East Anglia and the Cotswolds. The vastness of the wealth which wool provided can be judged from the more than 1,500 medieval churches in East Anglia alone, the great majority of which were rebuilt in the 14th and 15th centuries on the revenues created from woollen cloth.

Tudor poet Michael Drayton compared the Cotswolds and Welsh Border (now called Ryeland) breeds, favouring Cotswolds for greater numbers, but Ryeland for fineness of wool:

'T'whom Sarum's plaine gives place, though famous for its flocks;
Yet hardly does she tythe our Cotswolde's wealthy locks;
Though Lemster him exceed in fineness of her ore,
Yet quite he puts her downe for his abundant store'.

St Laurence's church, Ludlow, Shropshire.

The modern Ryeland breed of sheep from the Welsh borders

Later, in 1627 in his poem *The Battaile of Agincourt*, Drayton includes a phrase to sum up a number of the English counties represented at the battle. For Herefordshire he writes '*a golden fleece fair Hereford doth weare*'. Indeed, such was the popularity of this Welsh Borders wool that a pair of stockings given to Queen Elizabeth I as a gift, pleased her so much that thereafter she announced that she would only wear clothing made from Borders wool. The breed now known as the Ryeland was the 'Golden Hoof' animal of the Welsh Borders. During the 1700s the Ryeland was grazed extensively in the lower parts of Monmouthshire, Herefordshire and western Worcestershire, and was common in north-western Gloucestershire. It was so named as it was found in areas which grew large quantities of rye. Even King George III (1760-1820) kept a pure-bred flock of the highly-valued Ryelands on heath and bracken at Windsor, on the advice of his agricultural advisor Joseph Banks, of whom more later, after having tried unsuccessfully to keep Spanish Merinos.

'We got a beef steak pie, a couple of gooseberry tarts, and a leg of mutton from the hotel.'

Jerome K. Jerome (1859-1927)
Three Men in a Boat

By the end of the 16th century, many of the hallmarks of modern sheep farming had been established. Fitzherbert, writing in 1523, described the sheep farmers year in a way which would be easily recognised today.

However, the price paid by rural populations for this improvement in sheep farming was considerable. Several hundred entire villages were abandoned and disappeared through the enclosures. Sir Thomas More was appalled at the effect the enclosures were having on the rural people, as he wrote in his celebrated book *Utopia* in 1516:

'Your shepe that were wont to be so meke and tame, and so smal eaters, now, as I heare saye, be become so great devowerers and so wylde, that they eate up and swallow down the very men them selfes. They consume, destroye, and devoure whole fields, howses and cities . . . Noble man and gentleman, yea and certeyn Abbottes leave no ground for tillage, thei inclose all into pastures; they throw down houses; they pluck down townes, and leave nothing standynge but only the churche to be made a shepehowse.'

This opposition to early Tudor sheep farming methods culminated in at least two revolts in 1549 and around 1600 amongst the rural populace. Reacting to pressure, several Monarchs passed laws supposedly limiting the Enclosures, but the speed and severity of them continued apace. The resistance continued into the 19th century. It was the rural poor who lost the most from the enclosures. Even ancient rights exercised by cottagers such as turf cutting were denied them. In the 1770s at Maulden in Bedfordshire a report on the Enclosures recorded a conversation with one cottage tenant who claimed that *'... enclosing would ruin England; it was worse than ten wars.' 'Why?'* he was asked, *'What have you lost by it?'* He replied, *'I kept four cows before the parish was enclosed, and now I don't keep so much as a goose; and you ask me what I lose by it!'*

> *He loved mutton well that licked where the ewe lay.*
>
> English Proverb
>
> (referring to those who scraped or licked their dish after a good meal)

Despite the suffering of some rural communities, the arguments in favour of enclosing land were based on improvements in agricultural efficiency, with more food being produced for the country's burgeoning population. In Cumberland in 1794 there were still 150,000 acres of improvable common, which were said to be *'generally overstocked'*. Another report claimed that *'No improvement of breed was possible, while a man's ewes mixed promiscuously with his neighbour's flocks. If any part of the flock had the scab or other infectious disease, there was no means of preventing it from spreading.'* A high proportion of these common lands were said to be good corn-land. It was said in the reports to the Board of Agriculture that if enclosed, and part ploughed for grain crops, not only would there be an increased supply of corn, but instead of *'the ill-formed, poor, starved, meagre animals that depasture it at present,'* there could be *'an abundant supply of fat mutton sent to our big towns.'*

THE HIGHLAND CLEARANCES

The enclosure process reached its climax in the Highland Clearances in Scotland in the 18th and 19th centuries. Until then, Scottish farming and sheep in particular had changed little for several centuries. Little local demand for sheep meat (the first butcher's shop opened in Edinburgh in 1816), and small unproductive indigenous sheep was compounded by the general belief that the animals should be housed throughout the winter – a tall order for poor farming communities.

In 1729, William Macintosh proposed enclosing land with hedges, which he suggested would enable farmers to keep sheep outside. *'Why may they not keep them unhoused?'* wrote Macintosh. He considered that planting hedges would allow hay to be made for winter feed and act as shelter for the animals. He also claimed that outside wintering would improve wool production. It was not until about 1750 that farmers in Perthshire successfully out-wintered sheep. Indeed, as Macintosh had predicted, the sheep thrived on it.

With the defeat of the 1745 Rebellion, the traditional Highland Clan system of land tenure was swept aside, allowing greater security of tenure for farmers, together with amalgamation of farms. Demand for both sheep meat and wool in the lowlands and England, together with improved sheep breeds and development of feed crops such as turnips lead to a huge increase in agricultural output in Scotland, with sheep replacing cattle in many areas. Firstly the now extinct Linton breed, followed by the highly successful Cheviot replaced the small indigenous sheep, and numbers increased rapidly. However, the speed of the sheep invasion worried many, including engineer Thomas Telford, who predicted that the rush into sheep production would go too far, replacing both cattle and people in the Highlands. From 1770 this exodus did indeed take place. By the end of the century, Telford's predictions became reality. One Argyll Chieftain lamented in 1788 *'I have lived through woeful days. When I was young the only question was how many men lived on the estate; then it came to be how many black cattle it could keep; but now they only ask how many sheep the lands will carry.'* Although some historians suggest that depopulation of the Highlands would have happened even without sheep, the increased rents demanded by landlords for profitable sheep production certainly hastened the process.

Eviction during the Highland Clearances

In 1809 The Duke of Sutherland cleared his estate in Staffordshire. Ten years later he turned his attention to his lands in the north of Scotland. One witness to the action was the Rev. Donald Sage, missionary at Achness:

'To my poor and defenseless flock the dark hour of trial came in right earnest. It was in the month of April, 1819 that they were all, men, women and children, from the heights of Farr to the mouth of the Naver, on one day to quit their tenements and go – many of them knew not whither, for a few some miserable patches of ground along the shore were doled as lots without anything in the shape of the poorest hut to shelter them. They were supposed to cultivate the ground and occupy themselves as fishermen. Many had never set foot in a boat.'

By the 19th century, the removal of many thousands of crofters by apparently unfeeling landowners resulted in mass emigration to the New World of the British Empire and the Americas. This often left even greater poverty and suffering for those who stayed behind. Ironically, within a few years of the Highland Clearances, even the sheep, which had replaced the people, would have to a large extent disappeared. The vast areas of land, designed to produce meat for the urban masses, and wool for their clothing, were undercut by the very places to which many of the displaced crofters had fled – the grasslands of the New World.

CONSEQUENCES OF THE ENCLOSURES

The enclosures and clearances overall did have a positive impact on agricultural production, albeit with high levels of human suffering. The struggle to feed the burgeoning urban populations wrought great changes, both social and agricultural. Not only was mutton in demand, but sheep manure became an important input for arable crops – such was the demand for fertiliser that even sweepings from city streets were used in some places. In grassland pastures, the impact was no less dramatic, with yields of livestock increasing substantially.

The enclosures encouraged a different type of farmer. The Oxfordshire Reporter (1809) stated: *'If you go into Banbury market next Thursday, you may distinguish the farmers from enclosures from those from open fields; quite a different sort of men; the farmers as much changed as their husbandry – quite new men, in point of knowledge and ideas.'* In the same year, Arthur Young wrote in a rather inflammatory way of Oxfordshire farmers, who *'... are now in the period of a great change in their ideas, knowledge, practice, and other circumstances. Enclosing to a greater proportional amount than in almost any other county in the kingdom, has changed the men as much as it has improved the country; they are now in the ebullition of this change; a vast amelioration has been wrought, and is working; and a great deal of ignorance and barbarity remains. The Goths and Vandals of open-fields touch the civilisation of enclosures.'*

Gently stir and blow the fire,
Lay the mutton down to roast,
Dress it quickly, I desire;
In the dripping put a toast,
That I hunger may remove;-
Mutton is the meat I love.
On the dresser see it lie;
Oh! the charming white and red !
Finer meat ne'er met the eye,
On the sweetest grass it fed:
Let the jack go swiftly round,
Let me have it nicely brown'd.
On the table spread the cloth,
Let the knives be sharp and clean,
Pickles get and salad both,
Let them each be fresh and green.
With small beer, good ale, and wine,
O ye gods! How I shall dine!

Jonathan Swift 1667-1745

SHEEP NUMBERS

When Mrs Beeton was writing her famous cookery book in 1861, in which she extolled the virtues of mutton, the number of sheep in this country had increased from an estimated 12 million at the beginning of the 18th century, to around 20 million. Shortly after Mrs Beeton's book, the number rose to 30 million, which is approximately where it stood in 2013 in Great Britain. Including Northern Ireland, the 2013 total was 32.8 million – roughly half a sheep per head of human population in the UK.

From the mid-1880s, cheaper sheep meat from the prairies of the New World started to flood into the UK, depressing prices and sheep numbers on the country's farms. With dips in numbers during both World wars, rapid expansion of sheep numbers has taken place since 1945. Sheep populations peaked in the 1990s when EU subsidies changed from a payment system per head, which had encouraged farmers to keep as many animals as possible. Since then, numbers have declined as farming subsidies became more environmentally focussed.

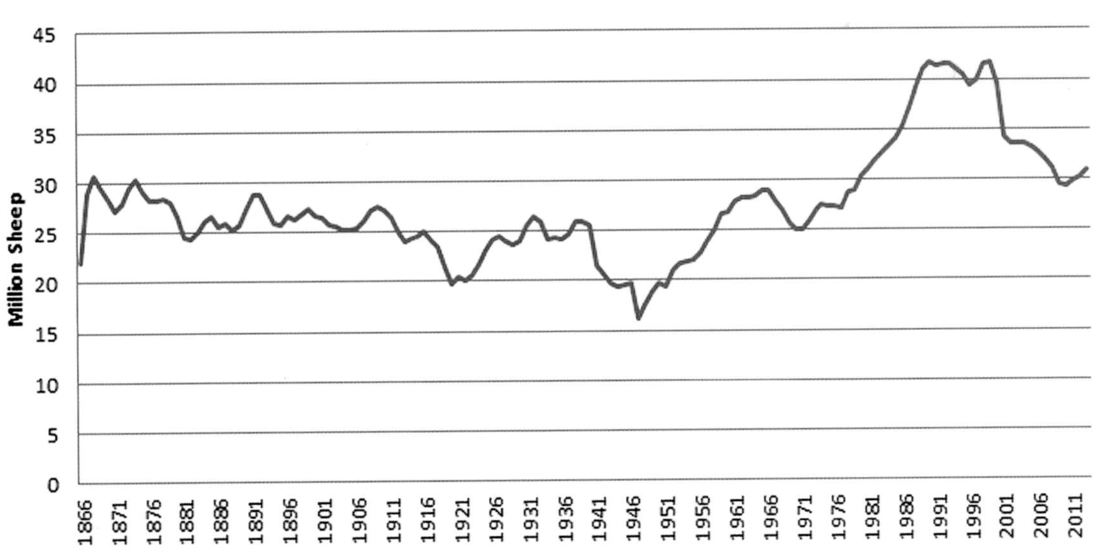

Demand and Supply for Sheep Meat

From the 12th to the 18th century, the primary reason for keeping sheep was wool. Manure and milk were secondary, and meat production was for much of the time a poor fourth. However, as the wool trade declined and towns began to grow in the 16th and 17th centuries, so the demands for meat increased, and the national sheep flock needed to be considered for mutton production as well as wool. There were many more mouths to feed from 1600, when the UK population was over 4 million. By 1700 it had increased to around 6.5 million, and by 1801 it was about 10 million. During the Victorian period the population rocketed to 21 million by 1851 and 37 million by 1901, and with it came an increased prosperity and an almost insatiable demand for more food. The task of feeding so many more mouths in a relatively short time was enormous.

The switch from wool to meat production was quite a task for sheep farmers. Breeding sheep for meat requires different characteristics from those which will produce plentiful wool. For a start, for meat you need the lamb to reach maturity early, to have a thick covering of lean meat, and a modest covering of fat. As we will see later, this systematic breeding over hundreds of years has given us a huge genetic pool of sheep traits and breeds – a valuable asset today in a world of changing climates.

From the 1600s there began an escalating change in emphasis from wool production to meat. Improved sheep farming management resulting from the Enclosures produced increased yields. Consequently, wool prices fell through over-production and fleece quality deteriorated as the mutton improved. The growing towns and cities demanded heavier animals for mutton and lamb, which were suited to enclosed pastures. Unfortunately, although new varieties of sheep produced more meat they gave coarser, poorer quality

Sheep Product Prices and Wages 1610 – 1910

(1910 = 1)

Source: G.Clarke, University of California 2010

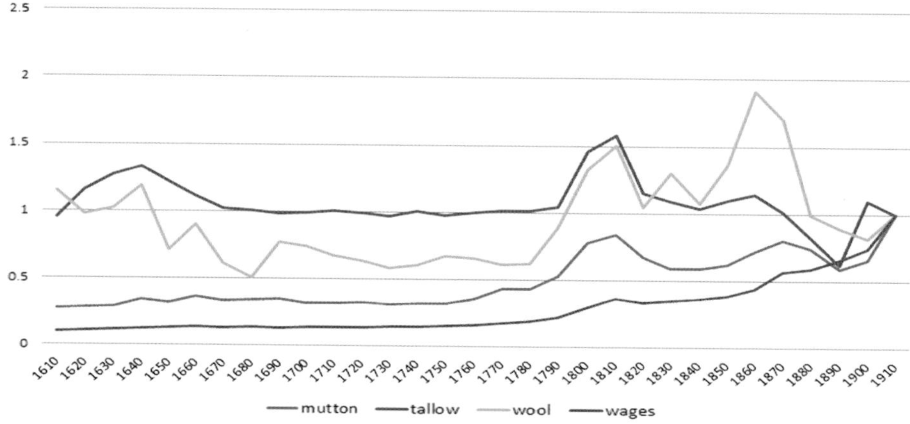

wool. English wool, once the premium product throughout Europe, now lost some of its glister. Although still commanding high prices, it was no longer indispensable for foreign weavers. This decrease in value of English wool slowed the rate of conversion of arable land into pasture, as much as did Acts of Parliament which tried to curb the enclosures.

An interesting piece of research carried out at the University of California, has pieced together prices of agricultural products (including wool, mutton and tallow), as well as wages from 1610 to 1910. The results of this research are shown in the graph *(see page 46 opposite)*. The stimulus for the increase in demand for mutton can be seen in the dramatic growth in the population of England and Wales, which increased 99% between 1801 and 1851 (from 9 to 18 million). Somehow this population had to be fed.

> *'He had one of the meat-tins between his knees, and sat with a large piece of cold Australian mutton between his fingers.'*
>
> Sir Arthur Conan Doyle (1859-1930)
> *The Lost World*

The relative prices of mutton started to increase substantially around 1800, the point at which pioneer sheep breeders such as Bakewell and Allman started to achieve significant results from their improved mutton breeds. All prices as well as wages increased substantially around 1810 during the Napoleonic wars. Mutton prices fell again after 1890, when refrigerated New World mutton started to arrive in Britain.

A second graph *(see below)* shows mutton prices, combining the University of California with UK government pricing data. Mutton prices stopped being recorded by the Ministry of Agriculture in 1966.

UK Mutton Prices 1610 – 1960

(old pence per pound)

Source: G.Clarke, University of California 2010

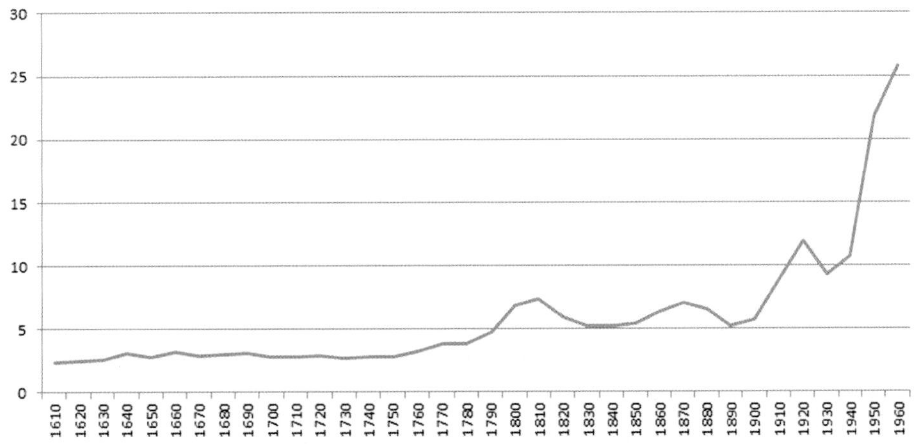

Mutton and the New World

The opening up of the vast pasturelands of Australia, New Zealand, and South Africa, as well as North and South America in the early to mid-19th century, led to rapid increases in the production of low-cost mutton. This allowed imported mutton and lamb to compete successfully with domestic production, to feed the rapidly increasing UK urban population. Initially these imports were of live animals, and until 1865 were of a very variable pattern, but reached their peak in 1870-1900. During the 1880s, Germany and the Netherlands led the list of exporting countries, followed by Canada, the USA and Denmark – hardly what we would expect in a list of sheep exporters today. In several of these latter years of the 19th century, over a million live animals arrived in British ports from across the world.

Two patterns soon emerged. Firstly, there was a shift to importing from the cheaper New World countries rather than from mainland Europe. Secondly, perhaps the most important development, from the 1880s refrigerated ships carried frozen sheep meat, rather than live animals. By 1889 imports from Germany were stopped, and by 1892 so had those from Denmark and the Netherlands, with the gap in imports being filled by Australia, New Zealand and Argentina. Live imports fell from over a million in 1895 to a mere 501 animals arriving on British docksides in 1913.

By 1900, 175,000 tonnes of frozen mutton was imported into the UK, and by the beginning of WWI, imports accounted for 44% of this country's sheep meat consumption, the majority of which was from within the British Empire and South America – with New

Zealand, Argentina and Australia supplying 96% of imports by 1913.

It was the availability of low cost lamb from the vast natural resources of the New World which was the beginning of the end of the reign of mutton as the main form of sheep meat in the UK. By 1923 only 50% of sheep meat imports were of mutton, and the rest was of lamb; a mere six years later in 1929, mutton accounted for only 37%.

Of course, cheap imports put additional pressure on British sheep producers. Life was becoming tough for them at the end of the 19th century. As author Henry Rider Haggard wrote in 1898:

'How are British graziers to compete against mutton at two-pence-halfpenny a pound? Moreover, as appliances improve and rates of carriage lessen, will it not come in at a still lower price from a country of endless and fertile pastures, where they pay their labour in paper and depreciated silver, which must be taken at face value, and are paid for their produce in good British gold? The prospect is so melancholy that I do not care to study it further. Perhaps the world may fill up, or perhaps drought and locusts will take a hand in the game. We must put faith in our old friend — the Unexpected – for we have no other.'

With refrigeration, supplies from outside the UK could be increased when supplies from domestic production were at their natural lowest, between March and August. This made lamb and mutton available year-round.

So, ironically, following the bitterness of the Highland Clearances, it was the grasslands of the Empire which eventually fed the urban workers of the British Industrial Revolution, not the Scottish Highlands, which in many cases became shooting estates for the few who had made money from the Industrial Revolution.

Interestingly, as we shall see, it was the French Revolution which was responsible for the Australian sheep industry.

NEW ZEALAND

'The whole of this great industry, and to a very great extent the general prosperity and advancement of New Zealand, hangs on the slender piston rod of a refrigerating machine'. This was how the sheep meat industry of New Zealand was summed up in an academic

Above: New Zealand tinned roast mutton label (1900-1920)
Opposite page: unloading frozen mutton from ship in London docks

paper in 1918.

The current £2 billion export industry had a rather inauspicious start with British explorer Captain James Cook bringing the first sheep to New Zealand on his second visit in 1773. A ewe and a ram from the Cape in South Africa were landed in Queen Charlotte Sound. They survived only a few days, hardly an inspiring start to the country's long association with sheep farming. Further attempts followed in 1814 and again in 1834 when sheep were put on Mana Island, near Wellington, to feed whalers. However, more followed, and by the 1850s New Zealand was a country of few people, exporting mostly wool and wheat.

In the mid-1800s wool was king, and New Zealand was well suited to its production. Initially large numbers of the fine-woolled Merino, a Spanish breed, were brought to New Zealand from Australia. Unfortunately, it was soon found that they were unsuited to the damp climate, and foot rot was a very serious problem; added to that the Merino carcass produces little meat. Farmers then started to import British sheep breeds which could survive in New Zealand's varied climates, particularly the areas with high rainfall. The Romney from Kent did particularly well, producing high good quality yields of wool, together with a good amount of meat on the carcass. Although improved over the generations, the Romney remains New Zealand's most popular sheep breed, with its 25 million sheep representing almost 70% of the national flock.

> *'A man of sense and education should meet a suitable companion in a wife. It is a miserable thing when the conversation can only be such as whether the mutton should be boiled or roasted, and probably a dispute about that.'*
>
> James Boswell (1740-1795)
> *Boswell's Life of Dr Johnson*

By the 1870s one main problem faced New Zealand. Whilst wool was valuable and easy to export, the meat from the sheep simply could not be consumed within the country, and they had no way of exporting the mutton to the main markets of Europe, on a long and sometimes hazardous sea voyage. As a result, most of the sheep, once past their best for wool production, were discarded, and the meat literally thrown away, or boiled up to make tallow for candles.

Frustratingly, there was high demand for mutton and lamb elsewhere. Within the burgeoning towns of the British Industrial Revolution, between 1850 and 1880, the price of meat doubled as the population soared from 28 million to 35 million. Meanwhile, in the new pastures of the southern hemisphere, in South America, Australia and New Zealand, sheep numbers grew from 230,000 in 1851 to 13 million by 1880, principally for the wool trade. With meat being wasted in the New World, and increasingly wanted in the UK, what was missing was a means of transporting the excess to the hungry mouths across the oceans.

In the 1860s-80s over 200 patents were registered for preserved meat processes. Canning of the best cuts began in 1869 in New Zealand with the rest of the carcass being boiled down for tallow. Such was the over-production of sheep, there are records of whole flocks being driven over cliffs into the sea *'...knocked on the head and thrown down a precipice as a waste product'*, as one despairing witness described it. Something had to be done.

The obvious answer was to freeze the meat, but no technology existed to do so on board a ship. In 1874 the first long-distance transport of meat took chilled beef in natural ice from the USA to the UK. Then in 1876 it seemed that a breakthrough had been made in Australia when Messrs Mort and Nicole developed a refrigeration system using pipes circulating cold brine, which were successfully installed on a ship, the *SS Northam*. However, disaster struck before the voyage began, when the pipes leaked. Eventually, a successful trans-Atlantic shipment of 80 tonnes of frozen mutton was sent in 1877-8 between San Nicolás in Argentina and Le Havre. Even so, the journey took seven months to complete, following a collision which damaged the ship. For Australia, the breakthrough came on February 2nd 1880, when the SS *Strathleven* sailed into London with 40 tonnes of frozen mutton and beef, practically all in excellent condition. What is more, it was sold at Smithfield for around 5½ d per lb; in Melbourne similar meat would have sold for 1½ d to 2d per lb. It all made economic sense. By 1881 a regular route had been established between Australia and the UK for frozen mutton.

With the unreliable technology of the day, and sailing ships taking three months to reach the UK, an extension of a refrigerated shipping service from New Zealand seemed logical, but by no means easy – indeed, many New Zealanders at the time said it simply couldn't be done.

The development of the railways in New Zealand from 1863 simplified transport to the ports, and helped to overcome the difficulties of exporting meat half way across the world, as did two enterprising businessmen, W.S. Davidson and Thomas Brydone. Simply transporting the carcasses from the new slaughterhouse on their farm to the port involved journeys by both horse and cart and steam train. They chartered a 1,320-ton sailing ship The *Dunedin*, and installed the very latest steam-powered refrigeration plant from Australia in her. Mutton carcasses were loaded and frozen on board. However, with about 600 carcasses safely frozen and stowed, disaster struck when the plant failed. Davidson and Brydone simply started again. Over a two-month period, they froze some 5,000 mutton carcasses on the ship, as well as some pork, quail, rabbit and butter.

The SS Dunedin in 1876

Eventually, on 15th February 1882, The *Dunedin* sailed. Many of the passengers who had booked to take the journey to the UK had cancelled their tickets, fearing that the refrigeration equipment would break and the crankshaft would pierce the hull; others thought the steam-driven equipment would set the sails alight. And other challenges weren't over yet. *The Dunedin* was becalmed in the tropics, and it was feared that the meat would defrost as the cold air was unable to circulate. The Captain crawled into the hold to drill more holes, which improved the efficiency of the refrigeration, the crew had to pull him out of the hold with a rope round his ankles and then resuscitate him, as he had nearly frozen to death.

After three months' sailing, The *Dunedin* reached London, with all except one mutton carcass in excellent condition. They sold at a good price. This achievement opened the floodgates to other New Zealand companies. By 1882 the *New Zealand Herald* claimed that *'Virtually, the exportation of frozen meat makes the colony of New Zealand as much a province of England, as easy a source of supply for the London market, as Yorkshire or Devon'* – a prophetic statement indeed. The entrepreneurial gamble by Davidson and Brydone had paid off.

Nevertheless, probably neither men could have foreseen the future impact of their venture. It created mass employment in New Zealand which would last until the present day, and profoundly changed the structure of farming there, together with the welfare of its people, as refrigerated exports offered a market for many family farms. Sadly, The *Dunedin* was lost on a voyage to Britain three years after her initial momentous success.

New Zealand sheep numbers peaked in 1982, at 70.3 million sheep. With a human population at that time of 3.2 million people there were 22 sheep per person. Since then, numbers of sheep have dropped, and the current ratio is nearer 7 to 1.

SOUTH AFRICA

In South Africa, mutton also has a long history. This is reflected in traditional mutton recipes such as Bobotie and Bredie (*see Recipe section*), both developed from the Malay culture, brought into the country by slaves and other immigrants since the 17th century. There remains a large Malay community around the Cape Town region today.

Colonel Robert Jacob Gordon

The Merino breed has had a large part to play in the development of South African sheep, both for wool and meat. The original Merino breed was developed in Spain, but until the end of the 18th century, the Spanish Guild of sheep owners, the Mesta, prevented any exports. However, the breed started to move outside Spain as the demand for fine wool increased with the beginnings of the Industrial Revolution. In the 1780s King Charles III of Spain donated two Spanish Merino rams and four ewes to the Dutch Government. Unfortunately, the animals didn't thrive in the cooler Dutch climate, so someone in the Dutch bureaucracy decided it would be a good idea to send them to their colony in the South African Cape, where the climate would be more akin to that of Spain.

Mutton Merino sheep in KwaZulu Natal, South Africa

Once there, the sheep were put into the care of Colonel Robert Jacob Gordon, the military commander at the Cape. Born in the Netherlands in 1743, Gordon was from a Scots family which had followed the Stuarts into exile in Holland. He had been brought up there, and joined the Dutch army. Posted to the Cape in 1774, by the Dutch East India Company, he became Garrison Captain three years later. He soon gained a reputation as kindly and cheerful, full of local knowledge, cultured and hospitable. He was a classical scholar, an avid reader, and a linguist who spoke French, Dutch and English, as well as the local languages of Hottentot and Xhosa. He warmly welcomed the odd assortment of writers, explorers and botanists who regularly visited the Cape. They must have given him the intellectual stimulation which life as a Dutch army officer would have lacked. He was a considerable explorer himself, and was responsible for naming the Orange River in South Africa after the reigning Dutch House of Orange.

The gift of wool-producing sheep in South Africa was not particularly welcomed by the farmers of the Cape, who at the time kept sheep only for mutton. So it was left to Gordon to find a home for them. He promptly sent them to an outpost in the back of beyond at Groenkloof. Gordon could have had no conception of the implications of this action, for it ultimately resulted in the development of major sheep industries in two countries. Out in the bush, the newly-arrived Merinos thrived. There were no other sheep around, and they started to reproduce as pure Merinos. Unfortunately, it seems that the Dutch had not read the small print in the documents accompanying the sheep from Spain, for two years later the Spanish demanded the flock back, on the grounds that they had left Europe, contrary to a sub-clause in the paperwork. One can just imagine the panic amongst the civil servants in The Hague, possibly along the lines of *'They want what!? .... Where are they??'*. It was fortunate for the Dutch officials that, not only had Colonel Gordon kept the flock intact and isolated, but he even had surplus pure-bred animals. So, no doubt to the huge relief of the bureaucrats in the Hague, Gordon was able to return to the Spanish the exact number of sheep originally sent, and he still had at Groenkloof the beginnings of a national flock of

Merinos for South Africa. Although it took some years for the local farmers to take to wool production, when they did, the population of Merinos expanded rapidly. They now account for 50% of the 25 million sheep in the country.

As part of the aftermath of the French Revolution, in May 1795 the United Provinces of the Netherlands became the French-influenced Batavian Republic. The British saw this alliance as a threat to their route to India, and occupied the Dutch Cape in June 1795. As Officer Commanding the Cape, it was Gordon who was required to surrender to the British. This, together with his realisation that the Netherlands had become a Republic, and his subsequent shunning by both Dutch and British society in the Cape, was all too much for the patriotic Gordon, who killed himself four months after the surrender.

Dorper sheep in Swaziland, southern Africa

Later, the SA Merino was improved by imports of other breeds, (including the delightfully named American Vermont, the Australian Wanganella and Peppin Merinos) resulting in a hardy yet efficient dual-purpose breed, producing both wool and mutton.

After WWI, South African farmers needed a breed which could be exported from the dry Karoo region, where the endemic local fat-tailed sheep would appear alien to the UK consumer. As a result, various British breeds were crossed with hardy breeds to find an exportable animal. By the 1930s a cross between the British Dorset Horn and Blackhead Persian breeds produced the Dorper (the name being part of each breed – Dor-Per). This seemed to fit the bill. Having little wool, it is described as 'easy care', meaning there was no need to annually shear the animal, and such wool as there is, is shed naturally in late spring. The breed soon spread to Australia, where it became the second-most popular breed.

Another popular, if slightly confusingly named South African cross is that between the Merino and British Dorset Horn, known as the Dormer.

Another import, confusingly called the SA Mutton Merino is in fact of German origin (Merinofleischschaf), and only appeared in South Africa in 1932. This prolific sheep can survive in poor conditions, yet produce a good quality carcass for meat.

AUSTRALIA

Australia has a lot of sheep – around 100 million. It is the largest wool-producing country in the world, accounting for over one quarter of the world's wool. It is also recognised as producing the world's highest quality woollen fibre – Australian merino wool. The development of this vast industry was possible due to the hard work and determination of one family, John and Elizabeth Macarthur.

John Macarthur, the son of a Devonian mercer and draper, and professional soldier, arrived in Sydney in 1790 with his wife Elizabeth. He was soon appointed paymaster of

Parramatta, 15 miles inland from the coast, and was allocated 100 acres of land. He received a second patch of 100 acres for being quick to farm the first, and named the combined landholding Elizabeth Farm (after his wife). In 1793 the Macarthur family moved into a permanent farm house. Soon after, Elizabeth wrote to her family in England *'Our farm, which contains from four to five hundred acres, is bounded on three sides by water. This is particularly convenient. We have at this time, about one hundred and twenty acres in wheat, all in a promising state. Our gardens, with fruit and vegetables, are extensive and produce abundantly. It is now spring and the eye is delighted with a most beautiful variegated landscape. Almonds, apricots, pear and apple trees are in full bloom.'* However, when it came to the Macarthur's move into sheep farming, this was fraught with frustration. When attempting to build a flock, all they could get hold of were *'some hairy Bengal sheep and an Irish ram'*.

John Macarthur (1767-1834)

Responding to the sheep shortage, a Captain Waterhouse took his ship *The Reliance*, in tandem with Captain Kent and his ship The *Supply*, to the South African Cape. They bought 40 local fat-tailed sheep for meat, and a further 26 Merinos. Each Captain took half the sheep. Unfortunately, none of the animals in Kent's care survived the journey, but about 10 of Waterhouse's did make it back to Sydney. Macarthur offered to buy them all, but was allocated only four Merino ewes and two rams. Critically, unlike other farmers, he did not cross-breed his Merinos, but kept them pure, which ensured that the wool was of the highest quality.

By 1800, Macarthur had started to produce enough wool to be looking for a market, so sent eight fleeces to Sir Joseph Banks in London for analysis. Banks was a hugely influential figure, President of the Royal Society, naturalist, explorer and founder of Kew Gardens to name but a few of his achievements. In 1768, he had joined Captain James Cook's expedition, to explore the uncharted lands of the South Pacific, which included a visit to Australia. Within the batch of Macarthur's fleeces was one from their Merino sheep, which Banks declared was almost as good in fineness and quality as that from King George III's briefly-held flock. In his report on the fleeces Banks posed the idea that *'could the colony* [in Australia] *produce such kinds of wools, it would be a great acquisition to our manufactory in England'*. This gave the Macarthurs added vigour in their sheep breeding endeavours. In 1801 John was sent back to England to face a court martial for duelling with his commanding officer, but was acquitted of the charge, and soon returned to Australia where he expanded his sheep farming activities. Unfortunately for him, in 1808 he was involved in the Rum Rebellion, an attempt to depose the colony's new Governor, Captain Bligh of The *Bounty*. Although he resigned his army commission, he was arrested and exiled to Britain for a further nine years. During his exile his redoubtable wife Elizabeth ran the farm. Such was her outstanding agricultural ability that the Elizabeth Macarthur Agricultural Institute opened in New South Wales in 1990.

Even the setback of exile did not deter the fiery and determined Macarthur, who in 1817 returned again to Elizabeth Farm, and together with his wife applied himself to improving their Merino sheep. In 1818 he rather despondently wrote to a friend '*My feeble attempt to introduce Merino sheep still creeps on almost unheeded and altogether unassisted. Few settlers can be induced to take the trouble requisite to improve their flocks or to subtract a few guineas from their usual expenditure – tea and rum – to purchase Spanish rams.*' Despite this, the Macarthur's efforts and determination paid off, and Macarthur is generally credited with being the founding father of the sheep industry in Australia. After the success with wool Merinos, the Australian sheep industry moved into sheep meat production towards the end of the 19th century, boosted by the development of refrigerated shipping.

> *'She took the leg of mutton and held it high above her, as though it were the head of John the Baptist on a platter'*
>
> W. Somerset Maugham (1874-1965)
> *Of Human Bondage*

And the source of those original South African Merino sheep sent to Australia? The sea captains bought them from Mrs Gordon, the widow of Colonel Gordon who had sent the original diplomatic gift of the small Spanish flock of Merinos out of harm's way to Groenkloof. After the Colonel's death, his widow was disposing of his assets just as the Australian sea captains came looking for sheep. As the suicide of Gordon was indirectly as a result of the French Revolution, maybe the Australians should be grateful to the likes of Robespierre for their sheep industry?

USA

The first domesticated sheep in the US were brought there by the Spanish, and have developed into the Navajo Churro which is the oldest breed of sheep in the U.S. Like many other countries in the New World, the modern sheep industry was built on British breeds, and a major industry it was too.

The portrayal of cattle, cowboys and Indians is well-known through Hollywood films, but in fact it was the shepherds of the USA who, although less glamorous, were at least as important as the cowboys. As ranching spread westwards, the first livestock into a new settled area was normally the sheep, and many hundreds of thousands were driven west in the mid-19th century.

In New Mexico the Apache and Navajo Indians were very practised at stealing sheep, which by the mid-1800s resulted in some 30,000 sheep a year being stolen from the settler farmers. In order to escape with their booty, the Apaches developed an ingenious way of moving the sheep quickly. The strongest sheep were lashed together in pairs, and these were then arranged on the outside of the flock, and tied end to end, to form a perimeter, enclosing the weaker animals in the middle. In 1863 the US Government decided to put a stop to this raiding, and sent in the army under Colonel Kit Carson and General James H. Carleton. Carson proceeded to operate a 'scorched earth' policy, destroying the Native Americans' means of livelihood, including the slaughter of many thousands of their sheep.

A writer from Ohio in 1910 considered British Downland breeds to produce the best mutton and lamb, particularly Shropshires, Southdowns, Hampshires and Dorsets. In fact the writer's favourite was the Shropshire. *'These sheep have taken the firmest hold of any of the mutton breeds in this country and Canada'* he wrote. He simply could not find fault with them and went on to praise their meat, wool, hardiness and ability to thrive in almost any climate, and the good mothering qualities of the ewes. He finally notes that the *'Hampshires are, I think, hardly as widely distributed as the Shropshires or the Southdowns, in this country, though they are very popular in the English colonies.'* Another glowing testimonial from William Phillips recorded in *Hints for American Husbandmen* of 1827 concluded *'To the excellence of the Southdown mutton, I can with pleasure testify, as well as several gentlemen whose judgement of the luxuries of the table, will not be doubted by those who know them – They were so well pleased with it, that they cordially gave the annexed certificate of their opinion of the saddle of an imported wether, which was a present to Mr David Lewis, who kept it upon his farm, on common pasture, without grain or any particular attention, and it was the finest saddle of mutton, in appearance, delicacy and flavour, I ever saw or tasted. It was greatly admired by many others. Their thriving properties, and tendency to become fat, are very important recommendations. I remain, with much esteem, Yours, William Phillips.'*

More about UK sheep breeds later.

Sheep production in the USA has declined from 50 million head in 1940 to 25 million in 2012. It seems the decline of mutton in the United States can be traced back to the tinned mutton sent overseas with the GI's during WWII. According to Erica Rosa of the Livestock Marketing Information Centre in Colorado *'They hated it, and when they came home they said they never wanted to see lamb or mutton on the table again.'* Poor cooking techniques and inadequate distribution have also hurt uptake of mutton in the US, she said.

Sheep and the Landscape

By the nineteenth century, UK sheep farming had evolved into three main types – extensive hill, grass downs and more intensive mixed lowland farms.

SHEEP ON THE HILLS AND MOUNTAINS

With little farming alternative to keeping sheep in the hills and mountain areas of the UK, specialist breeds had developed which survived the harsh conditions. Large numbers were kept in the hills and uplands of Britain, where they were stocked at very low density, often several acres per sheep. From this system, ewes produced lambs for a few years before they were sent to lower altitudes and an easier life in order to produce a couple more crops of lambs before being sold as mutton. Some of the lambs born on the hills were kept as wethers (castrated males) for a few years, supplying the farmer with a wool crop every year until they were sold as wether mutton. The rest of the lambs were sold to farms in the lower altitudes for breeding or fattening. Some ewes were sold off each autumn as ewe mutton.

Many of us, walking in the rolling hills of upland Britain, may imagine that we are enjoying glorious scenery which has evolved naturally to become the grass or heather-covered expanses which we see today. Stone walls or fences divide the view into interesting patterns, and sheep are often seen grazing, apparently at will.

However, looks deceive. This is a far from natural landscape. Rather it is one which is almost entirely man-made as a result of systematic grazing of cattle and sheep. Without this control, our best-loved landscapes would soon return to scrub and eventually to forest. Some people believe we should allow these areas to return to the true wild forest. However, not only would that deprive walkers of the very landscapes they enjoy, and reduce overall food production on our crowded islands, but it would also disrupt a system of managing the national sheep flock which has taken centuries to develop. Just as importantly, it would deprive many families of their livelihoods, and would undoubtedly result in depopulation, as the local population could no longer sustain a living without sheep.

Nevertheless, these often-windswept, cold and wet upland areas of Britain are very difficult to manage. Tough grasses, wild herbs and heathers are the only cropping alternatives to trees. Indeed, above certain altitudes, even hardy pines are unable to survive. Cattle find it difficult to live in the tops of hills and mountains. Even many breeds of sheep would not survive, and only careful breeding over many hundreds of years has ensured that we can produce any food at all from these upland areas.

Above: Typical mountain heft country
Opposite page: Clun Forest sheep in the rolling hills of the Clun valley, Shropshire

HEFTS AND HIRSELS

On the sweeping hills of Britain, such as in the Lake District, with grassland uninterrupted by walls or fences, sheep appear to be grazing entirely freely over vast areas. Again, this is a deception.

Over many centuries, in the unfenced uplands, sheep have learned the rather useful trick of having a home area from which they generally do not stray. This area is known in many parts of the north as a heft, and the ability of a family of sheep to keep within its open boundary is known as hefting or heafing. The word 'heft' is from the Old Norse word 'hefda' which means 'to acquire by right or prescription'. Indeed, some hefted flocks in areas such as Cumbria may go back to the time of the Viking invaders, who were the first to successfully farm these inhospitable areas of northern England. The Welsh word for hefted sheep is 'cynefin' (pronounced kinevin) meaning sheep 'with their own habitat'. In Wales, these areas are also known in English as Sheep-walks or Liberties.

The development of this system allows different farmers in an extensive landscape such as moorland to graze their sheep in different areas without the need for fences. Each ewe remains within her particular area, and returns there of her own volition after lambing

A Cumbrian upland sheep farm

or from other temporary periods away. Such behaviour is passed from ewe to lamb, much as African elephants remember the location of water sources through the generations. Indeed survival of the ewe and her lambs will depend entirely on the mother's knowledge of her heft. She will know where to go to find essential nutrition, such as the protein-rich seaonal new shoots of particular grasses or sedges, she will know safe routes across streams or bogs, and where to find enough shelter to survive the harshest of weather.

Traditionally, the area of open hillside for which a shepherd was responsible is a 'hirsel' or 'herding', each of which carries around 600-700 sheep. Each hirsel will contain a number of hefts, depending on the terrain. So, a heft is an area which defines a sheep group's territory, whereas a hirsel is a grouping of hefts, denoting a shepherd's area of responsibility. Depending on the quality of the grazing, the area of a hirsel may vary between one and five thousand acres, with each ewe needing between one and ten acres.

The boundaries are known by the sheep. Some old wether sheep, who knew the area well, would be kept to guard the hirsel boundaries from neighbouring flocks.

The practice of grazing hefted sheep on unfenced land is an ancient one, which requires minimal shepherding. The system had become more widespread in England after the Black Death in the 14th century. The huge losses of population due to the plague resulted in acute labour shortages, and therefore a system which required minimal labour was a major advantage.

Lambs learn all they need to know about the area of their heft from their mothers. It is therefore a crisis when, at times of widespread sheep disease (such as Foot and Mouth), entire flocks, and particularly the ewes, are removed from hillsides, and this 'local knowledge' is lost. Re-hefting sheep in areas which have lost entire sheep populations is a difficult, expensive and time-consuming process, even supposing sufficient numbers of suitable breeds of sheep are available. This was a problem in Cumbria after the Foot and Mouth outbreak of 2001, when many flocks were destroyed. When upland sheep farms are sold, it is important that the sheep are sold with the farm in order to keep knowledge of the local environment within the flock.

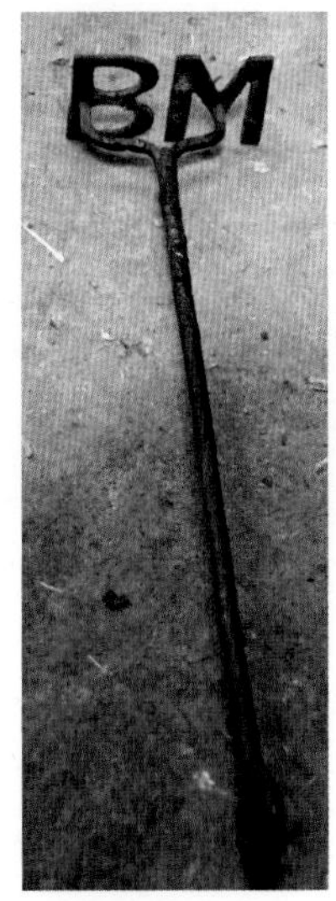

Sheep marker with farmer's initials

Of course, from time to time a few of these unfenced sheep will wander out of their heft. So, how do farmers know their sheep from their neighbours? They use a simple marking technique, used for centuries, either a simple design, or, more often, the owner's initials. A metal tool with the design on the end, like a branding iron *(right),* is dipped into tar, or today a proprietary colour marker. The ears are also used to identify the sheep. Today there are ear tags, which are required by law to identify sheep. Before, there were cuts in the ears, each farmer having his own pattern.

In 1878 the *Globe* magazine ran an article explaining how farming neighbours sorted out sheep when they strayed 'out of heft'. *'On November 7th the autumn gathering of the moorland shepherds of the north of England took place in the village of Saltersbrook, Yorkshire, and as an indication of the value of such meetings to farmers, it may be stated that no fewer than 121 strayed sheep were returned to their rightful owners. In the spring the farmers turn out immense flocks, sometimes numbering thousands, to nip the tender but scant herbage which the moors furnish. These sheep will wander about the whole of the summer, and it is the shepherds' duty to see that they do not stray. Occasionally animals will wander miles from the parent flock, to be picked up and kept by other shepherds until 'meeting time' comes round, when they are enabled by the marks stamped on their coats to return them.'*

A geographical shift in sheep production between 1900 and the Second World War had a significant impact on the visual landscape of Britain. As mixed farming with both sheep and crops died out, so sheep numbers became concentrated in the western and northern parts of the UK. Between 1900 and 1930, sheep populations declined by over 40% in 14 southern and eastern English counties, whilst numbers increased by over 40% in two Welsh and three Scottish counties. In many of the areas where sheep populations fell, downland and general mixed farming gave way to the plough and increasingly intensive arable farming. Exceptions to the rush to arable in southern England included Kent, where even in 1944, the county still boasted over 455,000 sheep due to its extensive marshes, where little else could be farmed. Numbers here fell by under 20% from 1900 to 1930.

Marking sheep

HILLS, TICKS, SHEEP, PEOPLE AND GROUSE

Another reason for hill walkers to be grateful to sheep concerns ticks. The tick found in the uplands is happy to feed on people, sheep or grouse, it seems not to mind which. The presence of sheep on the hills acts as a magnet to the ticks which reduces the number of hungry insects looking for a tasty lunch from a passing hill walker. Grouse-shooting businesses also appreciate the magnetic effect of the sheep on ticks, as it also keeps them off the grouse, which can be badly affected by the parasites.

Sheep on the Downs

The modern Downland breeds of Southdown, Shropshire, Oxford, Hampshire and Dorset are mostly creations of the 19th century, started, as we shall see, by the man who transformed the Southdown into the world's most popular meat-producing sheep. The downs themselves were originally the preserve of sheep which were '... *tall, light and narrow in the carcass, with a white face and shanks.*' They were kept mostly for wool, and as providers of manure. Until the Second World War the mostly chalk downlands of southern England were considered useful only for sheep grazing, as they had generally thin, infertile soils. When Britain faced the threat of starvation in 1939, vast areas of land, even the downs, were ploughed up to increase grain production. After this, combined with the introduction of chemical fertilisers, the need for sheep on the downs disappeared, and even the redoubtable Southdown's numbers soon dwindled.

Sheep on Lowland Arable Farms

During the 18th century, the main reason for keeping sheep, at least according to Thomas Davis of Wiltshire, writing at the turn of the 19th century, was the production of manure to fertilise crops *'The first and principle purpose [of keeping sheep] is undoubtedly the dung of the sheep-fold, and the second is wool.'* The improvement of the carcass was not considered a primary object. This was about to change dramatically.

Whilst the majority of sheep were kept on the hills and mountains of Wales, Scotland and northern England, many were also living on arable farms in lowland areas. This was due to the famous 'Four-course Rotation', which was a sustainable system of farming which maintained the fertility in the soil through the enclosure of sheep in pens, which were moved across the large open fields on a regular basis. This in turn had been made possible by the development of fodder in the form of higher quality root crops, such as turnips and swedes, which when fed to sheep produced improved levels of nutrition for the animals and their rapid growth. The rotational system of farming uses different crops on the same land in consecutive years, rather than the single crop monoculture which we generally see today. The classic Norfolk Four-course Rotation consisted of a root crop (such as turnip or swede), followed by barley, then a seed crop (often clover and grass), followed by a wheat crop. In terms of cropping, it is the cereals which the farmer produced for selling, which were the primary purpose of this system. Root crops were grown to feed the sheep, which as well as fertilising the soil, also compacted the lighter sandy soils of areas such as East Anglia for sowing the subsequent barley crop.

The sheep would eat the green leaves (the 'tops') of the root crops as well as the root itself. In an era when there was no artificial nitrogen fertiliser, the soil was 'fed' to produce the crops in two ways – sheep manure and a clover crop, which 'fixed' nitrogen from the air into the soil. This ensured both good soil fertility and high organic matter levels. Good levels of organic matter are essential for good soil structure and moisture-holding capacity.

Sheep eating root crop, Wales, controlled by an electric fence

Young sheep, often from the hills of Wales and Scotland, were brought into the lowland arable farms for a few months, helping to maintain soil nutrients, and then fattened quickly and sold as year-old lambs or older wether mutton into the markets and butchers of the surrounding towns and villages.

Sometimes permanent breeding flocks of sheep were kept within the arable rotations. By keeping a permanent flock of sheep the farmer could also benefit from a wool crop each year from the ewes, in addition to fattening the lambs within a year. As the ewes became too old to breed, they were sold as ewe mutton.

In 1906, J. E. Vincent wrote of his observations of 'folding' sheep on arable fields *'Substantially speaking, the Berkshire Downs are not grazed at all, although it may be conjectured that, if they were, the mutton would be passing excellent. Our Berkshire sheep are not of the hill-climbing type, and they are hardly ever allowed to graze at large. Except along the roads, which they spoil abominably with their cloven hoofs when they are driven from place to place, they take practically no exercise. The system is to pack them on good feed – grass, clover, turnips, or what you will – practically as close as possible, until they have eaten it bare, and then to pass them on to the next plot. Some years ago, for example, I had a rank after-math of about an acre and a half, which as a favour to me a farmer neighbour permitted his sheep to eat. He hurdled the little area off into two equal plots, put 300 sheep into one of them for one day and night, and to the next for the same time, and behold, every vestige of the grass had vanished. Had they all lain down simultaneously, no ground to speak of would have been visible. That is the way we feed sheep hereabouts, and one rarely sees the Downs dotted with sheep singly or in groups.*

> *"Go further away from the leg of mutton, or you'll be picking it, I know,' said Miss Sally.'*
>
> Charles Dickens (1812-1870)
> *The Old Curiosity Shop*

Herdwick flock, Wastwater, Cumbria

The Berkshire sheep lives between hurdles, and seldom knows freedom from the day when he or she is born in the sheltered lambing-yard, to that on which the Saxon sheep is converted into the French mutton.'

One agriculturalist, Professor John Wrightson, writing just before the First World War, measured the benefit on the output of an arable farm of keeping sheep in pens. He compared the yields of barley, hay and wheat with and without the use of sheep to fertilise the soil. He found yields of both barley and wheat increased 67%, and hay increased three-fold by using the sheep to fertilise the soil.

On some arable farms, a 'flying flock' (not what it sounds like) would be used, which meant buying older ewes from the hills every year, producing a lamb from them, then selling them fat as ewe mutton some weeks or months after the lamb was weaned. The advantage of this system was that it saved costs in keeping them throughout the year. However, these farmers did not selectively breed to steadily improve their flocks each year, so their returns from sheep depended almost entirely on buying good quality, healthy ewes every year.

There were many combinations and systems of keeping arable sheep, each dependent on a range of factors including the nature of the soils and the climate on the farm, as well as the farmer's own stockmanship or willingness to employ a shepherd.

The various systems of sheep farming across the country meant that mutton became available from different regions in different seasons, as a Ministry of Agriculture publication detailing mutton supplies to London's Smithfield Market in 1930 showed. From November to May came 'root-fed sheep from upland areas, mainly in the south and east of England'; from October to June was the season for animals from Scotland and the north of England; a few Irish sheep arrived via Birkenhead from Christmas to May, and from June to September came animals from South West England, Lincolnshire and Yorkshire, and from the Romney and Pevensey marshes in Kent.

'By my Christendom
So I were out of prison, and kept sheep,
I should be merry as the day is long.'

William Shakespeare (1564–1616)
King John

Through the various farming systems both on the hills, downs and in the lowlands, lambs, wether mutton and mutton ewes were produced until the middle of the 20th century, when farming began to change dramatically.

Shepherding

'The sheep has one main ambition in life, and that is to die.'
Common saying amongst shepherds

There is something rather special about shepherds, unlike any other branch of farming. Since Biblical times they have been idealised in the communal psyche. Writers over the centuries have romanticised the bucolic nature of the shepherd's life. Shakespeare saw the connection between the apparently innocent and carefree life of the shepherd and the world-weary life of danger and intrigue lived by kings, in Henry VI part III:

Gives not the hawthorn bush a sweeter shade
To shepherds, looking on their silly sheep,
Than doth a rich embroidered canopy
To kings that fear their subjects' treachery?
O, yes, it doth; a thousand-fold it doth.
And to conclude – the shepherd's homely curds,
His cold, thin drink out of his leather bottle,
His wonted sleep under a fresh tree's shade,
All which secure and sweetly he enjoys,
Is far beyond a prince's delicates,
His viands sparkling in a golden cup,
His body couched in curious bed,
When care, mistrust, and treason wait on him.

The urban view of the shepherd was often idealised in art and literature. Written with some envy of a life in the open air, was one anonymous mid-17th century English rhyme entitled *The Jolly Shepherd* which epitomised this romantic pastoral view. It was put to music in the 1930s by Peter Warlock:

The life of the shepherd is void of all care,
With his bag and his bottle, he maketh good fare;
He ruffles, he shuffles in all extreme wind,
His flock sometimes before him and sometimes behind.
He hath yon green meadow to walk in at will,
With a pair of fine bagpipes upon a green hill.

Later, in the late 18th century, William Blake included a short poem about the shepherd in his collection *Songs of Innocence*, although here he is calling on the strong Christian connection with the Good Shepherd and his innocent flock.

How sweet is the Shepherd's sweet lot!
From the morn to the evening he strays;
He shall follow his sheep all the day,
And his tongue shall be filled with praise.
For he hears the lamb's innocent call,
And he hears the ewe's tender reply;
He is watchful while they are in peace,
For they know when their Shepherd is nigh.

'I look at the sunlight coming in at the open door through the porch, and there I see a stray sheep – I don't mean a sinner, but mutton – half making up his mind to come into the church.'

Charles Dickens (1812-1870)
David Copperfield

Shepherds were often considered to be slightly apart from the rest of the community: by the nature of their work, they lived solitary lives. W.H. Hudson recorded a conversation with a shepherd in 1910.

'It is lonesome with the flock on the downs; more so in the cold and wet weather, when you perhaps don't see a person all day – on some days not even at a distance, much less to speak to.'

Indeed, when shepherds died, they were often buried with a piece of lamb's wool between their fingers – to explain why, as a shepherd, they had been unable to regularly attend church services – the needs of their sheep being always paramount.

'Oh, Lord, why did you make Cwm Pennant so beautiful
And the life of the old shepherd so short?'

Translation of lines by Welsh poet
Eifion Wyn (1867-1926)

This custom is described in some old verses from Wiltshire which ran:

Over the downs at lambing time
The bells of a Sunday call;
Whether or no I must bide from church
With my ewes and the lambs and all.
Fine folk passing shake their heads,
Good folk's kind hearts grieve,
I'd like to be doing my bit of praise
If my ewes would give me leave.
But He that took on Him shepherd's job
Still walks with my flock and me,
Every Sunday at lambing time
I can say my prayer at His knee.
And when my time comes place in my hand
A lock of wool from my sheep -
(Bury me where the down shall watch
Mother-like o'er my sleep) -
And when I come to the Gate of Heaven
Peter will not refuse
To let me in, though I stayed from church
Because of my lambing ewes.

In Biblical times, the Jews considered shepherds to be unclean, and unable to observe certain religious rituals due to their nomadic lifestyle. Their presence as the first at the nativity symbolises their importance and 'special' spiritual status. It is not hard to see why shepherds have often been associated with a spiritual life, not only through the obvious Christian connotations. Their lives were lived close to nature, with something of the hermit about their periods of solitude. The Rev. John Wilson, editor of the extraordinary four volume work of 1849 the *Rural Cyclopedia*, obviously understood the parallels between the shepherd's and the spiritual life.

He wrote in some awe of a Scots shepherd by the name of Hogg, who worked near Ettrick in the Borders *'A remarkable instance of how the tending of flocks may warm the heart and fire the genius and light up the whole intellect into a luminary; and, in spite of all the doubtfulness and darkness of his higher speculations, even he spake of the mountain shepherd, seeing God in the clouds, and being almost of necessity an intensely religious man. 'The daily feeling naturally impressed on the shepherd's mind' said he, 'that all his comforts are, so entirely in the hand of Him that rules the elements, contributes not a little to that firm spirit of devotion for which the Scottish shepherd is so distinguished'.*

Wilson continued by considering the fate of shepherds caught at the mercy of the elements through violent storms in their native glens *'There they are left to the protection of heaven, and they know and feel it. Throughout all the wild vicissitudes of nature, they have no hope of any assistance from man, but are conversant with the Almighty alone.'* Wilson obviously had shared the experience of these storms with the shepherds high in the hills, as he wrote after the passing of the storms that the shepherds *'... rise from their devotions with their spirits cheered and their confidence renewed, and go to sleep with an exaltation of mind of which kings and conquerors have no share... There we lived, as it were, inmates of the cloud and of the storm; but we stood in a relationship to the Ruler of these that neither time nor eternity could efface.'*

Whilst it is easy to romanticise the shepherd, we should not forget the reality, which was a physically hard and demanding way of life, for little financial reward, long working hours in all weathers, often living alone with the flock. These demands made the character of the shepherd a critical element in the success of a sheep farm.

Statue of shepherd, sheepdog and sheep, Royal Welsh Showground, Builth Wells

In Medieval times, the high value of the sheep flock made the shepherd one of the most important of farm servants. He was required to be a patient man, *'not overhasty,'* never to be absent without leave at *'fairs, markets, wrestling-matches, wakes, or in the tavern,'* and always to sleep in the fold together with his dog. Later writers even insist on the value of lameness in the shepherd, as a lame man was unlikely to overdrive his sheep. Yet throughout the nineteenth century, the shepherd's traditional calm, dignity and intelligence made them the most respected, independent and trusted of agricultural workers.

John Little wrote in 1815 on the wider qualities needed to be a good upland shepherd. *'The qualification required in taking care of a hirsel,* [flock] *is not in running, hounding, and training dogs, or in performing a day's work of any other kind; but to direct them according to the soil, climate, and situation of the farm, in such a manner as to obtain the greatest quantity of food at all seasons of the year. Their health and comfort should be carefully looked after by the shepherd; and if his exertions are made with judgment, they are of very great consequence to the farmer. It is not by walking much, and doing a great deal, that a shepherd is a good one, but it is knowing where to walk so as to disturb the sheep the least, and by doing at the time whatever is necessary to be done.'*

One hundred years later, in 1913, John Robson writes *'The hill shepherd holds a unique position amongst hired men. Practically his own master, he is never interfered with so long as he does his duty; he has the sole charge of stock worth £2,000 to £3,000 [£200,000 to £300,000 in today's values], and the trust reposed in him is seldom abused.*

He has no hours of labour; at some seasons he works from daylight till dark, at others he lives the life of a gentleman, and enjoys himself as he feels inclined, provided always that he is within reach of his hirsel should he be required. The shepherd must be a careful, regular man, as regularity is one of his best attributes, and a rough, careless man amongst sheep does incalculable harm. The shepherd and his dog are inseparable, but the less the latter is in evidence the better, for unless when being gathered for sortings, or in tup time, it is wonderful how little dogging is required.'

Medicine horn

In his recollections from a late Victorian childhood, Fred Archer reflects the high degree of respect given to shepherds by colleagues on the farm in his description of Cotswold shepherd Corbisley *'The old shepherd, as all the other men and boys on the farm called him, was one of nature's gentlemen, a man living very close to the soil and all living things except his fellow men. He only mixed at busy times; otherwise his life was lonely. It was considered an honour to help him out at his work and we boys looked upon him as something much more than a farm worker. There was something very stable about him and he seemed to have an inner peace and serenity which he had cultivated over the years. He was more or less his own boss over the sheep and his word was taken as law both by the other workers and usually by his employers.'*

Archer goes on to describe Shepherd Corbisley's appearance: *'To be in his company, a jolly man with an infectious laugh, was my ambition at holiday times from school. He dressed for his job among sheep. His cord trousers were known as fall-fronted or broad falls, fastened up the sides like breeches with buttons. We called them tailboard front. He wore a corduroy waistcoat with lots of pockets, one for his watch; this was an old turnip watch, almost as big as a small clock. His thick silver watch chain had a golden sovereign on it. One pocket was for his tobacco tin and so on. In the other no doubt would be a tin of Stockholm tar and some raddle [for marking the sheep]. His coat – when he wore it – was of dark-grey fustian, a hard-wearing cloth of heavy weft. I never saw him in anything else but an Oxford shirt with a blue stripe in it. Just below his knees he wore some leather straps called yorks. When I asked him what they were for he said, 'Oi, to kip the dust out of me eyes.' But I found out that their main purpose was to give the trousers a little fullness at the knee, and when he was sweating in the summertime and his clothes stuck to his body this would prevent his broad leather braces pulling the buttons off his trousers. At lambing time he wore something like a pinafore frock made of burden or sacking tied with binder twine around his waist. When he wasn't smoking it, he stuck his clay pipe under the band of his battered trilby; and his crook (which I still use) completed his make-up. Well-dubbined hobnail boots, of course. On Sundays when he occasionally came to chapel I thought he*

looked a little like the Aga Khan; his features were distinguished.'

Despite the hardships, living and working in such natural surroundings meant that the shepherd had an intimate knowledge of his environment, and its changing pattern through the seasons. In 1916, W.H. Hudson wrote of the early life of shepherd Caleb near Salisbury. *'Caleb's shepherding began in childhood; at all events he had his first experience of it at that time. Many an old shepherd, whose father was shepherd before him, has told me that he began to go with the flock very early in life, when he was no more than ten to twelve years of age. Caleb remembered being put in charge of his father's flock at the tender age of six. It was a new and wonderful experience, and made so vivid and lasting an impression on his mind that now, when he is past eighty, he speaks of it very feelingly as of something which happened yesterday.'*

Particular times of the year were busier than others for the shepherd, such as at lambing and shearing, and this required shepherds to work very long hours. Many shepherds lived in huts or caravans close to the animals, especially at lambing time, with little in the way of creature comforts or human contact. Thomas Hardy described such a hut in his Wessex novel *Far From the Madding Crowd* in 1874. *'The inside of the hut, as it now presented itself, was cosy and alluring, and the scarlet handful of fire in addition to the candle, reflected its own genial colour upon whatever it could reach, flung associations of enjoyment even over utensils and tools. In the corner stood the sheep-crook, and along a shelf at one side were ranged bottles and canisters of the simple preparations pertaining to ovine surgery and physic; spirits of wine, turpentine, tar, magnesia, ginger, and castor oil being the chief. On a triangular shelf across the corner stood bread, bacon, cheese and a cup for ale or cider, which was supplied from a flagon beneath. Beside the provisions lay the flute, whose notes had lately been called forth by the lonely watcher to beguile a tedious hour.*

Traditional shepherds' caravans in Shropshire and Somerset

The house was ventilated by two round holes, like the lights of a ship's cabin, with wood slides.'

Even with modern conveniences, many of today's sheep farmers would recognise the exhaustion of waking all hours, particularly at lambing time, as A.G. Street wrote of one shepherd in 1946 *'He woke at five a.m. He had done this every morning for almost as long as he could remember, winter and summer, Sundays and weekdays; and even forced himself to obey the new-fangled single and double summertime, that he hated and despised as something immoral. But if his sheep, or rather his master's sheep had to be tended, according to the altered clock, he, their shepherd, must fit his life to match theirs.'*

Mr Roper at the Coronation Pageant in Kington, Herefordshire, 22 June 1911

The dedication needed by generations of shepherds has continued into modern times. In Ronald Blythe's 1969 story of an English village 'Akenfield' in Suffolk, he records the story of a young shepherd, Anthony Summer, who was aged 23 at that time, and looked after 500 ewes. Even for a young man, his enthusiasm and pride were evident, particularly at lambing time *'I don't have to help a great deal with the births, only be there. This is most important. I never leave the flock then, I am with them all the time. I only call the vet if there is a big mishap, such as the womb coming out. I take each lamb away from its mother and do all the little odds and ends, like. You can't raise every lamb that is born, there must be some loss. It's easy on the farm against what it used to be. The old men wore their bodies to death but we only wear out a few machines. We all get on well together on the farm. Ages don't count. There is an old shepherd who still works here part time and he has helped me a lot. He lends me books and tells me many things. The young men are very fond of him because he is so interesting.'*

The sense of wonder and care of a shepherd remains to the present day. In his book about his life as a shepherd, modern shepherd David Kennard writes: *'Every shepherd must feel the same. And it doesn't matter how often I see it. Those first lambs of the year are something to be savoured. To watch how, within a few minutes of their birth, through trial, error and some*

> *'A shadow in his life had always been that his flock ended in mutton – that a day came and found every shepherd an arrant traitor to his defenceless sheep.'*
>
> Thomas Hardy (1840-1928)
> *Far from the Madding Crowd*

amazing instinct of survival, they've managed to find their mother's milk and suckle is a thing of wonder. In the darkness tonight, I witnessed it once more. Within five minutes each lamb had found the teat and, judging by the soon rounded bellies, had taken a half pint of milk from their mother's full-to-bursting udder.'

Not always were the shepherds' reputations entirely complimentary. For some reason those of Salisbury Plain had a reputation for being lazy, although it also seems they could display a stinging wit. Adelaide Gosset wrote of one encounter with such a shepherd in 1910 *'A gentleman saw one of them lying down near his sheep, and after talking with him for some time said: 'Well, my man, I do think you are as you are described; nevertheless here's a shilling for you.' To which the man replied 'Thank ye kindly, sir, but will ye jist get off your horse and slip it in my pocket.''*

Shepherding may have declined in relative economic importance, but the way of life continues in our sayings, such as *Red sky at night, Shepherd's delight; Red sky in the morning, Shepherd's warning*; or less familiar now in its original form: *If St Swithin's day (15th July) be wet, Thrice thirty days shall clouds their fleeces wet*; and now almost forgotten is: *A Leap Year is never a good sheep year.*

Left: Counting sheep by running them through a counting-pen, mid-Wales

Counting Sheep

If you count sheep to get to sleep, how do you count them? Almost certainly, one, two, three ….? Well that's not the way shepherds have counted across the United Kingdom for many hundreds of years. They used an ancient system, generally known as 'Yan, Tan, Tethera'. In areas such as Cumbria, the tradition is said to still survive. The Yan Tan Tethera system was also used for counting stitches in knitting.

The words are thought to derive from a Brythonic Celtic language, although modern Welsh uses some different numbers today for counting. The names used for each number vary according to region, and in areas such as Cumbria or the Yorkshire Dales there were even variations between valleys. One historian records over 100 variations of the words. The numbering system is said to have survived because it can be said much faster than 'one, two, three...' and when you're counting a lot of fast moving sheep, you need to count quickly. That may appear a strange statement when many of the words of Yan Tan Tethera are actually longer than one, two, three, but try saying the words out loud. They seem to slip off the tongue so much easier. Some examples from across the country for counting sheep from one to twenty are:

	Lincolnshire	**West Country**	**Lake District**
1	Yan	Hant	Yan
2	Tan	Tant	tyan
3	Tethera	Tothery	tethera
4	Pethera	Forthery	methera
5	Pimp	Fant	Pimp
6	Sethera	Sahny	sethera
7	Methera	Dahny	Lettera
8	Hovera	Downy	Hovera
9	Covera	Dominy	Dovera
10	Dik	Dik	Dick
11	Yan-a-dik	Haindik	Yan Dick
12	Tan-a-dik	Taindik	Tyan Dick
13	Tethera-dik	Totherydik	Tethera Dick
14	Pethera-dik	Fotherydik	Methera Dick
15	Bumfit	Jiggen	Bumfit
16	Yan-a-bumfit	Hain Jiggen	Yan-a-Bumfit
17	Tan-a-bumfit	Tain Jiggen	Tyan-a Bumfit
18	Tethera-bumfit	TotherJiggen	Tethera-Bumfit
19	Pethera-bumfit	FotherJiggen	Methera-Bumfit
20	Figgot	Full Score	Giggot

Above: A group of Welsh Mule ewes with lambs

The traditional sheep counting systems, like some other Celtic numbering systems, are generally based on the number twenty (vigesimal), and lack words to describe numbers above twenty. In counting to twenty, the literal English translation would be one, two, three, four, five, six, seven, eight, nine, ten, one-ten, two-ten, three-ten, four-ten, fifteen, one-fifteen, two-fifteen, three-fifteen, four-fifteen, twenty. For a shepherd counting a large flock of sheep, he would count in multiples of twenty (a score), counting each multiple by dropping a small stone into his pocket, making a mark on the ground, or moving his finger to another crooove on his crook. So, if he had five pebbles in his pocket by the end of the count, then he had 100 sheep. The counting system using 20 is older than our familiar decimal system based on 10. Old folk songs celebrate this ancient counting method, such as the *The Lincolnshire Shepherd*:

Yan, tan, tethera, tethera, pethera, pimp.
Yon owd yowe's far-welted, and this yowe's got a limp
Sethera, methera, hovera, and covera up to dik,
Aye, we can deal wi' 'em all, and wheer's me crook and stick?

There is even evidence that a similar counting system was being used just before the First World War in the Appalachian Mountains of the USA (een, teen, tuther, futher, fipps, suther, luther, uther, duther dix...)[12] Then again, there is some suggestion that the 'Hickory, Dickory Dock' from the Mouse ran up the clock nursery rhyme is 8,9,10 from a similar counting system.

A hybrid counting system was recorded in Sussex in 1907 by J. Bateman. He recalls as a young man standing by the farmer as he counted his sheep. The boy's job was to remember the number of twenties. The old man counted two animals at a time *'One therum, twotherum, cockerum, qutherum, setherum, shatherum, wineberry, wagtail, tarrydiddle, den.'*

12 Celtic Folklore Cooking by Joanne Asala, Llewellyn Worldwide, 1998

'Mr Swiveller, who was perfectly ravenous, and had had, all night, amazingly distinct and consistent dreams of mutton chops, double stout, and similar delicacies, felt even the weak tea and dry toast such irresistible temptations, that he consented to eat and drink on one condition.'

Charles Dickens (1812-1870)
The Old Curiosity Shop

Names of Sheep

Sheep production is an etymologist's delight, although probably a complete mystery to the layman. Names not only vary between ages and sexes of sheep, and whether the males still have all the breeding equipment they were born with, but the names also change by region of the UK.

The word 'Sheep' unusually, refers to one or many animals. A group of sheep is normally called a flock, but can also be a mob, down, drift, drove, fold or parcel. Adult female sheep are known as ewes, or in some regions, yows; intact males are rams or regionally tups; castrated males are wethers; and the youngest sheep are lambs. A number of other terms are used for each of the various life stages of sheep, such as lambing, shearing, and old age. This enables an exact description of animals to be used when buying or selling them. However, as nothing is straightforward, there are many regional differences both of the words used, and even definitions of the same word.

Examples of the variety of names for sheep:

From birth:
Female lamb: *Ewe lamb, cliver, or chilver lamb*
Male lamb: *Ram lamb or tup lamb*
Castrated male lamb: *wether or wedder lamb*

Traditionally, after lamb sales in July to September, or after Christmas:
Ewe lambs and wether lambs become *ewe and wether hoggets, hogs or tegs,* or in the Midlands and into Wales, *theaves.*
Ram lambs keep that name until after shearing the following spring.

After first shearing:
Ram lambs become *shearling rams* or *wethers.*
In the north, *shearling ewe lambs* for breeding become *gimmers*, until their first lambs are weaned.
Yearlings are lambs over a year of age.

Older sheep:
Later in their lives, sheep are classified according to the number of times they have been sheared, the number of teeth they have, or in the case of ewes, the number of crops of lambs they have had.

Teeth

Sheep can be defined in terms of their teeth:
There are two types of teeth in sheep – Molars (upper and lower grinding teeth) and Incisors (cutting front teeth in lower jaws only).

Through a sheep's life these teeth change, and this can define the animal:
A lamb has 8 milk incisors (represented as oooooooo)
At 1 year, 3 months the centre pair drop out and are replaced by permanent incisors – a 'two tooth'. (oooOOooo)
At 1 year 9 months, the second pair of incisors change –a 'four tooth' (ooOOOOoo)
At 2 years 3 months the 3rd pair change – 'six toothed' (oOOOOOOo)
At 3 years the final pair changes (OOOOOOOO)

By 7-8 years teeth loosen and may fall out – this is when the animal is 'broken-mouthed', or 'crone', at which point it is past breeding age and is normally sent for meat.

The age is measured in numbers of wool shearings the animal has had. So, a two-shear ewe is probably six-toothed and has had one set of lambs, and is 2 to 3 years old; a three-shear ram is 3 to 4 years old.

Ewe grazing

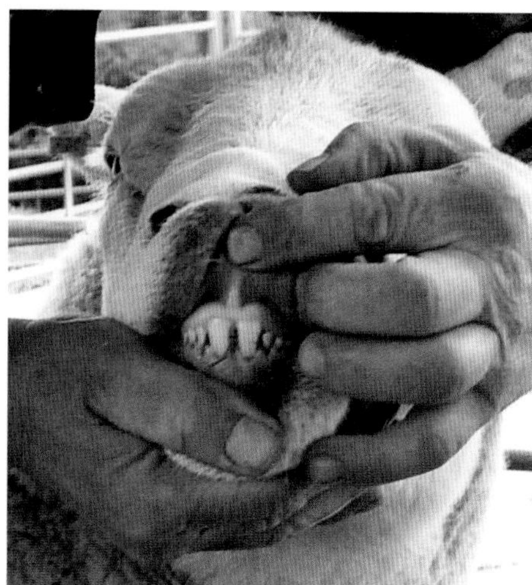

Teeth of a ewe

Shepherds' Equipment

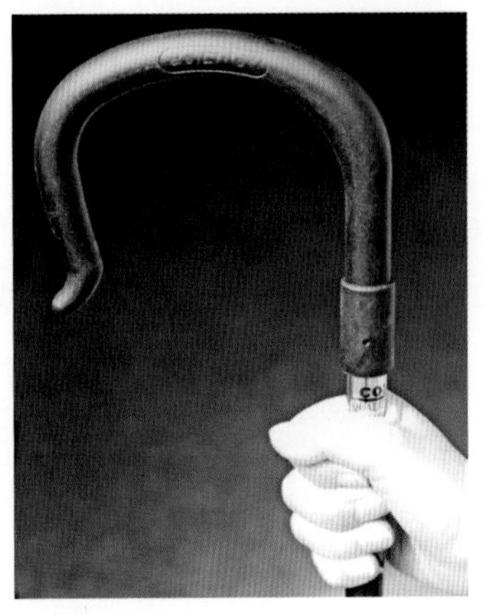

Modern neck crook

THE CROOK

The design of shepherds' crooks has changed little over millennia. Modern shepherds would recognise the crook in the hand of a statue of Pharaoh Tutankhamun from the 14th century BC.

There are two basic designs. One is essentially a metal hook on a stick, which enabled the shepherd to catch sheep by the leg. Whilst there was a standard design, it had many local variations, as can be seen by the illustration of three crooks from Herefordshire. A second type, often made from a ram's horn, was used to capture the sheep round its neck. Sometimes shepherds would make use of the natural curves of tree branches. This would be encouraged by bending back a thinnish branch of a tree and tying it to the main tree trunk, thus forming a tight curve. Once grown like this for a while, the branch would have adopted the crook shape and could be cut off. Such wooden crooks can be made from a variety of woods, including ash, oak and chestnut.

These days, many shepherds' crooks are mass-produced leg or neck types in metal or wood, and are imported. The last UK mass-producing crook maker was an old family firm of Coopers, in Goldalming, Surrey. When the factory closed in the late 1980s, most of the machinery was sold abroad, presumably then used to make crooks to export to the UK. However, there remains in the UK a strong crook-making tradition in the hundreds of craftsmen and women who produce hand-made bespoke crooks, often with a ram's horn or buffalo hooks. For most it is a hobby, but it is maintaining a centuries-old tradition of crook-making.

Stephens describes the design of a metal leg crook and its use in 1876 *'A crook catches the leg quietly and securely. It consists of a round rod of iron, bent in the form shown, terminating at one end in a knob, and at the other end in a socket, which receives and is fixed to a wooden helve, 5 or 6 feet long, according to fancy. The hind-leg is seized from behind the sheep; and as its small bone just fills the narrowest part of the crook, the leg cannot get loose backwards, and remains in the roomy loop of the crook until the shepherd has caught hold of the sheep, and allows its foot to slip through the loop. Some caution is required in using the crook, for should the sheep give a sudden start forward to get away the moment it feels the crook touch its leg, it may forcibly draw the leg through the narrow part, and strike the fore edge of the bone with such violence against the bend of the loop as to cause the animal considerable pain, and even occasion lameness for some days. On quietly hooking the leg from behind the ewe, the crook*

Victorian leg crooks from Herefordshire

should be quickly drawn towards you, so as to bring the bend of the loop against the leg as high up as the hock, and lift the foot off the ground, before the sheep is almost aware of the movement; and being thus secured at once, her struggles will cease the moment the hand seizes the leg.'

There are innumerable Christian images showing Christ as the Good Shepherd, with a symbolic crook. The Christian bishops carry a stylised crook in the form of a crozier, denoting his office as being the Shepherd of the flock of God.

The most accepted of the several possible derivations of the phrase 'by hook or by crook' first recorded in 1380, refers to the amount of firewood which a peasant could collect from the manorial forest being defined by what could be collected using a billhook or shepherd's crook.

Christ the Shepherd, stained glass from the Swansea School of Glass

SHEPHERD'S SMOCK

The countryman's smock was normal work wear for most farmworkers in the Midlands, southern England and parts of Wales, until the turn of the 20th century, similar in purpose to overalls today. Each region of the country would have their own characteristic material, style and even colour – blue in the Midlands for example, and olive green in East Anglia.

By the early 18th century plain smocks were being worn for work; while very ornate versions were worn to hiring fairs (when men sought work), for church or even for getting married.

The origin of the design of the traditional smock goes back to the Roman 'tunica' which survived into the Saxon period. Medieval illuminated manuscripts, such as the Luttrell Psalter, show agricultural labourers working in plain, loose garments which reached the knees, similar in design to the 18th and 19th century smocks which can be seen in museums today.

Often they were reversible, being the same design on the back and front, so that they could be turned round and worn back-to-front if they became dirty. Some were made waterproof by oiling, and most were made with several layers of cloth over the shoulders, with a large collar, somewhat like a cape, for extra protection against the weather and carrying loads.

Some experts believe that the embroidered design, especially around the collar, denotes the wearer's occupation – such as crooks, sheep and hurdles for shepherds, although there is some debate about this.

Smocking is a word which describes the charac-

'Wife, make us a dinner, spare flesh, neither corne,
Make wafers and cakes for our sheepe must be shorne;
At Sheepe shearing, neighbours none other things crave,
But good cheere and welcome like neighbours to have.'

Thomas Tusser (1557)
Five Hundred Points of Husbandry

teristic gathering of the fabric, which is held in place by stitching. There were regional styles of achieving this smocking effect. The gathering of the fabric in smocking enabled the wearer to enjoy both flexibility and strength of the material where it was most needed in the areas of the shoulders, chest and wrists. The garments were usually made by women, frequently from linen or rough thick cotton material, with the fabric cut into rectangles to avoid wastage.

> *'To wash pits where the willow shadows lean*
> *Dashing them in their fold-stained coats to clean.'*
>
> John Clare (1827)
> *The Shepherd's Calendar – June*

Thomas Hardy, in his novel *Under the Greenwood Tree*, wrote *' ... stalwart ruddy men and boys were dressed mainly in snow-white smock-frocks, embroidered upon the shoulders and chest with ornamental forms of hearts, diamonds and zig-zags'*. By 1874, Hardy had noted that *'long smocked frocks and the harvest home...nearly disappeared'*. As workers migrated to the new industrial towns in the mid-19th century, the smock was simply not practical, and was even a danger, as it would get caught in factory machinery. In Elizabeth Gaskell's novel *North and South* (1855) a character observes when she arrives at the fictitious northern manufacturing city of Milton from the rural south *'...there were no smock-frocks...they retarded motion, and were apt to catch on machinery, and so the habit of wearing them had died out'*.

Shepherd's smock from Herefordshire (19th century)

By 1880, it was suggested by Richard Jeffries at the time that the habit of wearing smocks in the countryside of Wiltshire was waning *'Some of the older shepherds still wear the ancient blue smock-frock, crossed with white 'facings', like coarse lace; but the rising generation use the greatcoat of modern make, at which their forefathers would have laughed as utterly useless in the rain storms that blow across the open hills. Among the elder men too, may be found a few of the umbrellas of a former age, which when spread gave as much shelter as a small tent. ... The aged men sling these great umbrellas over the shoulder with a piece of tar cord, just as a soldier slings his musket, and so have both hands free – one to stump along with a stout stick, and the other to carry a flag basket.'*

There was a fashionable revival of smocks (particularly for girls and women) in the 1970s, and smocking is still seen in clothing today.

SHEPHERD'S GAITERS

These leather protective leg guards are the equivalent of wellington boots today. They protected the shepherd from kicks and scrapes when working with their stock, and kept his trousers dry. Indeed, they were a common sight, being worn by most rural workers before rubber boots became available.

Rural gaiters, Herefordshire

'Suppose we get on with our dinner?' said Benjamin, resignedly. 'Here is a loin of mutton, my dear – an ordinary loin of mutton. Is there anything suspicious in that? Very well, then. Show me you have confidence in the mutton; please eat. There's the wine, again. No mystery, Valeria, in that claret - I'll take my oath it's nothing but innocent juice of the grape. If we can't believe in anything else, let's believe in juice of the grape. Your good health, my dear.'

Wilkie Collins, 1875
The Law and the Lady

The Sheepdog

The close relationship between a shepherd and his dogs is a wonderful thing to see in action. The dogs become almost a part of the shepherd, his arms extended through the animals to embrace his sheep and bring them to the desired place.

Man's relationship with the dog is ancient, particularly in the management and protection of domestic animals. Lucius Junius Moderatus Columella (AD 4-70) the Roman writer on agriculture, considered that sheepdogs should be white, so that they could be seen on dark mornings and distinguished from a wolf at dusk. The Venedotian Code of Welsh laws of the 13th century mentions three types of dog – the shepherd dog, the mastiff and the house cur. The need for protection of herds and flocks from wild predators such as wolves required sheepdogs of sufficient size to take on and overcome such attacks. However, as the wolf numbers declined, so did the size of the sheepdog. It was intelligence and speed that now mattered more than size. As John Keys, author of the first book on British dogs commented in his *Treatise on Englishe Dogges* in 1576 *'Our shepherdes dogge is not huge, vaste, and bigge, but of an indifferent stature and growth, because it has not to deale with the bloudthyrsty wolf, sythence there be none in England.'*

The key to using sheepdogs was the characteristic of sheep to cluster together in flocks. Our window back to the UK's original sheep, is the Soay breed, which scatters when chased, rather than bunching together as other modern sheep do. At some point this scattering characteristic was bred out of them, and from then on the dog and shepherd combination could move and control large numbers of sheep between them. By the 16th century, the dogs were controlled by whistles and calls from the shepherd, much as today. Control of the sheepdog was also described by Keys, writing as Johannes Caius in the 16th century *'This dogge either at the hearing of his masters voyce, or at the wagging and whisteling in his fist, or at his shrill and horse hissing bringeth the wandring weathers and straying sheepe, into the selfe same place where his masters will and wishe is to have the[m], wherby the shepherd repeth this benefite, namely, that with litle labour and no toyle or moving of his feete he may rule and guide his flocke, according to his owne desire, backward, or to turne this way, or to take that way. For it is not in Englande, as it is in Fraunce, [etc.] where the sheepe follow the shepherd, for heere in our country the sheepherd followeth the sheepe.'*

By the eighteenth century, two main breed types had developed as sheepdogs – the collie type in the north of the UK, and the Old English Sheepdog in the south. The latter has now disappeared as a working dog, and it is the Collie which is the mainstay of sheep handling. The Collie is believed to have originated in the hills of Scotland and Ireland, and the Border Collie is now most prevalent of all sheepdogs. Developed in the Scottish Borders, it is well-known for its agility, energy and intelligence. The breed's first written description dates only from the late 19th century, although they are thought to have become particularly popular following the Highland Clearances, when their speed and stamina were a great resource. There is a record of the introduction of 'Highland' sheepdogs into Wales from Cumbria in the middle of the 19th century.

As in the writings of John Keys almost 450 years ago, the sheepdog today is still commanded by the shepherd through a series of whistles, spoken instructions and arm movements. Over the years, a common set of commands has become recognised not only across the UK, but across much of the English-speaking world. Until recent times, the actual commands were not written down. Through the surprise television hit, *One Man and His Dog*, many of these commands are now familiar far outside the shepherding world:

Come-bye or **bye** – go to the left of the stock, or move clockwise around them, or go beyond the sheep. (In some areas it can mean go anti-clockwise)
Away to me, **Come away**, or just **away** or **'way** – go to the right of the stock, or anti-clockwise around them. (In some areas it can mean go clockwise)
Stand, Stop, Lie down – means what it says, although can sometimes mean slow down, especially if said quietly.
Wait, **(lie) down** or **sit** – stop or slow down.
Steady or **take time** – slow down, or give more distance between dog and sheep.
Get out or **get back** – move away from the sheep, giving them more room (used when the dog is working too close to the stock, stressing the sheep).
Look back – leave the main flock to gather a missed animal, or a group of sheep further away.
In here – when separating a flock into two groups, means go through a gap in the flock. Dog will often then move one separated group away from the others.
Walk up, **walk on** or **walk** – move in steadily closer to the stock or away from the shepherd, without frightening or scaring the sheep.
That'll do – stop working and return to shepherd.

Opposite page: Welsh National Sheepdog Trials, Penybont, 2013

Jess, a border collie sheepdog

Some shepherds use whistles. When using more than one dog at a time, each will be trained to react to a different set of commands to avoid confusion. There are stories of two dogs being operated on a farm in Scotland, one in English, and one in Gaelic.

In 1910, W.H. Hudson described the inevitable end of the complex relationship between the shepherd and his dogs. *'He told me that in all his shepherding years he had never owned a dog which had passed out of his hands to another; every dog had been acquired as a pup and trained by himself; and he had been very fond of his dogs, but had always been compelled to have them shot in the end. Not because he would have found them too great a burden when they became too old and their senses decayed, but because it was painful to see them in their decline, perpetually craving to be at their work with the sheep, incapable of doing it any longer, yet miserable if kept from it.'*

It is easy to underestimate the importance of the sheepdog in the development of the sheep industry. As James Hogg (1770-1835), shepherd and poet from Ettrick in the Scottish Borders, wrote *'Without the shepherd's dog the mountainous land of England and Scotland would not be worth a sixpence. It would require more hands to manage a flock of sheep and drive them to market than the profits of the whole were capable of maintaining.'*

The Shepherd's Year

The traditional shepherd's year was and is still dictated by the seasonal needs of his flock. The following is from various historical descriptions, and whilst a modern shepherd would recognise the pattern of seasons, there have been some significant changes in the shepherd's year brought about by modern technology, which has taken away some, though not all, of the back-breaking work of being a shepherd.

AUTUMN SORTING OF EWES

The shepherd's year begins in the autumn with the sorting of ewes. By this time, the lamb crop for the year has been weaned from the ewes, and mating for the next season of lambs must be prepared for. In early autumn, the shepherd will go through the ewes looking for weak ones, or those with insufficient teeth to continue for another year. In the hills, after a few lambings, ewes would be sent to easier lower pastures on farms where they would be mated with lowland rams, such as Blueface or Border Leicesters to produce the cross-bred lambs. The ewes which are removed from the flock either to be sent to easier climates or for ewe mutton are known as 'drafts' for breeding, or 'culls' for mutton.

A good shepherd will know each ewe, and her mothering ability. Lamb survival is dependent on the ewe's ability to look after her lamb, particularly in the uplands where the environment will be ruthless to a young animal exposed to the extremes of mountain weather. The shepherd will also know if a particular ewe had produced twins or even triplets. Today this information will be recorded on many farms on electronic ear tags. The shepherd looks at her udder to ensure that there is no damage, and be sure that the next crop of lambs can have plenty of milk. If the ewe failed to produce a lamb in the previous

Auctioning ewes at Knighton Market, mid-Wales

year, it may be given another chance, but these days, she is most likely to be culled, as feeding and looking after an animal for another year will be an expensive business.

The ewes are then sorted into groups of about 40, which is the number of ewes which a ram can 'cover'.

FLUSHING

From a fertility point of view, it is important that a ewe is in the right condition when she is mated. A fat or under-nourished ewe will be less likely to conceive, or produce twins compared with one which is in 'improving' condition. Once the ewe has reared its lamb, it is given sufficient food to live, but not to become too fat. Then, as mating or 'tupping' time arrives, in the late summer or autumn, the ewes are given extra food to improve their condition, and they start to lay down some fat reserves. This makes them particularly fertile for mating.

TUPPING

A ram or tup, will be run with around 40 ewes from about August to November, depending on when the farmer wants lambing to occur. The gestation period of a sheep is around 147 days or 5 months, so the farmer can adjust the tupping time and consequently lambing. Generally this is in October or November in the hills, which will mean lambing in March or April. Producing lambs at this time of year will give access to fresh spring grass when the lambs are weaned. Ewes come into season on a 17 day cycle and are fertile for about 36 hours.

Today, the ram is fitted with a 'raddle', a coloured marker on his chest, which transfers colour onto the back of any mated ewe, which allows the shepherd to see which ones have been mated.

Southdown Mutton
Hansard 18 November 1919

Earl Winterton
asked the Food Controller if his attention has been called to the fact that losses have been sustained by breeders of South Down sheep under the present grading system of the sale of meat, owing to the fact that pure-bred South Down mutton, where there is an open market, is invariably sold at a higher rate than other mutton of the same weight and age; and whether he proposes to take any action in the matter?
Mr McCurdy:
'Owing to the administration difficulties involved, it has been found impossible to fix differential prices for meat according to quality. I am aware that the present arrangement is not in every way satisfactory, but I am afraid that no alteration is practicable so long as the controlled distribution of meat, and guaranteed prices to the farmer are necessary.'

(see page 99)

Grazing Herdwick

SUMMER AND AUTUMN DIPPING

Sheep are very attractive to a plethora of parasites. If external parasites, such as 'keds', ticks, scab-mites or lice were a problem, then the flock was 'dipped' prior to mating. This involved immersing the whole animal in a solution containing pesticide which kills off the parasites. Often this would be done by damming a stream on the farm, but for obvious environmental reasons, this is no longer allowed. During the 19th century a number of preparations were used against parasites by rubbing them into the skin. Some of these were quite deadly to humans, let alone to the parasites or even the sheep. Concoctions included ingredients such as lime, mercury, tar, turpentine and arsenic. Even in 1945, the standard sheep dip mixtures contained either sodium arsenite, arsenic-sulphur compounds or tar acids and oils.

David Nixon worked on a number of farms before WWII. He describes dipping sheep in the Chilterns.

'We all wore oilskins or old rain coats, the old hands knew without any telling, but Harry warned Billy and myself that we would get drenched if we did not. The concrete sloped gradually up until it reached a long ramp, ribbed with shallow steps, and the ewes walked out. If a ewe failed to go under, she was hooked under the head by a posser and made to swim again to the deep end and ducked once more. Often there were three sheep in the dip and the hubbub and laughter mingled with the cries of the ewes. Occasionally a ewe would career past Billy and myself and take a flying leap into the dip, landing with a tremendous splash and showering everyone. ... After dipping the ewes stood for a while in the draining pens and the dipping fluid ran down the herring-bone pattern of channels in the sloping concrete and back into the dip.'

'The feast consisted of a pot-au-feu, which Miss Chalice had made, of a leg of mutton roasted round the corner and brought round hot and savoury (Miss Chalice had cooked the potatoes, and the studio was redolent of the carrots she had fried);... There was a pause while they waited for the leg of mutton, and Miss Chalice lit a cigarette.'

W. Somerset Maugham
(1874-1965)
Of Human Bondage

These days, 'pour-on' products are often used which are literally poured onto the animals' backs to get rid of the parasites. Not only is this less labour intensive, it is much less environmentally damaging. The disposal of large volumes of dipping solution is a serious environmental problem.

FEEDING

During the winter, most sheep are kept outside. Normally they would have been fed with hay. Today that has largely been replaced with silage, which is preserved grass, and sometimes 'concentrate' feed pellets may be used.

Some sheep would have been (and still can be) over-wintered on a root crop such as turnips or swedes. It is the shepherd's daily task, in winter and early spring, to bring food to the sheep, and check on their wellbeing.

WINTER WARMTH

Means of protecting sheep from the extremes of winter is a subject which has long vexed shepherds. Since the Romans, jackets have been tried, as has an insulating layer smeared over the wool. This practice was widespread in the hill flocks of Britain until the 19th century. Various mixtures were used, including tar and butter, or in Scotland pine tar and brown grease. Such practices were also used against the dreaded and contagious disease of scab. Today neither smearing nor jackets are used, with sheep left much to their own devices. During the winter, few if any animals are left on the highest pastures, as the weather at such altitudes can be fatal even to hardy breeds of sheep.

Top: feeding sheep on Iona, Scotland.
Above: sheep concentrate feed

Victorian coat for sheep

'For dinner we'll have a tureen of the hottest and strongest soup available, and we'll have the best made dish that can be recommended, and we'll have a joint (such as a haunch of mutton), and we'll have a goose, or a turkey, or any little stuffed thing of that sort that may happen to be in the bill of fare – in short, we'll have whatever there is on hand.'

Charles Dickens (1812-1870)
The Mystery of Edwin Drood

Texel cross Welsh Mule with lambs

Lambing

Traditionally, this crucial part of the shepherd's year was said to be determined by luck – it could be good, meaning that most lambs survive, or bad, when they don't. However, the biggest influence on a successful lambing is the management by the shepherd or farmer.

Lambing normally takes place in January or February in the lower areas, or as late as March or April in the very highest farms, to avoid the worst of the weather. Some farmers specialise in early lambing, in December, or, by using breeds such as the Dorset Horn, even earlier. These early lambing farms aim to have lamb ready for the market by Easter. However, as the demand for this traditional Easter delicacy has waned in recent years, fewer early lambing flocks are around, as without a higher price, early lambing is not economic, because the lambs have to be fed with expensive concentrate feed to fatten them before the new season grass has grown.

The pros and cons of indoor or outdoor lambing have been debated for hundreds of years in the farming community. The heyday of sheep housing was the Medieval period, and the farmer's willingness to build shelters for his sheep has reflected their value. Elaborate thatched wooden houses can be seen in illuminated manuscripts of the 15th century. Once wool prices dropped, sheep housing declined until the modern era, when government grants enabled most lambing to be done in relatively sheltered, airy barns or 'lambing sheds'.

A ewe about to lamb often separates herself from the flock, showing signs of restlessness, scraping the ground with her foot, bleating, and alternately lying down and standing up. For short periods she will peacefully graze or eat if food is available. Once lambing starts, she will lie on the ground on her side, raising her head as the contractions come and she strains. Once started, the process should be over within a couple of hours, and most ewes lamb without help. If lambing is prolonged there may be a problem, and the ewe might need help. A normal birth will be with the lamb's front legs forward (as if diving). The most common abnormal presentation is for just one leg to be forward, whilst the other lies against the body of the lamb. The shepherd will normally push the lamb back into the womb, feeling for the other leg, and ensure that they are both pointing forward, which enables the lamb to be delivered. Alternatively, both front legs may be beside the body, and the head only emerges. Again seeing this, the shepherd will gently push the lamb back, and move the front legs into the 'diving' position for normal birth.

Twins or triplets can add problems as well as being potential extra profit for farmers. If a farmer is aiming for a 'lambing percentage' (the number of lambs reared per 100 ewes) of say 150%, then around half of the ewes will have to produce twins. The biggest problem with multiple lambs is to ensure that only one comes out at a time, otherwise the pressures exerted through the birth process can damage both lambs and ewe.

Lambing pens on the marshes, Walton-on-Naze, Essex, c1930

Once born, it is essential that the lamb is given every bit of help early on, as this has an effect on its longer term survival chances. The mother should instinctively lick the lamb dry, to help it keep warm. It needs to be kept warm and dry, with access to its mother's milk as soon as possible, as this early milk (colostrum) contains antibodies to diseases to which the mother has been exposed. Today, the lamb will also be vaccinated against some common diseases. If a ewe has no milk, its lamb will be fostered onto another ewe, either one which has lost its lamb, or simply has plenty of milk and a single lamb. Sometimes a rather gruesome technique must be employed. If a lamb needs fostering by a ewe which has lost its own lamb, and she seems unwilling to take on the stranger, the dead lamb is skinned and the fleece placed over the orphan lamb so that the mother recognises it from her lamb's smell. The moving of lambs between ewes to ensure as many as possible survive takes a lot of effort by the shepherd.

Lambs start eating food (grass, silage or hay) as well as mother's milk after about two weeks. Then, as the weeks go by, the proportion of nutrition the lamb gets from the mother's milk reduces, as the lamb becomes weaned.

Owen Sheers, a contemporary poet, writes of lambing, based on his personal experiences on the family farm in Wales:

Lambing

My father gloves himself in her,
up to his elbow, on his knees,
head angled, cheek resting
on the sprung wool of her rump.
Looking for coins down the back of a sofa.
His invisible fingers work inside,
finding a tangle of swollen joints
and crooked legs.
The hooves, soft as plums.
And then the slow, hydraulic extraction,
Chinese eyes and long ears pulled back
by the g-force of the womb.
The tight cling-film of the amniotic sac,
the pre-packaging of birth,
which, when it comes,
falls, flat and bloody as road kill –
a glued body, trailing a placenta,
a still life, until, at last, the first breath,
which arrives from nowhere -
an electric shock
run across the railings of its ribs.

Owen Sheers, from the *Blue Book 2000* (by kind permission of the author)

TAILING, CASTRATING AND WEANING

Lamb tails have traditionally been removed for one very good reason. Being at the rear end of the lamb, if not removed, they are inclined to become caked in faeces. This attracts flies which lay eggs which hatch into maggots which literally eat the lamb alive. Removal of the tail is not so widespread at the highest altitudes, where flies are rarer and the tail can act as a shield against the weather. Today tail removal is done with a rubber ring applied an inch or two along the tail from the base. This restricts blood supply, and eventually the tail falls off, causing minimal discomfort to the lamb. Similarly, to improve growth rates, reduce the chances of accidental pregnancy, and avoid any possible testosterone tainting of the meat, males not required for breeding are castrated by the same method.

Weaning is done in groups, once lambs are taking less milk and are feeding mostly on grass, normally at three to four months of age, minimising the shock to the lamb. The flow of milk is normally gradually reduced by moving the ewe and lambs to poorer quality pastures so that the ewe produces less milk. Sometimes, early in the season, lambs are sold for slaughter before weaning. These are known as milk lambs.

WASHING

In the late spring and early summer, the washing of sheep before shearing was once an almost universal practice, hence the many place-name references to 'sheepwash'. Prior to shearing, the sheep were taken to a stream or washing tank where they were immersed in

Washing sheep on Knill Farm, Herefordshire c 1908

plain cold water. This removed most of the soil from the fleece, and perhaps surprisingly, a fair amount of the natural grease (lanolin) in the wool. The natural creamy colour of fleeces is due to a mixture of lanolin and water-soluble 'suint', from the sheep's sweat glands. The reason why the grease can be removed simply by washing is that the suint acts as a detergent. Indeed, when washing hands after handling sheep or their raw fleeces, no soap is needed to remove the lanolin.

It was customary to wait a week between washing and shearing, to allow a little of the lanolin (or 'yolk') to return to the fleece in order to make shearing easier. Traditionally, four men could wash about 400 sheep in a day, and whilst there was a cost involved in washing the sheep, not to say a risk of some sheep dying through the shock of being submerged, in the 1930s there was an extra 2d a lb paid for washed wool over unwashed, greasy wool. This had to be balanced against a weight loss of the wool, through washing, of some 12-20%. Costs involved have made this practice uneconomic today, and no sheep are washed in this way. The premium paid by the Wool Marketing Board for washed wool was abolished in 1979.

'It was customary to combine and collect the sheep off the open hills for washing, on the same day at one centre. The men were in the water for two or three hours, and it was thought necessary to provide them with some warm gruel with a liberal supply of gin added. The gruel was made with oatmeal boiled in home-brewed beer, with currants, spices, sugar, etc., and was served hot. This was very tasty and sustaining and the men ate it while in the washpool.'

from Llanfihangel Rhydithon (Dolau) 70 Years Ago, by W. Watkins, J.P. Proceedings of the Radnorshire Society 1932

Washing sheep, 1844

Shearing time on Knill Farm, Herefordshire, c.1906

Shearing

Traditionally shearing takes place in the early summer to lessen the risk of the shorn sheep catching a chill. The animals should be dry, as wet wool when rolled can deteriorate. In some areas even lambs were shorn, which avoided them being bothered by flies which lay eggs in dirty wool in the summer. Today only around 2% of lambs are sheared.

Hand-shearing, using manual shears is a very laborious task. Nevertheless, the world record for hand-shearing using blade shears was originally set in 1892 by the Australian Jackie Howe who sheared 321 sheep in 7 hours and 40 minutes. He had previously set a weekly record of 1,437 sheep sheared during a working week of 44 ½ hours. This aggregate record was not broken until 2005, even with modern machinery.

In 1870, Lady Mary Barker described the life on a sheep station in New Zealand. Of shearing she wrote *'A good shearer can take off 120 fleeces in a day, but the average is about 80 to each man. They get one pound per hundred, and are found in everything, having as much tea and sugar, bread and mutton, as they can consume, and a cook entirely to themselves; they work at least fourteen hours out of the twenty-four, and with such a large flock as this – about 50,000 – must make a good deal.'*

The introduction of machine shears made a huge difference to the output of shearers and the physical effort involved. Jackie Howe's daily record was broken using machine shears by Ted Reick in 1950. Various classes of world shearing records are recognised, and there is huge competition between sheep producing countries to break the records of others. At major agricultural shows worldwide one of the main attractions is competition shearing. Most world records are currently held by Australians, New Zealanders or South Africans.

Today, shearing speeds are actually quicker in the UK than in Australia or New Zealand. A combination of less face and belly wool, together with lighter and cleaner fleeces with less grit, means that a professional shearer using mechanical shears can cleanly remove a fleece in under two minutes, whereas Down Under it would take two to three minutes. A UK top professional shearer can finish 300-400 sheep a day; in Australia

Shearing competition at the Royal Cornwall Show
Below: traditional hand shears

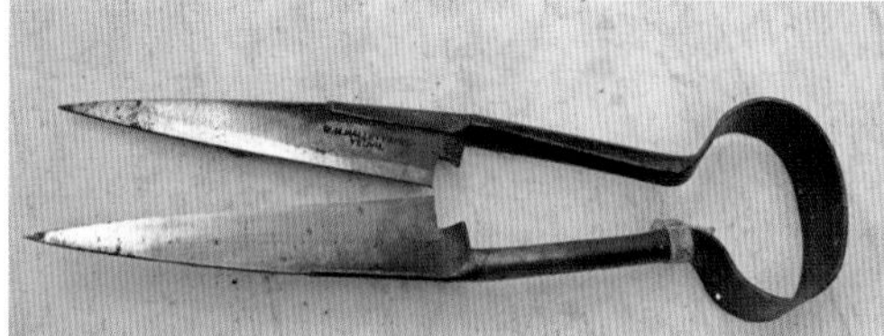

and New Zealand, the best shearers who shear or 'tally' more than 200 sheep per day are known as 'gun shearers'.

Historically, the annual sheep-shearing was probably the most important activity in the sheep farmers' calendar. This practical necessity was also a big social event and the skill of the farmer's wife was to cater for the greatly increased numbers of people working on the farm. Hand-shears were used until around the 1960s, and bigger flocks would require 15 to 20 men shearing on benches. A couple more men (the 'carriers') would bring in sheep to be shorn and take away those which were finished. Others would mark the shorn sheep with pitch, to identify the home of each animal. This was done with a recognisable identification mark, or initials, so farmers could readily find their sheep should they stray from home. The 'floor-man' had to keep the floor tidy and consequently the fleeces clean and look after any accidental injuries or cuts. He also distributed drink, usually cider, as well as tobacco and cigarettes amongst the workmen. The accounts of the Abbey-cwm-hir Estate in mid-Wales regularly showed purchases of cider through the summer months, 195 gallons at a time!

In 1898 Rider Haggard described a typical shearing day. *'The operator begins the task in the region of the belly, working gradually round towards her back until it is necessary to turn the animal on her side, when he ties the fore and hind leg together with a thin*

'After ewes and lambs are shorn, there is great confusion and bleating, neither the dams nor the young being able to distinguish one another as before. This embarrassment seems not so much to arise from the loss of the fleece, which may occasion an alteration in their appearance, as from the defect of that notus odor, discriminating each individual personally; which also is confounded by the strong scent of pitch and tar wherewith they are newly marked; for the brute creation recognize each other more from the smell than the sight; and in matters of identity and diversity appeal much more to their noses than their eyes.'

Gilbert White (1720-1793) *The Natural History of Selbourne*

cord. In the case of old and experienced ewes I am sure that they understand what is happening to them, as they look quite contented and struggle little – indeed the shearers say this is so. The moment that the thing is done – which seems to prove it – they spring up with blitheness, and, rushing from the barn, begin to bite hungrily at the grass outside.'

Once sheared, the fleeces had to be rolled up in a particular way to keep them intact. Mrs Mills from mid-Wales recalled how in the early years of the 20th century she would roll the fleece. *'You'd spread it all out, like if it was on this table; you'd turn this side in and that side in, and roll it up. And when you'd got to the end, you'd pull some of the neck wool and tie it round, and make a big knot.'*

From top: shearing by hand; rolling the fleece; a rolled fleece

In the outhouse the women would be busy with the preparation of the meals for the gathering, which would include neighbours, friends and relatives. A Mrs Wivell of Cumberland in the early 19th century recorded the importance of shearing *'In England on the day they began to shear their sheep a plentiful dinner was provided for the shearers and their friends. A table also, if weather permitted, was spread in the open air for the young people and children. The washing and shearing of sheep is attended with great mirth and festivity.'* Mrs Wivell also described making a Clipping Time Pudding, which with local variations was to be found all over the country. Essentially it was a rich rice pudding with dried fruit, cinnamon, bone marrow or suet, sugar and eggs. For hungry men on the shearing benches, this went down very well, and kept them going through the day.

Each farm had its own traditional day for shearing. The season started in the lower hill farms about mid-June, and continued every day until the end of July, all the time working further up into the higher hills, as the season progressed.

The system was one of collaboration, as neighbours worked together to finish each other's flocks. The main benefit was that it required little extra paid labour. The farmers and shepherds simply exchanged help, moving from one farm to another each day, as did their wives and daughters, helping with the housework and catering.

Shearing was a real social and festive occasion. Some finished with a football match in the late evening.

In the UK today the communal approach to shearing has almost vanished, with most shearing now done by specialist contractors, at a rate per head. Many shearers are from Australia and New Zealand. Working in both northern and southern hemispheres offers the chance of year-round work.

Welsh Mule crossed ewes

Good Breeding

There are places in the upland areas of the UK where only a few sheep breeds can survive; at lower altitudes other breeds can produce a lot of meat relatively quickly. Such has been the fine-tuning by farmers over the centuries, that in the UK we have a priceless genetic resource: a suitable breed or two for every environmental niche found in these islands. This versatile gene pool, together with the bonus of 'hybrid vigour' from cross-breeding, optimises the production of sheep meat in all our varied environments.

Sheep breeds developed in Britain over the centuries, firstly to survive in different environments, and then to produce plentiful supplies of either milk, wool, manure, fat or meat. Most reflect their geographical origin, many with names which resonate with the landscape which produced them – Derbyshire Gritstone, Swaledale, Hill Radnor, Hebridean or Southdown. Then there are the more bizarre names such as Badger Face Welsh Mountain, Bluefaced Leicester, Lonk, Scotch Mule and Jacob.

There are currently more than 60 indigenous breeds of sheep in Britain – more than in any other country. The physical variation between breeds can be enormous, in terms of size of the animal, wool quality, numbers of lambs born to, and the maternal instincts of the ewes. Each of our native sheep breeds has developed for a reason, whether it was ability to survive and thrive in local conditions, the quality of its wool, or the quality of its meat.

Generally, native sheep from Scotland and western UK are descendants of those brought here in Neolithic times from Scandinavia, the 'Soay-type' of sheep: the Cheviot and Welsh Mountain breeds for example. The exception to this in the North are the sheep of the Lake District, the ancestors of the modern Herdwick, which are likely to have been from Norse invaders. However one local theory claims that Herdwick are progeny of forty animals which staggered ashore on a sandy bay near Drigg from a wrecked Spanish ship of the Armada, and were claimed by the lord of the manor. The name Herdwick is a derivation of the Norse for 'sheep pasture'. Southern sheep spread up from the near continent.

By the middle of the 17th century, few individual breeds were recognised, and fewer still for the quality of their meat, most being kept for their wool-producing ability. Here and there, some local breeds were particularly famous for the quality of their mutton, such as that of Banstead or of Bagshot in Surrey, Portland in Dorset, Clun Forest in Shropshire, or the mountain sheep of Wales. However, there was great local variation, and few fixed traits – not what we would recognise today as distinct breeds.

This was soon to change in a remarkable way, through some quite remarkable individuals. And the driving force for change was the developing demand for meat to supply the burgeoning urban populations. It was time for sheep to change direction from wool producers to meat producers.

Robert Bakewell & John Ellman

Above: Robert Bakewell
Below: New Leicester ewe and lamb

One man credited with being a revolutionary pioneer of livestock breeding was Robert Bakewell (1725-1795), an English agriculturalist whose stockbreeding methods helped transform the quality of Britian's sheep, cattle and horses.

Bakewell was the son of a tenant farmer in Leicestershire. On the death of his father in 1760 Robert took over the tenancy of the family farm. When journalist Arthur Young first visited the farm in 1770, he found the 440 acres divided into one quarter arable, using a rotation of corn/turnip/grass; and 330 acres of permanent grass pasture for his livestock which included 600 sheep. Young commented that Bakewell *'brings up stock with amazing gentleness'*. Bakewell set to work on the farm with gusto, with such innovations as pioneering irrigation of his grassland, and establishing experimental areas to determine the best manure and flooding methods.

In fact, Bakewell was probably not quite the pioneer which history has crowned him through the enthusiastic writings of Young. However, with Young's help (which Bakewell privately resented) he was a good showman and self-publicist. With his Dishley Leicester sheep, he followed on the work of breeders such as Joseph Allom. Nevertheless, Bakewell did have a significant impact on sheep breeding, if only to show what could be done with systematic inbreeding to 'fix' desirable characteristics. He popularised serious livestock breeding. Previously livestock of both sexes were kept together in the fields which resulted in a very random form of breeding, with unpredictable results - *'the haphazard union of nobody's son with everybody's daughter*' as it has been described. Bakewell enabled his stock to be deliberately and specifically mated with particular animals by separating males from females. Furthermore, by inbreeding his livestock ('in and in') he fixed and exaggerated those traits he thought were desirable. In particular, as demand for meat was increasing in the growing towns and cities, he wanted to improve the meat-producing ability of his sheep. And with good cause.

'He was so polite as to stop at a public-house, expressly on our account, and entertain us with broiled mutton and beer.'

Charles Dickens (1812-1870)
David Copperfield

The wool-producing breeds had become very prone to producing plenty of wool, but also plenty of fat. A Teeswater sheep was killed at Darlington at Christmas 1779. Bearing in mind that a modern lamb carcass weighs around 20 kg, this animal, once butchered, weighed 113kg, and 8 kg of fat was removed from the carcass before cooking. Even by the tastes of the time, this was just not a butcher's animal. Something had to be done if the workers of the Industrial Revolution were to be adequately fed. John Lawrence in 1809 describes a meal he had where 'a leg of prize mutton' weighed 17lbs (8kg). '*At my desire, the fat which dripped in cooking was measured, and it amounted to between two and three quarts* [2.3 to 3.4 litres]; *besides this, the dish was a mere bog of loose, oily fat, huge deep flakes of it remained to garnish that which we called, by courtesy, lean, being itself so thoroughly interleaved and impregnated. It struck me forcibly that ... an exchange of seven or eight pounds of fat for lean meat, would have contributed much to the ... good character of the joint.*'

Top and bottom: Leicester Longwool sheep

Bakewell used another longwool breed, the old Lincolnshire, which through his methods of selective and deliberate breeding, was developed into what became the New Leicester breed. These were large yet delicately-boned animals, with a good quality fleece and an improved degree of lean meat. Once the results of his revolutionary methods became known, he began hiring out his prize rams to other farmers to improve their stock. By the 1780s Bakewell was renting out his rams by the season for the equivalent of £88,000 each in today's values. The New Leicester breed died out after his death in 1795, and Bakewell's breed became known as the Dishley Leicesters. The nearest current breed to the Dishley Leicesters is the

Leicester Longwool, but many other breeds benefitted from improvement by cross-breeding with Bakewell's breed. Many modern breeds benefitted from Bakewell's work.

However, not everyone at the time saw what a revolution Bakewell had unleashed. In 1840, Clark Hillyard, a Northamptonshire sheep farmer criticised the fatness of Bakewell's improved Leicesters *'.. most of the Leicestershire tups* [rams] *can only waddle amongst the ewes, and are often seen with many round them waiting to be served* [mated]*.'* Others described the Dishley breed as *'barrels on four short legs'*.

Despite Hillyard's misgivings, many of the world's major sheep breeds have Dishley blood, and Bakewell's contribution to food production is inestimable.

John Ellman, breeder of the Southdown sheep

The most celebrated sheep breeder who followed Bakewell's example and turned the Downland sheep into mutton breeds without compare was John Ellman (1753-1832) from Glynde in Sussex. He took the local speckled-faced heath breed which had grazed the Sussex Downs from time immemorial, and made the Southdown breed one of the most sought-after mutton breeds in the UK, and beyond – in direct competition with the Dishley Leicesters. Although it is not recorded exactly how Ellman went about his breed improvement (like Bakewell, he kept details of his methods secret), he talked to local butchers to find out what they wanted in a sheep carcass. He then bred for those characteristics, using selected good quality rams from within his flock to 'breed out' the poor aspects of even his worst quality ewes. As a result he rarely got rid of any ewes. His methods worked. He followed Bakewell's example of hiring out his rams to other farmers, and in 1802 one ram was sent to the Duke of Bedford for two seasons for the rent of 300 guineas – some £73,000 in today's values.

Arthur Young, the agricultural writer, was a great publiciser of both Bakewell and Ellman. He wrote in 1813 of the breed on the South Downs of Sussex *'The amazing number they keep is one of the most singular circumstances in the sheep husbandry of England'.* In 1817 he described why the Southdown was such a popular butchers' sheep *'The South Downs are thicker in their hind than in their fore-quarters; and when fat, the hind-quarters are frequently two or three pounds heavier than the fore. Mr. Ellman considers this a great merit in the breed, as the butchers have a ready sale for the former, at an advance of 1d. per*

Early examples of Southdown sheep

pound over the other; in which case he entirely agrees with Mr. Bakewell, that the criterion of breeding is flesh, not bone; and the true point, to throw the greatest weight upon the most valuable quarters of the carcass.'

The Southdown breed was a revolution, but eventually it was overtaken by breeds better suited to contemporary needs. After WWI the breed declined quite quickly. The typical Southdown animal became smaller following demands in the USA, and the traditional system of penning sheep on downland to increase fertility gave way to artificial fertilisers and labour shortages. The Southdown had lost its pre-eminent position as one of the top mutton breeds.

Nevertheless, the reputation of the Southdown persisted into the 1970s when the standard agricultural textbook of the time was still eulogising that *'No other breed in the whole world can challenge the Southdown in carcass quality; in this breed, the fineness of bone and texture of its dense flesh are supreme.'*

Modern Southdown

The work of Bakewell, Ellman and others extended well beyond these shores, and helped establish the sheep industries of the New World, which within a few decades would make a vital contribution to feeding the vast urban populations of the British Industrial Revolution.

The improvement work of such pioneers as Bakewell was designed to produce more meat from the previously wool-dominated sheep of Britain. However, this spelled doom for some of the high wool-yielding breeds. They either had to produce more meat for feeding the workers of the Industrial Revolution, or disappear. One such example was the Ryeland, which was known in the Medieval period as 'Lemster Ore', due to its hugely valuable fine wool, and being centred around the town of Leominster in Herefordshire. As mutton prices rose, the Ryeland began to be crossed with other breeds to try and increase its size. Dorsets, Southdowns and most commonly Leicesters, as well as Shropshires, Radnors, Cotswolds and Lincolns were all used. Although the size of animals was increased, many people complained that the taste of the mutton had diminished. In addition, the 'improved' sheep was more susceptible to disease and the quality of the wool deteriorated. Merchants started to favour longwool breeds, which gave much heavier clips of wool per ewe. It also became apparent that the offspring of a Ryeland and Leicester cross had an unacceptably high mortality rate. By 1903 only fifteen pure-bred Ryeland flocks remained. There were winners and losers in the rush to produce more meat.

Some lamented the changes which this breeding revolution was producing. In Scotland the Blackface and the Cheviot were replacing the old endemic sheep. This was a source of regret to Dr James Anderson who wrote in 1790 that the old breed with its sleek, deer-like countenance, and under fur of a *'sort of soft down over-topped by long, straight, rigid hair, somewhat like the coat of the beaver'*, was being 'debased' and pushed out of existence by the 'coarse-woolled sheep' from the south.

However, the improvement in sheep breeds was an undoubted success story. The results from the work of the early sheep breeding pioneers such as Bakewell and Ellman was simply astonishing. Between 1710 and 1795 the average live weight of sheep sold at London's Smithfield meat market increased almost three-fold from 28 to 80 lbs (11 to 32 kg).

Farmers discuss breeds at livestock shows

Individual breeds, developed from the late 18th century, started to be organised into societies from the 1880s, when the idea of Flock Books, recording pedigree animals, was imported from the USA. The definition of a breed goes very much on the physical looks of the animal. John Robson in 1913 described his method for selecting his Blackface rams (tups). Firstly a good even covering of wool for winter protection *'as to colour, I prefer a white-faced Cheviot with black nose, clear eyes, well-covered ears, and white legs with clean bones. But in commercial stock a little lightness about the nose and dun on the legs can be forgiven.'* The black tip of an ear or nose can thus be the source of heated debate, but it was, and is, suitability to local farming conditions which is most important – the breeds evolved to exploit the local environment most efficiently, producing optimum levels of wool, milk or meat.

Breeds Today

UK breeds are generally grouped into different types, depending on the environment they are most suited to, their purpose and their origin. Broadly speaking these are Mountain, Hill, Downland, Long wool, Primitive and Cross-bred (*see page 195, UK Stock Breeds*).

Scottish Blackface

MOUNTAIN

Spread across Scotland, Wales and the north of England, Mountain breeds include the Scottish Blackface, Welsh Mountain, Cheviot, Herdwick and Swaledale. The mountain breeds are small, hardy and have an excellent reputation for the quality of their mutton. In the southern Pennines, a related breed is the Whitefaced Woodland. In south-west England the descendants of the original West Country Mountain sheep include the Exmoor Horn, Dartmoor and Devon Closewool.

HILL

Tan-faced primitive sheep were the original inhabitants in the hill areas of Britain. After the improvements of the 18th and 19th century, these changed to the more recognisable sheep of today. The original upland sheep of Dorset and Wiltshire were horned and white faced. A second group of hill sheep developed around the Welsh Borders into such breeds as the Clun Forest, Hill Radnor and Kerry Hill. The internationally-widespread Shropshire was a result of crossing these hill breeds with the Southdown.

Above: Beulah Speckleface hill sheep

Below: Oxford Down

DOWNLAND

The downland breeds, also known as the short wools, were originally found on the Downs of Oxfordshire, Hampshire, Dorset and Shropshire. The spark which ignited the revolution to transform the localised downland breeds into some of the most popular and important mutton breeds across the western world, started with John Ellman's improvement of the Southdown in Sussex. By transforming this breed into a dual purpose mutton and wool animal, Ellman enabled breeders to cross the Southdown with other Downland breeds to pass the great improvement in mutton quality well beyond Sussex. Foremost amongst these breeds was the Shropshire, which was described in 1911 as the *'most ubiquitous breed extant'*. The Shropshire thrived and multiplied in the USA, Canada, South America, Russia, France, Germany, Australia, New Zealand, South Africa, Jamaica and the Falkland Islands. The improvement of the Shropshire was followed by the Oxford Down, which became a mutton version of the ancient wool-producing Cotswold breed. The Suffolk, Dorset and Hampshire breeds followed.

LOWLAND

The original development by Bakewell of the New Leicester breed led to a number of other improved breeds, all suited to the English lowlands. These included the Border Leicester and Bluefaced Leicester. The 'Golden Hoofed' Ryeland of the Welsh Borders was classified as a lowland breed. Other lowland breeds included Norfolk Horn and the Lleyn and Llanwenog from Wales.

Border Leicesters

Left to right: Wensleydale, Manx Loaghtan ram, Welsh mules

LONGWOOL

Developed for the quality of their wool, the original Longwool breeds consisted of improved varieties of marshland sheep found in Lincolnshire, Somerset and Kent. These animals may have been descendants of sheep introduced by the Romans. These are the breeds whose ancestors powered the golden age of British wool production from the medieval period to the 18th century. Such breeds as the Cotswold and Lincoln were Britain's most valuable asset for several hundred years. Although the breeds have been adapted in the past 150 years for better quality meat carcasses, their popularity has waned since their heyday. Following breeding improvements in the early 18th century, which produced breeds such as Lincoln, Leicester, Teeswater, Romney Marsh, Wensleydale and Cotswold, these were ideal for use on arable farms fertilising the fields and providing high yields of wool. They were large sheep, slow to mature, but which produced excellent fleeces, with wool fibres over a foot (30cm) long.

PRIMITIVE & PARKLAND

These breeds have changed relatively little since the first animals arrived from Scandinavia or the continent. They generally are found on the western fringes of the UK, such as the island of Soay, part of the St Kilda group off the west of Scotland, and the Isle of Man. These animals are small, hardy and lean with good flavoured mutton. Adelaide Gosset described this group of sheep in 1911. *'They are very hardy and picturesque, make excellent mutton, and except in very cold climates yield wool of exceptional quality.'*

There are three groups of Primitive and Parkland sheep:

Primitives – descendants of the earliest sheep in the UK, between the Neolithic and Iron Age – 2,000-4,000 years ago. Include Soay, Orkney (North Ronaldsay) and Shetland;

Four-horned – Their ancestors were probably brought with the Viking invaders, around 1,000 years ago. Include Hebridean, Manx Loaghtan and Jacob;

Parkland – Castlemilk Moorit, a recently developed breed from Dumfriesshire.

HALFBREDS & MULE

Halfbreds are where the mountain breeds meet the lowlands. Ewes from the mountains are bred with Blueface or Border Leicesters to produce Mules or Halfbreds, also crosses with the Cheviot breed. This produces such animals as The Welsh Halfbred, Scotch Mule, Scottish Greyface and Shetland Cheviot.

Flock of Ryland sheep

BREED NUMBERS

Rather surprisingly, nobody really knows how many sheep of each breed there are in the UK. The closest we can get to knowing is probably through the yield of wool, which is recorded by the British Wool Marketing Board (BWMB). By using their data on average breed fleece weights, together with total wool yields by type of wool, a fairly close approximation can be made to the numbers of breeding ewes of the main breed types. According to the latest estimates from the government of the national flock size, there were 14.3 million breeding female sheep in the UK in 2012. Based on the 2012 Wool Marketing Board data, the breed types as a proportion of the national flock, and the corresponding numbers of breeding ewes this would represent is:

Bluefaced & Border Leicester & halfbreds	44.6%	6,371,000
Mountain	24.0%	3,435,000
Hill	17.6%	2,521,000
Downland	10.9%	1,565,000
Lowland	2.4%	343,000
Primitives	0.3%	43,000
Longwools	0.1%	20,000

The combined uplands of Britain constitute about a third of the land area, with around three-quarters of Scotland being rough upland grazing, much of it only suitable for sheep production. It is not surprising then that the mountain breeds and their cross-bred progeny dominate the breed league tables. One result from these figures which is particularly striking is the degree to which the once mighty Longwools have diminished in number.

MIXING THE BREEDS

As we have seen, a reduction in the importance of wool to British farming coincided at the dawn of the Industrial Revolution with increased demand for meat. In reaction to these fundamental changes, and the efforts of breeders such as Bakewell, distinct breeds developed from the late 18th century. The use of wether sheep to produce both wool and meat declined as the focus changed to producing meat as quickly as possible. The question then arose what to do with the wethers which had been grazing in the uplands, and hitherto producing wool? Somehow these had to be fattened much quicker, which meant moving them to the lowlands. So, over the 100 years between about 1750 and 1850, an integrated system of sheep production evolved which made the most of all the various environmental niches and the breeds which occupied them. This system became known as stratification.

Welsh Mule at Royal Welsh Show

At first glance, stratification seems ridiculously complicated. It involves moving animals up and down hills, and cross-breeding on an apparently bewildering scale. In fact, if it is borne in mind that the process is simply wringing out the last drop of benefit from the principle of the right breed of sheep in the right place, it does become a little clearer. The following explanation has nevertheless been somewhat simplified. Let us assume that farms in the UK are divided into three groups, depending on their altitude – mountain, hill and lowland.

THE MOUNTAINS

(300 metres altitude and above)

On the very highest hills, only very hardy sheep can survive, so they stay there to happily breed amongst themselves. These breeds (such as Scottish Blackface, Welsh Mountain, Herdwick, Swaledale and North Cheviot) are generally good mothers, have a covering of rough, thick wool, but are small animals, and produce fewer

A Lakeland fell, Cumbria

and smaller offspring than the larger breeds of lower altitudes. A lamb from these breeds will have a carcass weight of around 8 to 16 kg. This compares with modern market demands for animals with weights of 14 to 21 kg.

In the past, castrated male lambs would have been kept as wethers. Today, once sufficient ewe lambs have been kept back to become future breeding stock, the remaining lambs are transferred to the lowlands as 'store lambs' where they are fattened or used for breeding by crossing with other breeds. Older ewes which have already lambed several times are moved to the milder climate of the hill areas where they are bred with rams from upland breeds.

THE HILLS (150-450m)

At these altitudes, some hardiness is needed, but with a kinder climate than the mountain tops, larger, less hardy breeds will survive. Once a mountain ewe had produced a few lambs, she is unable to withstand the winter conditions on the top of the mountains, so is 'semi-retired' down to the middle altitude of the hills for a couple of years, where she is crossed with the longwool breeds (mostly Blueface or Border Leicesters) to produce 'half-bred' or 'mule' lambs. For a very long time, it had been noticed that there were particular benefits from mating different sheep breeds. Firstly, such matings produced a 'cross-bred' lamb of more uniform shape and size, and secondly the cross-bred lamb showed increased vitality – known as 'hybrid vigour'.

If male, these cross-bred lambs are moved to the lowlands to be finished for the butcher. The female lambs also go down to the lowlands, but are bred with bigger lowland breed rams to produce larger lambs for the butcher. Having produced these half-bred lambs, the mountain ewe is sent off for ewe mutton, as is the half-bred ewe, once she has produced several crops of lambs.

Above: Hills at edge of Radnor Forest, mid-Wales
Below: Lowland at Leintwardine, Shropshire

THE LOWLANDS (below 300m)

Finally, in the lowlands the main business was to produce fat lambs for the butcher. Lowland breeds are of larger size, and normally have the best shape (conformation) for meat. Being more fertile than upland and hill breeds, lowland ewes would be expected to rear an average of at least 1.5 lambs, compared with one lamb reared from mountain breeds.

The hill half-bred ewe lambs were crossed with lowland rams, such as the Southdown, or Suffolk to produce the ideal butchers' lambs that could be fattened on grass over the summer.

'Store' lambs from the mountains and hills joined the locally born lambs to graze the lush pastures and turnip/swede crops, and fatten quickly over the summer and autumn whilst adding fertility to the soil. Cereal crops could later be grown on the fields.

That is how the system of stratification originally developed. The final challenge for sheep farmers has been to overcome the demise of the mixed arable/sheep farms in the lowlands. Artificial fertiliser has made the sheep's soil-fertilising role redundant, so land is needed for pure crop production. The solution has been a general move to produce fat lambs at higher altitudes than before, so that even on the uplands, the sheep breeders have again adapted the versatile sheep into producing lambs which will fatten within a year. Two developments have enabled this – the increased availability of bought-in 'concentrate' feeds and the use of multipurpose breeds such as the relatively hardy Texel, which produces a well-fleshed carcass, with plenty of meat even in some of the difficult upland areas.

THE EVOLUTION OF BREEDING

The 'primitive' breeds of sheep differ from the more developed breeds in one significant physiological trait - they develop fat inside their bodies, rather than on the outside. So a primitive breed such as the Soay or Manx will store any surplus energy as fat inside its body cavity, leaving the butchers' carcass lean. On a typical Manx Loaghtan lamb, for which data is available, the carcass will have 5% fat content rather than the 28% for a typical modern commercial breed. To modern tastes, the leaner primitive sheep have attractions. Indeed, to the Victorians, they were also a favourite source of good quality mutton. However, for the farmer, the fat in a primitive breed is lost, as being inside the body cavity, it cannot be sold. This means that control of fat production for a primitive sheep is a crucial issue for the farmer.

Research has also shown that the 19th century 'improved breeds' did not have an advantage over the primitives when it comes to the question of meat yield. Bones, as a proportion of body weight, are higher in the improved breeds in general compared to the primitives, who have finer, thinner bones. Indeed, when comparing total meat yield in a carcass, the primitives win over the improveds due to their lack of fat and finer bones. However, primitive breed carcasses are small. The most widely-used modern meat breeds such as the Texel have redressed the balance to an extent by increasing the amount of lean meat, whilst offering an ideal size of carcass for the mass market.

The stratification system will no doubt continue to evolve. There is a move to reduce the amount of concentrate feed used to fatten sheep. When grass could, in theory fatten an animal for the table, why import expensive grain and protein crops, using additional cash and CO2? This move towards on-farm growing of feed may mean a revival of some of our native breeds which have been in decline. Either way, the great asset which is the gene pool contained in our unique variety of breeds must not be lost.

A group of mixed-breed upland ewes

In the past, genetic stock has become extinct when breeds lost their commercial value. Between 1900 and 1970, 26 UK native breeds of livestock became extinct. Who knows whether in the future, some of their characteristics will be in demand again?

In a rapidly changing farming world, the vital importance of these native breeds as custodians of great genetic variety, has been shown in a new research paper from the University of York[1] analysing the genetics of upland breeds in northern England – the Herdwick, Rough Fell and Dalesbred. The results revealed *'surprising and high levels of distinctiveness'*, which clearly showed *'the continued existence of rare gene pools that may provide useful adaptive fitness traits to increase the sustainability of livestock agriculture in a changing climate.'* If we lose any of these breeds it now seems we lose a hugely valuable genetic resource. Foremost in conserving our native breeds is the Rare Breeds Survival Trust (RBST). Thanks to its efforts, since its foundation in 1973, no British breeds of livestock have become extinct. In 2014, the RBST listed 23 native sheep breeds on its critical status Watchlist, which includes breeds with fewer than 1,500 animals. In a changing world, a wide genetic pool is essential. The loss of any of these breeds would be a serious loss to us all. The sheep breeds considered to be 'at risk' by the RBST are indicated on the listing: UK Sheep Breeds *(page 195).*

1 *Genetic Distinctiveness of the Herdwick Sheep Breed and Two Other Locally Adapted Hill Breeds of the UK.* Diana Bowles, Amanda Carson, Peter Isaac. January 29, 2014.

The process of cross breeding and indeed breed development continues today, including commercially developed composite sheep breeds which attempt to create an all-purpose sheep which can thrive in most environmental conditions. Whilst new breeds are to be welcomed, there is a danger here. The ideal for supermarkets is to have a consistent, uniform product available all year round, and with expected worldwide shortages of meat supplies, they are increasingly seeking to tighten their grip on the supply chain. This can be largely achieved using a system of 'vertical integration' in which the retailers and their processors dictate and control much of the production process through supply contracts, with farmers increasingly becoming simply hired hands. This has been largely achieved in the pig and poultry sectors, with the result that there are now few commercial breeds of either species. Were supermarkets to encourage the widespread use of the modern composite breeds, particularly as part of an integrated supply chain, and if the companies producing the breeds were to control the use and sale of the animals on the farm through licence agreements, there would be several serious concerns on a number of levels. The advent of Genetically Modified sheep increases the likelihood of this coming about. By narrowing the genetic variability of the national sheep flock, resistance to disease may in the longer term be threatened, and systems will become more homogenised and less diverse, taking less account of the natural conditions of the farm and region. Consumer choice is diminished as has happened with chicken, pigs and apples, to mention but a few foods. It would be a calamity if the unique variety of sheep breeds available to the UK were consigned to the farm museum and rare breed status.

'A little English beef and mutton will soon make a difference.'

George Eliot (1819-1880)
Middlemarch

Indeed, it would be far preferable if supermarkets gave the consumer information to enable them to make an informed choice by stating on the pack the breed of the animal and where it was produced. This could stimulate interest for the consumer in comparing the merits of our different breeds, and knowing where the animal had lived. This information is available to the supermarkets' packers, and is already displayed by many small suppliers *(see label)*. It remains to be seen whether the supermarkets would want to supply information on variability, when their focus is on consistency. Why complicate it with interesting information, when they can get away with the message to the consumer simply 'this is lamb'?

For mutton, the same dangers apply, as the ewe mutton could become restricted to fewer breeds, as dictated by the large supermarket supply chains.

Traceability Details

Farmer: **David Pugh**
Near: **Knighton**
Breed: **Beulah**

To learn more about this farm and others in the Graig Farm Producer Group visit:

www.graigfarm.co.uk/p1.htm

Born and Reared in the UK
Slaughtered in the UK at: 4102
Cut in the UK at: UK7074N

4 8 4 7 7

Above: A traceability label for a pack of mutton from the author's former meat company

Changes in Sheep Farming

Sheep farming has changed hugely since WWII. The old systems of arable sheep, mixed farms, four course rotations, and even the sheep breeding system have disappeared, to be replaced by more specialist and intensive sheep production. Gone are virtually all the wether mutton producers and effectively all butchers' lambs are now finished in under a year. Whilst the shepherd's basic seasonal tasks remain unchanged, a number of developments have led to a transformation of the sheep industry.

WOOL

As already discussed, the wool price has suffered since the 1960s following competition from oil-based synthetic fibres and textiles, which has removed a vital income from sheep farming.

SILAGE

The development of silage in bags has transformed beef and sheep farming. In order to make grass available to ruminant (grass-eating) animals all year round, some of the grass grown in the summer is preserved to feed through the winter. Originally, there was only one way of doing this, and that was by producing hay.

Hay is simply dried grass. Historically, it would have been dried loose in the field and then moved and piled into a haystack; then along came mechanical balers. Initially these baling machines produced small rectangular bales, and more recently the now familiar 'big round bales'. Of course in our maritime climate, the most difficult bit of producing hay is the small matter of drying the grass. If not done properly, moulds can develop in the hay which may be harmful to both man and animals. It is easy to make hay when the sun shines, but sometimes it simply doesn't. Historically, this unreliability of production has meant that in some years there was insufficient food to take animals through the winter. The discovery of a new, much more reliable preservation method, effectively pickling the grass as silage, was a major step forward.

Silage is grass or other 'forage' crops such as clover which are 'pickled' by excluding air, allowing natural microbes to create an acid environment to preserve the forage without completely drying it. In early systems of

Top: cut grass
Middle: baling and wrapping
Bottom: wrapped bales of silage

Haymaking, Welsh borders, probably early 20th century

silage production, from the first half of the 20th century, grass and other forage crops were harvested and brought from the field into large towers or clamps. Then, when the silage was needed in the winter, the clamp or tower was 'opened', and the silage was cut out, using special large-bladed tools. Later, this was mechanised with tractors. The silage then had to be carried to the animals in barns or outside in fields – all very labour-intensive operations. No real surprise then, when a review of agriculture by Viscount Astor and Benjamin Seebohm Rowntree (a sociological researcher, social reformer and industrialist) in 1939 dismissed silage. *'Interest in silage was never great in this country, and is now on the wane.'*

Bagged silage took off in the UK in the 1980s. Machines take large round bales of forage, and wrap them in plastic (mostly black) sheeting to exclude the air. Modern machines cut, roll and wrap all in one movement. Then, the bagged bales are taken on trailers to a convenient place on the farm, not even necessarily under cover, where the fermentation process preserves the forage. When needed, a large 'bale spike' on a tractor skewers the bale, and takes it to the animals, where the plastic is stripped off and the silage can, in the simplest systems, be fed to the animals by merely unrolling the bale. Silage is one of those natural processes which can be judged by the simple smell of it. A pleasant sweet/sour smell suggests a good fermentation, and therefore good preservation. The feeding quality is determined by the crop, and time of harvest. Crucially, as the protein level changes through the season, the secret is to make the silage as the crop reaches the optimum point between high protein and maximum yield. As the crop becomes older, so the protein and digestibility of the silage decreases. Timing, as with much of farming, is everything.

CHEMICAL FERTILISER

Spreading chemical fertiliser

The third factor which has changed in modern sheep farming practices was the introduction of manufactured fertiliser, particularly of nitrogen fertiliser, a product of the oil industry which produced cheap, clean crop food. This bagged fertiliser was a greatly simpler and less bulky system than using compost and animal manure. Bagged chemical fertiliser meant that the use of sheep to fertilise the soil was no longer thought necessary in this new modern mono-cropping age. Monoculture, or continuous cropping of cereals was now possible, especially with the use of chemicals to control pests and diseases. The traditional role of sheep as a supplier of fertility was, for the time being at least, over.

Modern Breeds

The recent increased use of multi-purpose sheep breeds such as the Welsh Lleyn, French Charollais and Dutch Texel means that now a meat-type animal can survive harsh upland conditions and still produce an excellent butchers' lamb. These recently popular breeds also have a high level of lean meat, and produce a fairly consistent shape of carcass for the supermarkets.

LLEYN

Developed in the 19th century by a landowner on the Lleyn peninsula in north Wales, the Lleyn was until recently a relatively unfamiliar breed of sheep in the UK. However, over the past 10 years the breed has become extremely popular across Britain and Ireland for its easy management combined with hardiness and prolificacy. Whereas many breeds achieve 1.5 reared lambs per ewe per year (a 150% lambing percentage), the Lleyn is capable of achieving 1.8 to 2 reared lambs. It is a medium-sized lowland breed, weighing up to 70kg. The Lleyn fits into many farming environments and its versatility suits both lowland and upland grazing.

THE TEXEL

Over the last 30 years the Continental Texel breed has had a significant impact on sheep meat production. The British Texel Sheep Society is now the UK's largest pedigree sheep society, with 2,000 registered pedigree breeders, which considering the first animals were only imported into the UK in the 1970s, is an extraordinary speed of development, especially in the rather conservative sheep breeding world. The main reason for the dramatic rate of adoption of the Texel is its ability to produce a type of lamb which is required in the meat market – plenty of meat and little fat. Whether the taste is quite up to traditional domestic breeds is still hotly debated. The breed has proved to be very adaptable, and able to live in many upland areas. This hardiness has resulted in upland and hill producers using the Texel to breed store lambs and cross bred females of a better meat yield than traditional upland, hill and down breeds.

The Texel breed originates from the island of Texel, off the north-western coast of Holland, where the ancient native sheep was known as Pielsteert (Pin-tail, because of its thin short tail). To this original breed on the island, far-seeing breeders at the end of the 19th century used several British breeds such as Lincoln, Leicester and Wensleydale to improve the prolificacy, growth rate and size. This target was largely achieved by the beginning of WWI, when the breed had developed into animals we would recognise today as being Texel.

"That's good. What'll you have?'
'Fish pie,' said she, with a glance at the menu.
'Fish pie! Fancy coming for fish pie to Simpson's. It's not a bit the thing to go for here.'
'Go for something for me, then,' said Margaret, pulling off her gloves. Her spirits were rising, and his reference to Leonard Bast had warmed her curiously.
'Saddle of mutton,' said he after profound reflection; 'and cider to drink. That's the type of thing. I like this place, for a joke, once in a way. It is so thoroughly Old English. Don't you agree?"

E. M. Forster (1879-1970)
Howards End

Large grass bales, Clun Valley, Shropshire, for hay or bagged silage

Sustainability of Mutton Production

The watchword today is sustainability, a word our forebears would possibly not have understood, but would have done naturally. Mutton production is part of the overall sheep industry. Here, then are a few considerations about sheep in general.

According to government figures, agriculture causes 9% of the UK's greenhouse gas (GHG) emissions. This is made up of:

- Nitrous oxide (around 55%), which is produced by the use of synthetic and organic fertilisers
- Methane (around 36%), which is created through the digestion processes in livestock animals and the production and use of manure and slurry
- Carbon dioxide (around 9%) from energy used for fuel and heating

However, sustainability is about more than just GHGs. Mutton is a product of sheep farming, its sustainability needs to be looked at within the sheep sector.

FERTILITY OF THE SOIL

Traditional upland sheep farming uses little or no artificial fertilisers. Where animals are housed over the winter, the farmyard manure produced will be cleaned out of the buildings in the spring, composted to break it down to be better absorbed by the soil, and then spread, particularly on the better land of upland farms. Traditionally on lowlands, sheep were used as manure machines. Confined by moveable fences, they were moved across arable fields to add fertiliser to the soil before ploughing for the next crop. As oil and therefore chemical fertiliser prices rise, the system of natural sheep fertiliser may again have a place in British lowland arable farming.

Clun Forest sheep in the Clun Valley, Shropshire

USE OF 'PERMANENT PASTURES'

Grass fields, also known as pastures or leys, can either be ploughed every few years and re-seeded (short-term leys), or simply left to their own devices, when they are called permanent pastures.

Whilst modern arable crop production uses plenty of artificial fertilisers to feed the crops, grass production for sheep uses far less. This is important in sustainability terms, as artificial nitrogen fertiliser in particular uses a great amount of energy in its manufacture, which means the production of high levels of greenhouse gases such as CO2. In addition to low levels of artificial fertiliser, grassland is fed in two ways, both of which require no additional inputs. Firstly, most grass seed mixtures contain clovers, which are legumes. This group of plants have nodules in the roots which convert nitrogen in the air into soluble nitrogen in the soil, which plants can then use to grow. Secondly, grazing sheep return most of the nutrients in the grass which they eat, manuring and fertilising the soil as they go. Sheep have been central to highly productive permanent grassland and arable and grass farming systems for centuries, using minimal inputs. Such systems are as sustainable as can be.

In addition to this lower use of artificial fertiliser, it is now being discovered that permanent pastures hold large amounts of carbon from the atmosphere through a process known as sequestration. It is now recognised that pastures lock up large amounts of carbon and that pastures continue to sequester more carbon from the atmosphere as the soil organic matter levels build up, although there is still some debate about the amounts that are accumulated each year. Grasslands, unless ploughed up after a year or two, are therefore an important accumulator of carbon.

LAND USE

The choices for agricultural use of upland areas are very limited. The two main options are to grow grass for cows and sheep, or to plant trees. With today's climate change concerns, feeding grass to animals rather than feeding them crops which humans could eat, is patently preferable.

Sheep are able to live in more extreme climates, at the top of hills and mountains, where often cattle or even trees cannot survive. To achieve any food production from such areas in the form of sheep meat, when there is no other option, is a positive contribution to the UK's food production. Because the UK sheep industry has such a wide variety of breeds, the land can be used by those best suited to the particular environmental conditions, to maximise efficiency.

Sheep on common land, Penybont, mid-Wales

MAINTAINING THE VIEW

Our upland landscapes are enjoyed for their aesthetic beauty and as places to walk, cycle, or horseride. Without sheep constantly grazing these areas, the natural habitat would be transformed within a few years to scrubland and eventually woodland in the lower areas. This would have a dramatic impact on the landscape, and reduce the access and enjoyment there for many people.

Hebridean Blackface sheep, Isle of Lewis

WOOL PRODUCTION

Naturally-coloured knitting wool

Woollen building insulation

The decline in the price of wool since the middle of the 20th century was a result of the introduction of oil-based synthetic fibres, at a time when fossil fuels were relatively cheap. As a natural fibre, wool has many advantages, including fire resistance, pest resistance and insulation value. Its production is also relatively low in carbon, compared with synthetically manufactured materials, and unlike crop-based fibres such as cotton, it is low in fertiliser use. Sheep can convert low quality pastures into useful fibre crops with little external input. We also still have the genetic resources within our native breeds to produce large quantities of high quality wool. Perhaps with a little additional genetic assistance from the Merino breeds, that quality could be increased still further.

Whilst wool's insulation properties are starting to be harnessed in buildings, there are other characteristics which could yet be exploited, such as its hydroscopic (water-holding) quality, and even within medicine its ability to help blood to clot. It also has bacteriological properties, and even Hippocrates advocated greasy wool's use in dressing wounds. Wool's unique ability to arrange its fibres into felt could be used more widely as a natural fabric.

Future of the Family Sheep Farm

Rising worldwide populations and their demands for meat are already beginning to put strains on agriculture's ability to meet demand. The solutions proposed range from vegetarianism to more intensive livestock production. The call for intensification of food production is predicated on a continuing supply of cheap oil, which provides fertilisers and controls the pests of agriculture. However, because of the dangers of climate change we know that we cannot continue to use fossil fuels as we have in the past. So how do we solve this food demand/environmental damage conundrum? The answer will undoubtedly lie in a range of solutions, including a reduced dependence on oil in agriculture, and more sustainable farming systems, combined with increased efficiency of production, and a realisation that we cannot continue to look at meat as a cheap source of protein.

Just how sustainable is the current situation? Using high levels of fossil fuels and inputs, protein and energy crops are grown and shipped round the world to feed intensively-reared cattle, chickens and pigs in the UK, which in turn feed us. All this at a lower cost than the sheep and cattle simply grazing our hills and pastures. Whilst it works in today's economic system, there is something intrinsically unreal and unsustainable about this.

Increased efficiency is normally defined as increasing the scale of agriculture – large

Family livestock farm near Coniston, Lake District

mechanised farms employing fewer people seems to have worked in the past. However, this solution can have a devastating impact on the social fabric of the countryside. As farms become larger, so traditional family farmers are displaced, and their houses become holiday or commuter homes. Then the amenities, schools, shops and pubs become 'uneconomic' and close, reducing the attraction for young people who see farming as too isolated. Little wonder then that the average age of farmers in Britain is around 60.

However, there is an alternative to 'bigger is better'. The economies of scale created by combining farms can be achieved another way, by greater co-operation *between* farms. Yet, for some reason, the prevailing view amongst farmers in Britain is that they are still all yeomen who deal with the market as individuals. It is only the French who do this collaboration stuff, they say.

One example illustrates the efficiency benefits of traditional farmers working together and also brings us back to mutton. While genetics companies develop expensive new breeds, it seems our existing sheep breeds have by no means run out of steam when it comes to their potential for improvement through traditional breeding. The trick seems to be to gain scale by several farmers working together, then making use of modern technology.

A group of upland farmers in mid-Wales proved just that with their flocks of Welsh Hill Speckleface sheep together with individual identification and recording of each animal.

Most upland sheep breeds produce purebred lambs that are too small for the main UK market, which looks for carcasses from around 14-20kg. Most of these smaller lambs must be sold on the export market which is unreliable and produces volatile prices. This group of farmers decided to work together to increase the size of their lambs by selectively breeding from within their own sheep. Weights were regularly recorded and, using scanners, body fat and muscle sizes were also measured for each individual animal. All this data was fed into a computer programme. Finally, when slaughtered, weights and meat yields completed the picture. Recording was made easier on some of the farms by use of electronic tagging, enabling fast accurate recording of data from a large number of animals. This may sound like common sense, but it is still very much the exception in sheep farming. Armed with this equipment and data the mid-Wales farmers selectively bred their flocks with remarkable results.

Between 1999 and 2006, the average weight of the lamb carcasses on some of the farms increased by about 3 kg. In some cases this represented a staggering 25% increase over the six or seven years of their improvement work. What is more, this weight gain was predominantly muscle weight, seen when the farmers measured the 'eye' muscle found in a lamb chop, as well as monitoring the amount of fat on the animals' backs. The cost to the farmers of this extra production was minimal, as the sheep still grazed the same hillsides, and had virtually no extra feeding. According to one of the farmers, Nigel Elgar, an unexpected bonus was in the temperament of the ewe. *'A stressed and timid ewe would not give as much milk to the lamb as a calm mother. As a result the lambs that performed well in the early stages of life reflected the amount of milk from their mothers, and generally came from calmer ewes, making handling and recording easier. These offspring*

Three generations of Thomas' on their Radnorshire farm: Richard (left) with his father John and his sons Jonathan and James

then became replacements in the flock, passing on the trait.' Success also depended on the farmers working together and having a large enough 'pool' of animals to select from. By using the same ram on different flocks (through artificial insemination of the ewes as well as through natural mating), any variability due to management or environment could be eliminated.

Nigel explained that the traditional obsession with breed characteristics of the sheep can also be catered for with such a system *'With the large numbers of animals involved there were sufficient numbers of high performing animals to further select on other criteria, even the facial markings, and other personal preferences of each farmer could be kept, even though this made no material difference to the yield of meat.'*

The biggest benefit of all was the market value of the animals. With the small Speckleface sheep, the normally 'under-sized' lambs are often not suitable for the mass market. However, by this careful breeding programme, many more lambs were large enough for the supermarkets, and could therefore avoid the price penalty of producing small lambs or for a volatile export market. Importantly, there was no noticeable difference in flavour of the larger animals.

> *'It is not so much that farmers think that the system of individual marketing brings a greater collective profit than a collaborative system would. .. It is in the bone of their bone to compete with one another in marketing ... – almost every farmer nourishes a secret belief that in this competition he manages to do just a little better than his neighbour.'*
>
> From *'The Farmer and his Market'* prepared for the Liberal Party Land Policy, 1927

Modern ear-tags for livestock

In terms of mutton, this means a breed famous for its superb mutton flavour like the Speckleface can now produce more profitable, hardy lambs, as well as great mutton. Surely this practical experience in mid-Wales is a lesson which could be followed by more groups of farmers? Greater collaboration in a range of activities could have a revolutionary impact on both farmers, the rural economy and food production. Why leave it to the French?

Family-run upland sheep farms like that of the Thomas family (three generations pictured on previous page) in mid-Wales, are the backbone and life-blood of the rural economy and structure. The full value of their contribution in maintaining the rural community has never been measured. We risk losing these custodians of the uplands of Britain at our peril.

The Drovers

Two Welsh drovers

With the growth of urban populations from the 17th century came two problems for the supply of sheep meat. Most of the production was in the west and north of the UK, but the growing towns tended to be in central, east and southern parts. The other problem was that the upland areas which were producing much of the cattle and sheep destined for the town butchers, were not suited to 'finishing' (fattening) the animals, ready for the butchers – the environment was simply too harsh.

As a result, animals for slaughter, predominantly cattle and sheep (for mutton) and to a lesser extent pigs, but even geese and turkeys, were literally walked from the producing regions in Scotland, Wales, Ireland and elsewhere in England, to the fattening areas and markets of England.

This task was for the drovers. By the third quarter of the 18th century, London's Smithfield Market alone received around 100,000 cattle and 750,000 sheep, all of which were walked there by drovers.

Covering 10-12 miles a day with sheep, and more for cattle, these mass migrations of stock were undertaken by specialist stockmen known as drovers. Fragments of many of the original drovers' roads still exist. In Wales and parts of England, the old drovers' roads can still be plotted through small clumps of non-native Scots Pine trees, which were planted originally to mark the routes and to show that the drovers were welcome. Being locally unusual trees, they could be seen from a distance to keep drovers on the correct path to London or wherever they were headed. On the chalk downs of southern England the signpost tree was yew, and in parts of Buckinghamshire, Portuguese Laurel marked the way for the drovers.

Apart from clumps of trees and drovers pubs, modern indications of drovers roads include road names including the words 'Welsh', 'Halfpenny' (the fee charged for an overnight stay for livestock), 'Drove' or 'Drift'.

Ancient drovers' roads in Wales. Note Scots Pines denoting a welcome resting point

Along the British drovers' roads were frequent stopping places where both drovers and animals could be refreshed, fed and watered. Farmers along the routes were only too pleased to take in the drovers and their animals, for the free manure the sheep and cattle gave. Occasional drovers' pubs can still be found (eight *Drovers* were still open for business in England in 2011, plus *Drovers Arms*, *Drovers Call* and *Drovers Rest*). At the *Drover's House* inn in Wales there is still a notice in Welsh on the wall saying 'seasoned hay, tasty pastures, good beer, comfortable beds'. These hostelries were places where thirst could be quenched and other needs met along the long journey to London or elsewhere. However, the bucolic view of drovers wandering around the countryside enjoying local hospitality is as far from the truth as was the view of some writers of the time that all drovers were thieves and scoundrels. In reality of course the majority of drovers were at neither extreme. It was far from simple to become a drover. Since Tudor times, would-be drovers had to be licensed, over 30 years of age, married and a house owner.

Cattle and sheep tended to travel in separate droves. Sheep flocks could be 1,500 to 2,000 strong. On their journeys, drovers faced dangers from highwaymen and footpads, threats from storms and floods, and the regular inconvenience and cost of tollgates on a very inadequate road system. No roads had been built in the UK between the departure of the Romans and the turnpikes of the 18th century. The routes the drovers took encompassed a variety of ancient ways, from the Roman roads to ancient packhorse trails. Often detours and river crossings were required to avoid the expensive tolls on the turnpike roads. Drovers had to be both fit and quick-witted to survive, with their livestock intact. Night stops required places which provided suitable accommodation for the animals. Drought and animal disease epidemics such as Foot and Mouth and Rinderpest were added hazards from which the animals had to be protected by the vigilant drover.

When arriving at an inn for the night, a drover's first concern would be food for his dogs. So close was the relationship man to dog that on the road the drovers often shared

Kings Head Inn, Llandovery, where the Black Ox Bank was formed

even their oatmeal porridge with their dogs. One recorded memory of an early 19th century childhood in the north of Scotland describes how she would often pass solitary collies on the road, making their way north. These animals belonged to Scottish drovers who had decided to stay in England for the harvest after their journey south and had sent their dogs home by themselves. The animals simply returned home by the same route they had come, stopping at the same inns and farmhouses as they had stayed with their masters. When the drover himself returned home, he paid the same innkeepers and farmers for feeding his dogs the previous year. In Wales, author Hugh Evans told of drover Clough and his dog Carlo, who travelled to Kent with some sheep. Whilst there, Mr Clough decided to sell his pony and return home by coach. But what to do with the faithful Carlo? He tied the pony's harness to the back of the dog, with a note asking that the inn-keepers en route feed and water Carlo, and sent him on his way. Carlo set off for home in Wales, and visited every inn they had stopped at on the way to Kent. At each he was looked after, and arrived home safely a week later. A description of just how essential the drover's dog was to him was recorded in Scotland in the early 20th century *'The ordinary drover's dog's business is on the roads...He goes ahead and blocks the side-roads, he keeps the flock in hand and sees they don't go too fast, he guards open garden gates. And he does it all so methodically, and without being told to do it, that one can see he is quite an expert in his business.'*

The drovers acted largely on trust, collecting animals mostly from smallholder farmers, and making payment to them on their return from the urban markets. A crooked drover could therefore spell disaster for a trusting smallholder and his family, for whom the sale of a few livestock was their annual income. However, many drovers were trusted with taking more than livestock on their travels. Between Wales and England they carried 'Ship Money' collected in Wales by officials in the time of Charles I, as well as Welsh gold and silver for the Archbishop of York. It was the fact that they often carried large amounts of cash or other valuables that prompted several Welsh drovers to found banks in order that they could avoid the dangers of carrying such tempting luggage. In the 18th and 19th centuries, banks in Wales and England could issue their own bank notes, together with cheques, which the drovers frequently used rather than cash. The Black Ox and the Black Sheep were two drovers' banks. The Black Ox Bank, or Banc yr Eidion Du in Welsh was started at the Kings Head Inn in Llandovery, West Wales by a drover by the name of David Jones in 1799. The native cattle to the area were, and still are, black (The Welsh Black breed). Indeed, such was the popularity and trust imparted locally by the Black Ox Bank, that even into the 19th century, Bank of England notes were treated with great suspicion in

Two Drovers' Inns. Left: Howey, mid-Wales. Right: Inverarnan, near Loch Lomond

much of West Wales. The Black Ox was taken over by Lloyds Bank in 1909, and the Lloyds branch in Llandovery still has the initials of David Jones over the doorway.

There was good money to be made by landowners on the Scottish borders as hosts to the drovers and their livestock, especially as cross-border trade flourished after the unification of England and Scotland in 1603. Mostly this was with cattle, as until the late 18th century there was a misconception amongst the sheep farmers of Scotland that sheep could not be driven long distances. By the late 17th century the droving trade was causing great hardship to many Borders farming tenants, who were driven off the land to make way for the equivalent of the motorway services of the droving world.

Not all droving traffic from Scotland was destined for English markets however. With increasing populations employed in the new industries of the central belt of Scotland, the movement of Highland stock to the expanding urban centres of the Scottish lowlands became a significant source of income to the Highlands, where skilled drovers were in great demand. The drovers had to carry much of what they would need as, especially on the uplands of Scotland, sources of provisions were scarce. Porridge was a staple food, as was oatmeal which was sometimes mixed with blood taken from their cattle to produce black pudding. In Sir Walter Scott's *The Two Drovers*, of 1827, the Highland drover travelled south with just *'... a few handfuls of oatmeal and two or three onions renewed from time to time, and a ram's horn full of whiskey, used regularly but sparingly every night and morning.'*

Lloyds Bank, Llandovery, which still carries the initials of David Jones over its front door

The drovers enjoyed singing along their way. Many of the songs were bawdy, others acted as blessings, to ward off evil spirits. One such was called a *Sain for Sheep* (a sain being a sign of the cross), and it reflects the wide range of dangers which the drovers faced on their journey:

'The Sain placed by Mary
upon her flock of sheep
Against birds, against dogs,
against beasts, against men,
Against hounds, against thieves,
Against polecats, against marten-cats,
against eye, against envy,
Against disease, against 'Gaoban',
In the hollow of your meeting,
Be yours the aiding of God;
On the hillock of your lying, Whole be your rising.'

Drover's statue, Llandovery, mid-Wales

One early 19th century farmer in Northamptonshire specially bred his Leicester sheep for the long walk to London by crossing with a 'horned tup', which gave the offspring *'longer legs and less wool* [to] *travel better to the London market.'*

Once at Smithfield, the drovers would have been met with an extraordinary sight, as Dickens vividly described in Oliver Twist in 1838: *'It was market morning. The ground was covered, nearly ankle deep, with filth and mire; a thick steam perpetually rising from the reeking bodies of the cattle and mingling with the fog, which seemed to rest upon the chimney-tops, hung heavily above. All the pens in the centre of the large area, and as many temporary pens as could be crowded into the vacant spaces were filled with sheep; tied up to posts by the gutter side were long lines of beasts and oxen, three or four deep. Countrymen, butchers, drovers, hawkers, boys, thieves, idlers, and vagabonds of every low grade were mingled together in a mass; the whistling of drovers, the barking of dogs, the bellowing and plunging of oxen, the bleating of sheep, the grunting and squeaking of pigs, the cries of hawkers, the shouts, oaths and quarrelling on all sides; the ringing of bells and the roar of voices, that issued from every public-house; the crowding, pushing, driving, beating, whooping and yelling; the hideous and discordant din that resounded from every corner of the market; and the unwashed, unshaven, squalid, and dirty figures constantly running to and fro, and bursting in and out of the throng, rendered it a stunning and bewildering scene, which quite confused the senses.'*

Individual drovers were valued and trusted by most farmers because the task of droving required fine judgement based on experience. They had to know the land and the weather and to understand just how hard to push the livestock. Move too slowly and they could miss the market, but drive the animals too fast and they would lose weight and fetch a lower price when sold.

As we will see later, droving declined with the increased use of coastal shipping in the early 19th century, and was dealt a final blow with the growth of the railways in the mid-19th century. Yet, like so many aspects of livestock farming, we still use the word in colloquial English when people go somewhere in droves, meaning large numbers.

The movement of sheep from high ground in sparsely populated areas to lowland farms for fattening continues, but transport is now by lorry. Within living memory, in the Essex marshlands, sheep were brought from Wales to be fattened for the London market. When ready, the animals were put on barges and carried down to slaughterhouses in the capital. The boats would then be loaded with horse manure for the return journey, to grow more grass for feeding more sheep.

NEW ZEALAND'S DROVERS

In New Zealand one sheep drover became a legend, and although few facts are known about the true exploits of James Mackenzie, a statue commemorating him and his dog Friday stands in Fairlie, near Canterbury, South Island. As his biographer writes *'Mackenzie's exploits won him the admiration of those on the margins of society. He was a hero to many would-be farmers of small means. Those who resented the power of wealthy landowners also identified with him, and his rebellious spirit inspired many who did not fit easily into genteel Canterbury society.'*

Having been working as a sheep drover, in March 1855 Mackenzie was found in a pass in the upper Waitaki River with 1,000 sheep which had been stolen from a nearby farm. He denied the theft, claiming that he had been hired by the owners to move them. Although arrested, he soon escaped and walked 160km to the small port town of Lyttelton, where he was recaptured within days. He was tried in April by the Supreme Court, found guilty and sentenced to five years' hard labour. He twice escaped, albeit briefly, from the convict road gang, in May and June 1855. After the second recapture he was clamped in irons and closely watched. In September his luck changed. A new investigation of his case found errors in both the police enquiry and the trial. After his pardon, nothing more is known about Mackenzie, and it is assumed that he returned to Australia from whence he had come after leaving his native Scotland. However his legacy was great. The remote area where he was found with the sheep was soon being grazed by farmers' sheep, and the region was even known locally as the Mackenzie Country. According to his biographer, his pardon won popular sympathy in a frontier society still engaged in establishing its social and political norms. His life took on legendary proportions. His almost superhuman strength and a 'fabulous' dog saw him held up as shepherd, drover and thief extraordinaire.

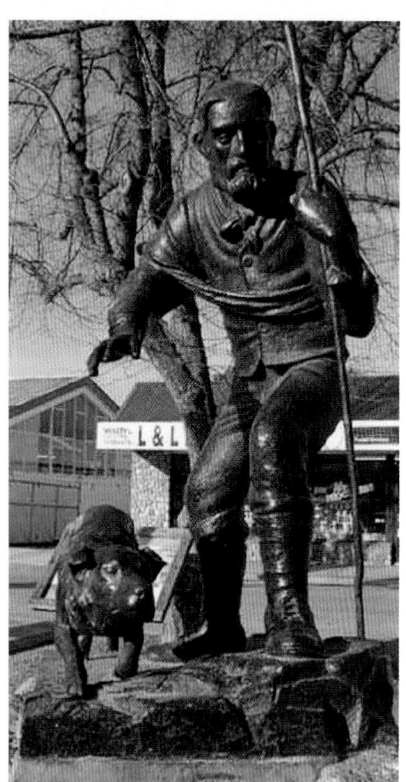

Statue of James Mackenzie in Fairlie, New Zealand

Opposite: Sheepdroving in the Australian outback by Walter Withers (1912)

AUSTRALIAN DROVING

In Australia droving still continues in some areas when the sheep follow the availability of feed across the vast expanses of Australian sheep country – known as Travel for Grass. However, modern-day motorised droving is a far cry from the days of horseback droving, which continued into the 1950s.

Sheep droving was not the romanticised world of Waltzing Matilda. It was described by one drover Peter Rake, as '*boring, mundane, mind-numbing work. The conversation level drops to an all-time low with nothing to stimulate the mind. The same thing day in and day out seven days a week.*' The sheep were expected to travel six miles a day, and in the heat of the Outback, the flock was started out early for the day's drove. '*The drovers would get a good breakfast into themselves and a hot black pannican of tea, saddle up and catch up with the mob of sheep, which the boss would have let out of the break half an hour ago. The mornings, being the cool time of the day, we would move the sheep along a bit to be in range of the next water by afternoon.'* Generally the animals would be taken along Travelling Stock Routes, but occasionally the trail led through private property. Here *'the grazier on the property would send his blokes down to keep his stock away from the droving mob.'* Just as in the UK, word went ahead of the drove to ensure that farmers kept their animals secure to avoid them being swept up into the flock of animals passing through. The tension between drovers and farm or ranch stockmen was as intense in 17th century Britain as in 20th century Australia.

During Peter Rake's long days droving in the Outback, *'At about mid-morning the sheep would look for a bit of a rest, and after they were 'Road Broke' they would all pick the same time every day to rest. The drovers would then catch up on a bit of kip under a shady tree if available or on the shady side of the horse.'*

Food for the drovers was the ubiquitous cold mutton and damper bread, washed down with a large mug of tea. The 'mob' of sheep moved in this way was often measured in thousands.

DROVING USA

Droving was also big business in the USA, with vast numbers of sheep being moved west during the 19th century. Droves of three to six thousand animals were the norm. With such numbers, they couldn't be individually counted, so with each group of 100 sheep, a black one was added, so that when they needed to be counted the drovers simply counted the black sheep. From 1865 to 1885, most of the sheep were older animals, but from 1885 to 1901, the majority were wethers. Like their fellow drovers across the New World, American drovers rode horseback, covering some 10 miles a day, with provisions being carried in covered wagons.

THE ARRIVAL OF THE RAILWAYS

The arrival of the railways in the early 19th century had a revolutionary impact on the farming and food industry of Britain and abroad.

We have a fascinating insight into the transforming impact the arrival of the railways had on livestock farming, on the very cusp of the railway age, from a book written in 1840 by Clark Hillyard, a farmer from Northamptonshire. Hillyard warmly welcomed the coming of the railways to transport his sheep and cattle to the London market of Smithfield. He viewed it overall as the *'... means of adding to the supply of meat for the London market by preventing some loss of weight, which has hitherto been in driving sheep and beasts to Smithfield .... In complaints of prices obtained in London, many forget the loss of weight by driving; it is not only the loss of weight of meat prevented by beasts being carried instead of driven a great distance to the London market, but the superior quality of the meat, from the beasts not having been killed when in an exhausted and wasting condition.'*

Droving, whilst achieving the task of moving animals across the country, had a number of drawbacks. It was slow, and depended for its success on animals eating sufficient food

Loading sheep onto trains at Kington, Herefordshire, in the 1920s

en route to market or fattening farm that they did not lose condition or weight – a difficult and not always achievable balance, at least according to Hillyard. Having often walked his own animals from Northamptonshire to London's Smithfield Market, he knew what he was talking about.

Taking weights of his animals on farm and at Smithfield, Hillyard measured the weight losses of his livestock driven the sixty miles from his farm to Smithfield, and found '... *on the average a loss of half a stone in the carcass of each sheep.'* That is some 3 kg on a sheep weighing on average at the time some 30kg, which is a 10% loss. Hillyard states that 1.5 million sheep were sold at Smithfield annually, and calculates the total value of annual weight losses through the process of droving sheep and cattle to London as £240,000 annually (some £20 million at today's values).

Hillyard's local railway station was Roade, built in 1838 as the main station for Northampton. It was part of the London and Birmingham Railroad Company (L&BRC), which had started in 1833, and was merged with the London and North Western Railway (L&NWR) in 1846. Roade station survived until Dr Beeching's axe in 1964. L&BRC quoted Hillyard £2 (£200 in today's values) for a carriage from Roade to London, which would accommodate 20-30 sheep. The cost for droving sheep by road to London from Northamptonshire was 1/6d per head of sheep (£7.50 in today's values). Taking all his costs into account, Hillyard calculated that the railway would cost an extra shilling (5p) - £5 today - over the cost of droving. Nevertheless, he felt confident that this would be a worthwhile cost as *'There cannot be doubt but that the additional value of each beast and sheep will be much more than this.'* Hillyard also argued that the railway would level out supply of animals to the London market, as *'Monday is the principal market day in Smithfield ; the report of Friday's market will be known in the country before the time of sending off beasts or sheep to Smithfield: thus the market is likely to be more equally supplied than it hitherto has been.'* In other words, the railway would result in better market intelligence for farmers, allowing them to avoid periods of glut in Smithfield, when prices drop. From London's butchers' point of view, according to Hillyard, they too would benefit from steadier prices and more continuity of supply – a major economic and probably unforeseen advantage of the new railways. No doubt the calculation being made by Hillyard as to the advantages from this new idea of moving livestock to market by train was being made by many others across the country. Little surprise then that this marked the nadir of droving. From now on it would see a steady and terminal decline. Even by 1845, there were over

Knighton market, Welsh borders

100,000 animals transported by rail on the Liverpool and Manchester line alone.

The railways were not the only nail in the coffin of the traditional droving system. From the 1830s London had been supplied with 'very fine' Scots beef by steam ship from Scotland. This too had a dramatic effect on the quality of livestock entering the London market. The relatively quick steamer journey, which would allow food and water to be available to the livestock, compared to a walk of several hundred miles, was inevitably going to improve meat quality, and quantity. In a reported London dinner party conversation before the arrival of the steamships, a Scotsman remarked *'Ye are indebted to my country for this fine beef;'* to which a wag at the party had replied *'For the bones, not for the beef'*. As Hillyard wrote *'Such a retort could not now be aptly applied to such an observation'*, such had been the improvement in meat quality when the animals had not walked to London.

UK postage stamp 1980: sheep travelling by rail in 1830

The 1980 postage stamp shows a railway carriage carrying sheep in purpose-built double decked vehicles (mainly found in the North and particularly in Scotland). Presumably these are similar design to that offered to Hillyard.

As the transport of livestock by rail became more popular, so facilities were built to handle them. Sometimes sidings were devoted to livestock. There were other benefits too for the sheep farmer. Local rail journeys to market towns from outlying branch lines became the accepted method of livestock transport for many farmers. The railways enabled breeding stock as well as fat stock to be moved easily around the country, which meant the practical logistics of arranging cross-breeding became very much simpler.

Soon carcasses, as well as live animals, were moved by rail. A major switch to transporting fresh killed meat in the 1930s resulted in a steady decline in the livestock traffic. The final blow to moving livestock on the railways occurred in 1962 when British Railways reduced the number of stations open for livestock from over 2,500 to just over 200. The service was finally closed in 1975.

Today, all sheep are taken to market or abattoir by road.

THE END OF THE DROVERS' ROAD

The coming of the railways caused a fairly sudden end to the drovers' way of life. The last man to use the drove roads of Wales bought 100 bullocks in Tregaron in 1870 and drove them to Hereford, taking a week to cover the distance. The last drove of Welsh mountain ewes took place in 1900. Dugald MacDougall was the last Argyllshire drover to pass away in April 1957. He was born in 1866. Many of his relations had been drovers, and he had driven cattle to the famous Falkirk Trysts, or fairs, which were the largest of their kind in their heyday.

Modern cattle lorry loading sheep at a livestock market

As one ex-drover put it *'The droving days are over, and more's the pity. Nowadays the animals are loaded into a big truck, up goes the tailboard and that's the last you see of them.'*

It was not only the drovers who were out of work when the railways and then lorries took their livelihoods. The inns and pasture owners, the blacksmiths, and all the other supporters of the drovers work had to find other forms of income.

The *Yorkshire Post* carried a postscript to the drover on 30th August 1961 *'Last Drover is 100. Mr Edward Know, believed to be the last of England's cattle drovers, celebrated his 100th birthday at South Croydon yesterday. He received congratulatory telegrams from the Queen and the Federal President of the Meat Drovers' Association of Australia.'*

When to market?

It is vitally important for a farmer to understand when an animal is fit for the butcher and our plates. As the young animal develops, firstly as a foetus, and later after birth, it first establishes its nervous system, then bone and then muscle. The bones and muscles continue to develop until physiologically the animal has reached its predetermined adult size. At this point it will develop a layer of fat on its body. The crucial job of the livestock farmer in producing good quality meat is to carefully manage this last fattening stage. He must judge when the optimal amount of fat has been put down, referred to as 'putting a finish' on it. At this point the finished animal is ready to be sold to the butcher before the meat becomes too fat.

How do farmers know when that point is? It's mostly a question of touch, and practice. The farmer with experience will feel how much fat there is on the animal in three places: the tail root or dock, the loin and the ribs *(see pictures below).*

It is very important that this process is done correctly, because the farmer's income can depend on it. The animal has to have just the right level of fat – too much or too little and the farmer will suffer price penalties. If he sells direct to his customers, they will soon vote with their feet if his animals are too fat or too lean.

When selling any livestock into the mass market through one of the large abattoirs, the price the farmer receives will depend on conformation of the carcass (its shape and distribution of muscle), and fatness. Each animal is assessed after slaughter on these two criteria, and given a score on both. Fatness is scored from 1, too lean, to 5, too fat. Generally, the best price is for a sheep with fat scores of 2 or 3. The conformation is strangely classified on a scale of E U R O P (E a lot of muscle, to P with very little meat). The ideal target here is E to R, although mountain sheep are often classified as an O, and will still make very good eating.

Checking for fat at the tail dock

Checking for fat at the loin

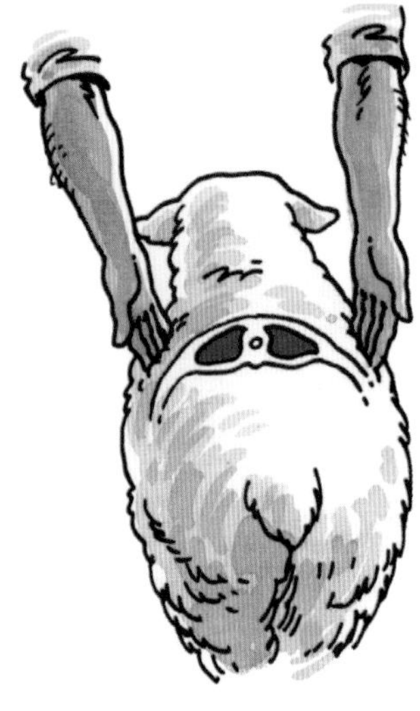

Checking for fat at the ribs

Abattoirs

There are three main stages in the journey an animal takes from a field to your dinner plate. At the beginning is the farmer, with whom we are fairly familiar. Buying the mutton, through butchers, farm shops, markets or direct from the farmer is similarly straightforward. It's the bit in the middle, the slaughtering of the animal, that most of us know little about, yet abattoirs are not only a vital link in the meat supply chain, but are also major contributors to local economies.

In the 1930s there were some 30,000 abbatoirs in the UK, many attached to the local butchers. In more rural areas the system was fairly simple. Farmers brought their livestock a short distance to their local abattoir, where the animals were slaughtered, butchered and sold to the local inhabitants. Cities were more complicated, as the animals were either brought into the larger conurbations alive, or in the form of carcasses. Often (as old photos show), butchers' shops would take whole carcasses, and cut them up on the premises. By the late 1980s the number of abattoirs in the UK had shrunk to about 1,500; by 1999 there were barely 350, and by early 2014 numbers stood at 279.

Boning-out mutton shoulder

There are several reasons for this dramatic decline. The major impact has been the shift in shopping habits with most meat purchased in the large supermarkets, which are supplied by a few very large abattoirs. One such establishment was the largest area under one roof in Europe when it was opened in 2000. This centralised system requires animals to be transported to a designated supermarket's abattoir from across the UK. A second cause for the decline in smaller abattoirs is that rules for legislation are often drafted with large businesses in mind. Smaller players in the meat industry have been hit disproportionally with the costs of legislation.

We have ended up with three groups of abattoirs. The handful of large plants, primarily dedicated to the supermarkets; the middle-sized group of abattoirs which fill in the gaps in supply to the first group, and supply caterers, and other retailers; and the smaller plants which continue to supply local farmer retailers, local butchers and caterers. Only the smaller meat plants are set up to process meat for farmers or smaller traders. The large plants neither want to, nor are able to keep all the meat from one animal separate from the others.

One of the smaller abattoirs is A.H. Griffiths. Doug is the second generation of his family to run a combined slaughterhouse and butcher's shop in the village of Leintwardine, together with another shop in nearby Ludlow in rural south Shropshire. Doug and his staff take a particular pride in the way they operate. One inspector who had many years' experience in the meat business, and who visited the Leintwardine plant, said that he had never seen a better set-up in terms of animal welfare (a stockman carefully guides the animals into the abattoir, with little noise or other stress). He was particularly impressed with the very high quality of meat leaving the slaughterhouse. The business takes animals from farmers in a 30 mile radius, both for the Griffiths' shops and for returning meat to farmers and others for sale elsewhere. A number of farm shops and suppliers to farmers markets, as well as other butchers' shops rely on the Griffiths' abattoir. Were he to stop operating there is very little alternative particularly for the specialist farmer retailers. With the dramatic decline in abattoir numbers, there are already many areas of the UK which are too far from an abattoir for a farmer to contemplate selling his own meat.

If the likes of Doug Griffiths were to disappear, we would, as a society, lose more than a few rural businesses. As the smaller meat plants close, so the essential infrastructure which enables alternatives to the supermarkets (eg farm shops) to operate becomes increasingly threatened. It is essential that the variety of sizes of abattoirs continues to exist. They all have their role. This knife-edge survival of alternative infrastructures to the supermarket food supply chain can be seen in other food sectors apart from meat – fish and vegetables for example now have very few independent wholesalers, and small, specialist retailers are often dependent on just one supplier.

The solution of course lies with the consumer. By supporting specialist food suppliers, we keep alive an alternative and maintain a genuine choice in what we eat. We will miss them when they're gone, and by then it's too late.

Doug Griffiths, butcher at Leintwardine, Herefordshire

Part Three
MUTTON IN THE KITCHEN

Choosing your Mutton

Whilst there is no such thing as 'just' a bottle of wine, so it is with mutton. As we have seen, there are many variables – breeds, feeding, the environment where the animal was grown, the hanging of the meat, and so on, all of which contribute to flavour. One cannot make generalisations about quality and flavour of all mutton. In 1954 Dorothy Hartley had some characteristically sound advice *'Do not treat all mutton in the same way, and always differentiate between lamb and mutton by quality, not size. Nowadays the hirsels[13] upon the mountains keep the natural grouping and it is sometimes possible to buy the genuine lamb and elderly mutton, but the bringing down of the castrated rams to the lower pastures and finishing them off for meat is much more general... Even under this rearrangement the mountain breeds never put on fat like the Lowland mutton, and the spicy thyme and herb fodder of the hills makes them much the best mutton obtainable.'*

Firstly, a major debating point, as we have seen, concerned breeds. In its heyday, before the Second World War, there were grades of excellence of mutton breeds, from what many considered to be the rather tasteless and fatty English Longwool breeds; to the incomparable Downland breeds, especially Southdown; the mountain breeds such as Welsh Mountain, Blackface and Herdwick; and the primitive, oldest established breeds, such as the Soay.

Then there is the question of the sheep's diet. Many believed the flora found on Britain's hill and mountain tops was a major contributor to the flavour of the meat. The diet also

13 A hirsel is the entire stock on a farm or stock under the charge of a shepherd.

Mixed sheep breeds in mid-Wales

controls the speed of growth which many people consider affects the quality and flavour of the meat. In addition, the salty grasses of the coast of England and Wales produces the famous Salt Marsh mutton, with its characteristic flavour.

The traditional ageing of the meat through hanging the carcass was considered obligatory by most people until the advent of the supermarkets. The discussions would be over not whether, but for how long, to hang the carcass.

Finally, the optimum age of the animal – 2, 3, 4, 5 and more years – all had their advocates, as did those who preferred wether animals, and others who thought nothing bettered the older ewe mutton.

With all these variables, how did people choose their mutton in the past? Everyone had their opinion on what made the best type. In the sixteenth century, Thomas Moufet (1553–1604) had no doubt. '*The best mutton is not above four years old, or rather not much above three; that which is taken from a short, hilly and dry feeding is more sweet, short and wholesome. Great, fat and rank fed sheep, such as Somersetshire and Lincolnshire sendeth up to London, are nothing so short and pleasant in eating as the Norfolk, Wiltshire and Welch mutton; which being very young are best roasted.*'

According to William Kitchener in 1817, fat mutton was the best, and the finest was from a 5-year old wether.

'It was a noble dish of fish that the housekeeper had put on table, and we had a joint of equally choice mutton afterwards, and then an equally choice bird.'

Charles Dickens (1812-1870)
Great Expectations

Eliza Acton agreed. Author of one of the first cookery books for non-professionals in 1845, and the inspiration for Mrs Beeton 15 years later, she considered that *'Mutton is not considered by experienced judges to be in perfection until it is nearly or quite five years old.'*

WHICH BREED?

Mrs Beeton had no doubt about the importance of breed to the flavour of mutton. *'The difference in the quality of the flesh of various breeds is a well-established fact, not alone in flavour, but also in tenderness.'* Both she and many other Victorian connoisseurs of mutton were convinced that sheep breeds, age and diet were all factors in determining the eating quality of the meat. There was also general consensus in the choice of favourite types of breeds, although this did not stop heated debate about the virtues or otherwise of specific ones. The Victorians were agreed that the best mutton breed types were the Mountain, Scottish island (primitive) and the Down breeds (reared originally on the chalk downlands of southern England).

> *'What's a joint of mutton or two in a whole Lent?'*
>
> *Henry IV, Part 2*
>
> William Shakespeare (1564-1616)

The most popular Mountain and so-called 'Forest' breeds included the Welsh Mountain, Welsh Speckleface, Scottish Blackface and Herdwick from the Lake District; Scottish island breeds such as the Hebridean, and Shetland; amongst the Downlad breeds were the Southdown, Portland, and Shropshire.

In 1912 Professor Wrightson described the mountain and forest breeds of mutton as having *'... small joints, the legs weighing only 4-6 lbs; the flesh resembles venison, only it is distinctly better; the grain is short and tender, and partaking of it seems to increase the appetite. Butchers contrive to leave a little wool attached, to prove origin by the carcass. The Scottish Blackface is said to taste of heather, just as grouse acquire the same flavour.'* Professor Wrightson went on to explain that the mountain and forest breeds all give mutton of fine quality because they are of small size, are mostly fed on natural herbage, and *'attain their growth gradually without being forced.'*

The often quoted opening lines of *The War-Song of Dinas Vawr* by Thomas Love Peacock (1785–1866) are in rather indirect praise of mountain mutton:

'The mountain sheep are sweeter,
But the valley sheep are fatter;
We therefore deem it meeter
To carry off the latter.'

For a long time, one of the most popular types of mutton was from Wales. Whilst 16th century writer Gervase Markham was not a fan of Welsh wool, he was a great advocate of Welsh

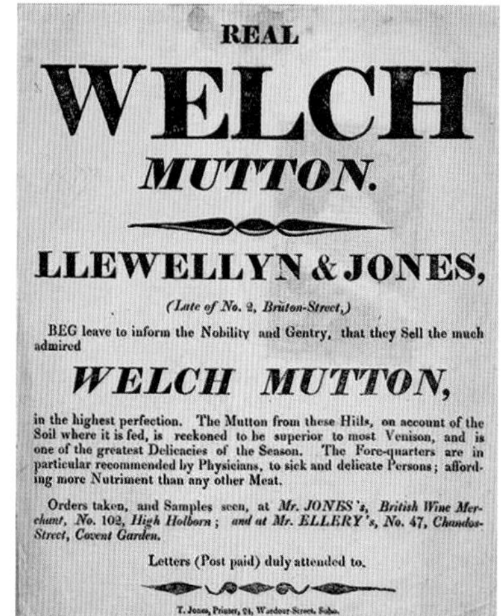

Advertisement sheet for Welsh mutton, in London

mutton. He described Welsh sheep as being *'praised only in the dish, for they are the sweetest mutton.'*

Travel writer George Borrow

Travel writer George Borrow travelled through Wales in 1862, and was hugely impressed by the Welsh mutton he was served in a cottage at Llangollen:

> *'For dinner we had salmon and a leg of mutton; the salmon from the Dee, the leg of mutton from the neighbouring Berwyn. As for the leg, it was truly wonderful; nothing so good had I ever tasted in the shape of a leg of mutton. The leg of mutton of Wales beats the leg of mutton in any other country. Certainly, I shall never forget the first Welsh leg of mutton I ever tasted, rich but delicate, replete with juices derived from the aromatic herbs of the noble Berwyn, cooked to a turn, and weighing just 4 pounds.*
> *'O its savoury smell was great,*
> *Such as well might tempt, I trow,*
> *One that's dead to lift his brow.'*
> *Let anyone who wishes to eat leg of mutton in perfection go to Wales...'*

Clark Hillyard, writing in 1840 agreed with Borrow, and thought Welsh mutton '... *to be superior to Scotch; it is also thought, that the finest flavoured is that which is produced on the Welsh mountains.*' Hillyard also recorded that Lord Spencer '... *for mutton to be consumed for his table, keeps Welsh sheep two years in Althorp Park, and thus has meat of the finest flavour.*' Finally, he talks of a butcher, Mr Giblett, of Bond Street, London who '... *feeds a great number of Welsh sheep on peas, meal, and cut hay at Bayswater; and his customers speak highly of the flavour of his mutton.*'

Whilst travel writer George Borrow and farmer Hillyard were extolling the virtues of Welsh mutton, Lord Cockburn disagreed. He was a strong supporter of Scots mutton, writing in his journal:

> '**Braemar, Scotland, 28 September, 1853**
> *I think it my duty to record the unmatched merits of a leg of mutton we had today at dinner. It was a leg which stands out even amidst all the legs of my long and steadily muttonised life. It was glorious. A leg of which the fat flats of England can have no idea, and which even Wales, in its most favoured circumstances, could only approach. It was a leg which told how it had strayed among mountains from its lambhood to its death. It spoke of winter straths and summer heights, of tender heather, Alpine airs, cold springs, and that short sweet grass which corries alone can cherish. These were the mettle of its pasture. It left its savour on the palate, like the savour of a good deed on the heart.'*

Sheep breed pens at the Royal Welsh Show

The downland breeds were strongly favoured by many, with Southdown the firm favourite, including with the indomitable Mrs Beeton. In her famous cookery book of 1861 she wrote *'Mutton is undoubtedly the meat most generally used in families. And, both by connoisseurs and medical men, it stands out first in favour, whether its fine flavour, digestible qualifications, or general wholesomeness be considered'.* On the subject of the best mutton she had strong views *'Of all mutton, that furnished by the South-Down sheep is the most highly esteemed; it is also the dearest, on account of its scarcity, and the great demand for it.'*

However, other Down breeds had their advocates. Mr P. Hedworth Foulkes, writing in 1913, described the Shropshire as having a large proportion of lean to fat. *'Butchers commend the breed for its quality and flavour, and in comparing it with its rival, the Southdown, contend that while quality is equal, the Shropshire has the advantage in the heavier weights attained.'* The Down breeds were preferred to the longwools as they produced smaller-sized joints, which were *'not overloaded with fat'* as one writer described them, and were *'shorter in fibre, richer in colour when cooked, produced better gravy, and a more appetising flavour'.*

One mutton breed which enjoyed royal patronage was the slow-growing Portland from Dorset, which had been recorded on Portland Island in the Domesday Book. In the late 18th century, on his visits to Weymouth, the sheep-keeper King George III ('Farmer George') always demanded Portland mutton for himself and his staff. This reputation of the Portland was confirmed in the Rural Cyclopedia of 1849 *'They are fed upon a rocky soil; and their flesh is so far superior to that of any other, that their mutton generally fetches a shilling a pound in the Weymouth market.'* Even by 1911 the breed retained its reputation for great mutton, with Adelaide Gosset remarking that *'Their chief characteristics are their hardiness, and the fact that they make excellent mutton'.* Today the Portland breed is an endangered rare breed, and its mutton is included in the Slow Food Movement's Ark of Taste collection of the World's Rare Gastronomic Delights.

'And it all ended, at last, in his telling Henry one morning that when he next went to Woodston, they would take him by surprise there some day or other, and eat their mutton with him. Henry was greatly honoured and very happy, and Catherine was quite delighted with the scheme.'

Jane Austin (1775-1817)
Northanger Abbey

The Whiteface Woodland breed was less well-known, but had powerful supporters, including friends of King George III. A breed of the Derbyshire High Peak, their ancestors had roamed the moors and hills of the Pennines, where they were kept for the quality of their wool and mutton. John Farey wrote of them in 1811 *'Aged sheep of this breed, however poor, when brought in, are in great repute, after well fattening, to furnish Mutton for the tables of the higher classes. Sir Joseph Banks annually has a score of these sheep sent to be fattened in his Park in Revesby in Lincolnshire and sometimes jocosely remarks to his guests, 'Here is Derbyshire bone and Lincolnshire Mutton'.'*

Sometimes breed enthusiasts looked rather subjectively at the evidence.

One anecdote from the turn of the twentieth century may have broader resonance. A Mr Beale-Brown of Andover Ford in Gloucestershire was a keen breeder of the Cotswold sheep. The Cotswold is a breed which developed from sheep of that area in Roman times. The Cotswold was greatly prized for its excellent quality long staple wool during the Middle Ages. The wealth they created was reflected in some of England's finest churches, built on the sale of Cotswold-breed wool. Many writers at the time considered Cotswold mutton, however, to be coarse and inferior to the sublime Southdown or mountain breeds – quite understandably, as it was a wool breed not a meat breed. Nevertheless, Mr Beale-Brown was obviously a passionate advocate of the Cotswold's eating qualities. He invited a group of his friends and neighbours to his farmhouse one evening, where he presented his guests with two legs of mutton – one of the Cotswold breed and the other of the impeccable Southdown. The result, presumably to Mr Beale-Brown's delight, was that his dining friends could not tell the difference between the two legs. Still, history tells another story and maybe the fact that the Cotswold is now considered a Rare Breed may just be a clue.

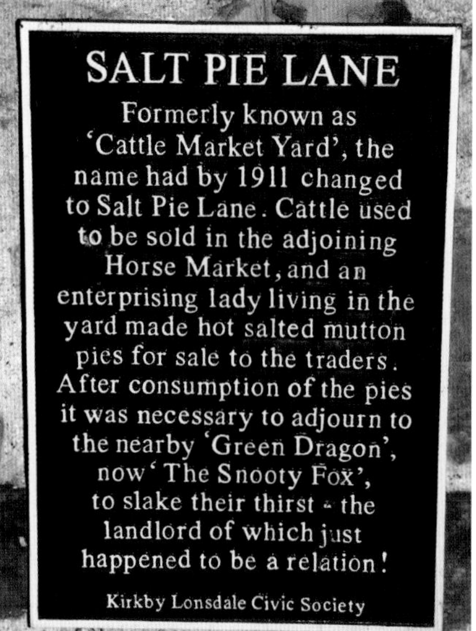

Sign at Kirkby Lonsdale, Cumbria

OPINIONS ON AGE

Changes in farming were accelerating by the middle of the 19th century. With mutton and lamb being produced at younger ages, there was resistance from those who liked their mutton at least five years old. So much so that Philip Pusey, MP and farmer, felt the need to write to *The Times* in 1851 almost apologising for producing young lamb for the table. He explained that on his farm he was producing sheep meat at one year old and added *'Your readers, who like myself remember that, in their youth, butchers were required to furnish five-year old mutton, may not like this*

> *'Oh yes, a good dinner – cold mutton and I don't know what.'*
>
> George Eliot (1819-1880)
> *Middlemarch*

'As she trod the staircase, narrow, but carpeted thickly, as she entered the eating-room, where saddles of mutton were being trundled up to expectant clergymen, she had a strong, if erroneous, conviction of her own futility, and wished she had never come out of her backwater, where nothing happened except art and literature, and where no one ever got married or succeeded in remaining engaged.'

E. M. Forster (1879-1970)
Howards End

rapid production; but it is required by the increase of our population.'

Nevertheless, older wether mutton remained a firm favourite of the housewife, and was produced in abundance by farmers for a few more decades, as can be seen from the reminiscence of Mr W. Watkins of Radnorshire, recalling rural life in Wales in the 1860s *'Wether sheep were kept until the age of four or five years, mutton being in demand at that period, and when wool was making a good price it was profitable to keep large flocks'.*

Writing in 1912, Professor John Wrightson asked if his readers remembered the high prices which were paid for four-year-old Southdown wether mutton – considered by some to be the amongst the best eating of any mutton. Indeed, his readers could possibly have remembered the 1850s when the Southdown commanded the highest price for both wool and meat. He asked if the 'modern' farming practice of producing sheep meat at 14-16 months had meant it had deteriorated in quality compared with the older mutton animals. He concludes that although some younger animals can be *'eaten with gusto'*, and young lambs may be very tender, they will not have the strength of flavour of older animals.

SOME EFFECTS OF FEED

Apart from the benefits of the plant diversity of old established pastures, which we have already discussed, other factors concerning feed can affect the flavour of meat. Professor John Wrightson, writing about sheep production just before WWI warns against ewe mutton which has been fattened rapidly and concludes that the *'best quality of meat is the result of slow feeding, accompanied by muscular development, rather than of rapid fattening on oleaginous foods, such as cake* [cereal-based concentrate feeds] *....it will be observed that the best qualities of butchers' meat are found in animals which have lived a natural life – as, for example in Scotch mutton grazed in deer forests. A free life during youth, with a variety of food during fattening, influence the quality of beef and mutton, as is proved by results. Nothing beats grass-fed beef or mutton.'*

Not to be left out, Cornwall's claim to producing the best mutton appeared to be based on the sheep's diet, as A. K. Hamilton Jenkin wrote in 1934 *'More aristocratic than these so-called mongrel breeds, was the sheep found on the north coast* [of Cornwall], *whose flesh and fleece were good. This superiority was ascribed to their liking for the small snails which appear on the sandy surfaces of the towns morning and evening.'* Indeed, some 180 years earlier, in 1758 William Borlase, wrote '... *the sweetest mutton is reckoned to be that of the smallest sheep, which usually feed on the commons where the sands are scarce covered with the green sod, and the grass exceedingly short; such are the towens or sand-hillocks in Piran-sand, Gwythien, Philac, and Senangreen near the Land's End, and elsewhere in like situations. From these sands come forth snails of the turbanated kind, but of different species and all sizes, from the adult to the smallest just from the egg. These spread themselves over the plains early in the morning, and whilst they are in quest of their own food among the dews yield a most fattening nourishment to the sheep.'* Such a mollusc-based sheep diet spread into the Scilly Isles whose native sheep William Borlase also described. *'In the Isles of Scilly sheep thrive exceedingly, the grass on these commons being short and dry, and full of the same little snail which gives so good a relish to the Senan and Philac mutton in the west of Cornwall.'* However, the idea of sheep eating snails which improved the quality of the mutton was the subject of some debate. In 1910, H. L. F. Guermonprez wrote a paper on snails in the sheep diet. He confirmed some shepherds claimed that the Southdown breed in its native habitat in Sussex, like its Cornish cousins, had a snail diet which added to the mutton's excellent quality. Guermonprez seriously doubted however that the animals seek the snails, as he comments on the Cornish situation *'In parts of Cornwall the species Helix acuta is very abundant, and here the shepherds say that the sheep seek for the snail, browsing on those parts very often at the edge of the cliff, where this snail is more numerous. This may, however, be just as well accounted for by the grass here being longer, as being less accessible, or otherwise more desirable...'*

'...our barons of beef, our noble sirloins, our exquisite haunches, saddles, legs of Southdown mutton, our noble rounds of boiled beef, and those haunches of British venison, the envy and admiration of the world.'

Joseph Breigion & Anne Miller
The Practical Cook, 1845

SALT MARSH MUTTON

There were, and still are, specialist types of mutton. One is from the famous salt-marsh sheep of Kent, Harlech and the Gower Peninsula in Wales, the Somerset Levels and Morecambe Bay. These areas produce exceptional meat, due to the salt-tolerant grasses and wild herbs such as samphire, sparta grass, sorrel and sea lavender, which are to be found in these wetland grazing areas. Salt marsh mutton and lamb is also popular in France, where is it called agneau de pré-salé. According to Dorothy Hartley in 1954, *'Salt-grazed or marsh mutton is flavoured by the salt grass and weed of its sea-coast pastures, and requires pungent condiments, such as samphire or laver, to make the distinctly iodine flavour pleasant. The principle is that as the sheep grazes on the iodine-and-salt weeds, its meat is slightly flavoured with them. Therefore if as a condiment you use some of the weed direct, at full strength, it will cover, and blend with the slighter flavour of the meat.'*

THE IDEAL MUTTON CARCASS

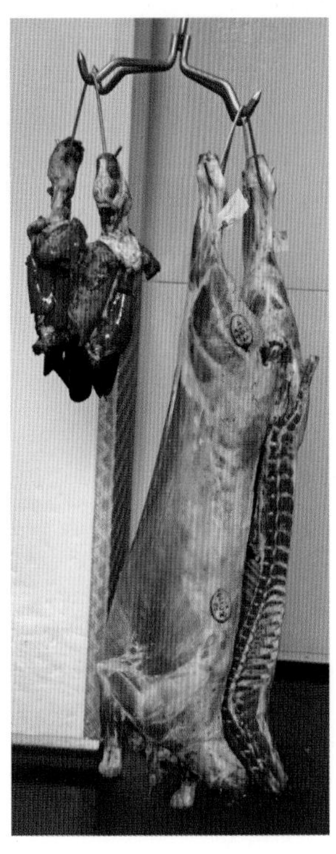

How does a customer buying mutton know how old it is? John Ellman, the celebrated sheep breeder had some practical advice on that. *'Observe the colour of the breast-bone when a sheep is dressed, – that is, where the breast-bone is separated, – which, in a lamb, or before it is one year old, will be quite red; from one to two years old, the upper and lower bone will be changing to white, and a small circle of white will appear round the edge of the other bones, and the middle part of the breast-bone will yet continue red; at three years old, a very small streak of red will be seen in the middle of the four middle bones, and the others will be white; and at four years, all the breast-bone will be of a white or gristly colour.'*

In 1950, the textbook *Modern Farming* described an ideal mutton carcass. *'The bone of a good carcase must be fine and the flesh of a lightish pink colour – not dark red. The carcase should be compact and relatively heavy in the hindquarters where the more valuable joints lie; the loin and leg for example should be well developed and the latter fleshed almost down to the hock. The fat should be firm, white and not more than half-an-inch thick. The popular size of carcase and the quantity of fat acceptable to the community differ somewhat in different parts of the country; in areas where most of the labour is employed in heavy industry, the joints may be larger and fatter.'*

HISTORIC ADVICE ON BUYING MUTTON

There is a considerable amount of historical advice on buying and using mutton. There are even instructions on reviving a dead sheep, which is probably best not tried at home.

In the days before pre-packaged standard meat from supermarkets, buying meat required considerably more knowledge than today. Mrs Beeton in 1861 considered the best joint of mutton to be a saddle *'Although we have heard, at various intervals, growlings expressed at the inevitable 'saddle of mutton' at the dinner-parties of our middle classes, yet we doubt whether any other joint is better liked, when it has been well hung and artistically cooked.'*

A. M. Ude, writing in 1849 had simple advice on buying the best mutton *'Always choose mutton of a dark colour and marble-like appearance.'*

Slightly later, in 1881, one US Professor Henry Harshorne of the University of Pennsyl-

> *'This lady lodged at a bird-fancier's, next door but one to the celebrated mutton-pie shop'*
>
> Charles Dickens (1812-1870)
> *Life and Adventures of Martin Chuzzlewit*

vania had firm views on the best mutton *'From the age of four to six years, and fed on dry pasture, is an excellent meat. It is of a middle kind between the firmness of beef and the tenderness of veal. The lean part of mutton, however, is the most nourishing and conducive to health; the fat being hard of digestion. The head of the sheep; especially when divested of the skin, is tender; and the feet, on account of the jelly they contain, are highly nutritive.'*

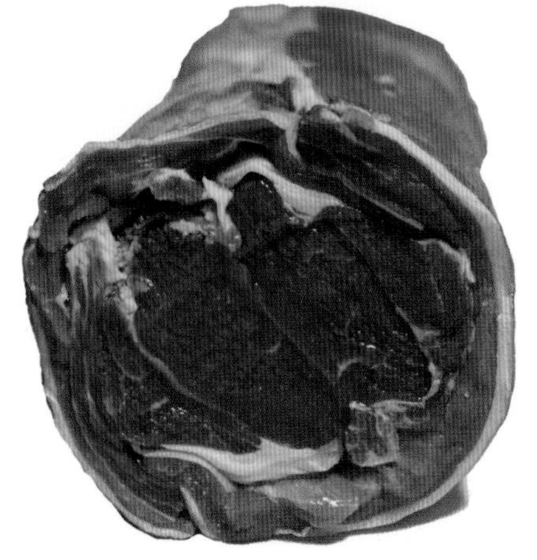

According to *Selfridge's Household Encyclopaedia* of 1929, *'The flesh of mutton should be fine grained and firm, paler in colour than beef; the fat white and firm. Mutton is at its finest when between four and five years old; but it is seldom met with. Sheep are generally killed when between two and three years old.'* In a 1930s cookery book, the buying advice was that *'The flesh should be dark-red in mutton, pink in veal ....'*.

'Never you mind about the piece of needlework, the tambouring and the maps of the world made by her needle. Get to see her work upon a mutton chop, or a bit of bread and cheese, and if she deal quickly with them, you have a pretty security for that activity, that stirring industry, without which a wife is a burden instead of being a help.'

William Cobbett
Advice to Young Men, and, Incidentally, to Young Women, in the Middle and Higher Ranks of Life, in a Series of Letters, 1829

REVIVING 'BAD' MUTTON

Before the days of widespread domestic refrigeration, keeping perishable food was a considerable problem. When meat did start to go 'off', the cost to the household was significant, and so all steps were taken to remedy the problem, rather than simply throw the food away. Indeed, this is said to be the reason for the development of curries, to mask any off-flavours. Again, the 1929 *Selfridge's Household Encyclopaedia* had the answer *'Wash with vinegar everyday, and dry thoroughly before hanging. In hot weather rub it with sugar and sprinkle it all over with pepper and ground ginger to keep off the flies.'*

HOW TO REVIVE A DEAD SHEEP

To a small farming family, the untimely death of an animal could spell disaster. Depending on how the animal died, its meat could in fact be perfectly safe to eat. As early as 1270, Walter of Henley offered advice on averting a crisis in his *Treatise on Husbandry*. *'If a sheep die suddenly they put the flesh in water for as many hours as there are between midday and three o'clock, and then hang it up, and when the water is drained off they salt it and dry it. And if any sheep begin to fall ill they see if it is because the teeth drop, and if the teeth do not fall out they cause it to be killed and salted and dried like the others, and then they cut it up and distribute it in the household amongst the servants and labourers... But I wish they would not do this.'*

In Scotland especially, fresh mutton was only available between August and Christmas. For this reason the Martinmas Fairs, held around the 11th November, were used in the 1720s by *'such of the inhabitants who are anything beforehand with the world, salt up a quantity of beef'* to sell at the fairs. Indeed, salted meat from the Martinmas Fair and 'Braxy' sheep, which had often died, of 'The Braxy', or colic, were the only butchers meat eaten by the poor at the time. *(see page 150).*

Mutton Ham

Mutton ham is an endangered species of British cookery. It was particularly popular in Scotland, reflecting the relatively low numbers of pigs and abundance of sheep. In the 1700s mutton hams were a famous Scottish border speciality and a major export overseas from Glasgow.

Mutton ham is simply the mutton equivalent of pork ham – a cured leg or shoulder of mutton. Known for centuries as a way to keep sheep meat over the winter, when farmers could not feed their animals due to lack of conserved feed, the 'curing' process, often together with smoking, preserved the meat to last all winter if necessary.

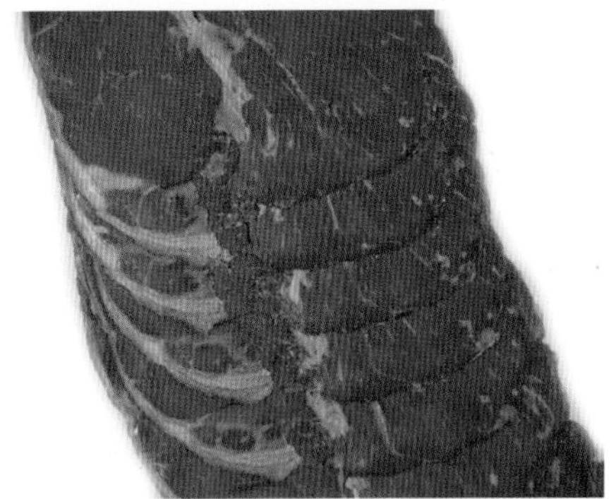

Mutton ham

As with any ham production, there are two methods – wet and dry curing. For a wet cure, salt, saltpetre and other ingredients are dissolved in water making a brine, and the meat is immersed in the mixture for some days. The modern way is to inject the brine mixture into the meat. In dry curing, the salt/saltpetre mixture is simply rubbed into the meat, repeatedly over several days, turning the meat daily. The meat is then left for several weeks or even months for the mixture to fully permeate through the joint. As the effect of dry-curing is to remove moisture from the meat, many older houses had salting slabs of stone or slate which had a groove around the edge, to catch the juices from the salted meat.

Saltpetre is added partly to turn the meat the familiar pink colour, and partly to kill the bacterium *Clostridium botulinum,* which cases the potentially deadly disease botulism.

One eighteenth century Scottish recipe described how to make wet-cured mutton ham. *'Cut it like a Ham and take 2 oz salt-petre and rub the Mutton all over and let it lie a day and make a Pickle of Bay Salt and spring water and put the Mutton in and let it lie 8 days and take and hang it in a chimney for 3 weeks, and then boil it till it is tender. The proper time to do this is in cold weather.'*

MAKE YOUR OWN MUTTON HAM

A modern version of the traditional Scottish dry-cured mutton ham is to take:

A shoulder (or leg) of mutton
15g saltpetre
60g bay salt
60g black pepper and some juniper berries
250g common salt
125g brown sugar

Pound all the ingredients together, heat them, and rub about half into the mutton. After two days warm the other half and rub that in. Turn the meat every day for a fortnight. It should then be smoked, and will keep well for three or four months.

When preparing the cured ham to cook, the crucial point is to remove as much salt as possible, otherwise the meat can be too salty. One option, just prior to cooking, is to bring to the boil, then discard the water, and repeat the process. Cooking would be the same as for a pork ham.

Mutton hams were well-known in popular culture, for instance in Robert Louis Stevenson's *Kidnapped* of 1886 *'Duncan Dhu made haste to bring out the pair of pipes that was his principal possession, and to set before his guests a mutton-ham and a bottle of that drink which they call Athole brose, and which is made of old whiskey, strained honey and sweet cream, slowly beaten together in the right order and proportion.'* Mutton ham would have been a common meal in poorer Scottish households for hundreds of years when John Gibson Lockhart published his novel *The History of Matthew Wald* in 1824, in which he writes *'In short, I found a comfortable and happy family, established in a small and snug dwelling; and nothing could surpass, in their several species of excellence, the tea, the barley scones, the eggs, the mutton ham, the kippered salmon, and the Athole brose of Biddy.'*

As ham is made from the leg or shoulder of an animal, so bacon is made from the central part, the back and ribs area. Whilst bacon usually refers to cured pork, the Scottish version of cured mutton bacon was known as macon – the Herdwick breed was also used for this purpose. There was an attempt early in World War II by the Scottish MP Frederick Macquisten, to gain government support for the mass production of macon. He

> Traditional Island Weddings (Outer Hebrides)
>
> *'The greatest chore for a wedding was the plucking and cooking of innumerable hens presented for the party by friends of the bride and bridegroom from all over the island. A delegation was formed just to deal with this part of the feast which consisted of cold chicken, roast mutton, scones and bannocks, fresh and salt butter, new cheese and many another special delicacy of the island, with the ever-present tea, and whisky and port wine for the toasts.'*
>
> Written on Canna in 1955 by Margaret Fay Shaw (1903-2004)

told the House of Commons *'If the Parliamentary Secretary to the Minister of Food will consult with any farmer's wife in Perthshire, she will show him how to cure it.'* However, despite wartime food shortages, Macquisten's rallying call failed, and macon never really captured the imagination of the people. In fact, even in 1822, William Cobbett remarked that although he knew of mutton bacon, he hadn't himself actually tried any *'Very fat Mutton may be salted to great advantage, and also smoked, and may be kept thus a long while. Not the shoulders and legs, but the back of the sheep. I have never made any flitch*[14] *of sheep-bacon, but I will, for there is nothing like having a store of meat in a house. The running to the butcher's daily is a ridiculous thing.'*

All parts of the mutton carcass can be cured. In his 1871 book, William Kitchener includes a recipe for Mutton, Venison Fashion: *'Take a neck of good five or six year old down mutton cut long in the bones; let it hang at least a week: two days before you dress it, take allspice and black pepper ground and pounded fine, an ounce each, with a quarter of an ounce of saltpetre, and a large spoonful of brown sugar; rub them all well together, and then rub your mutton well with this mixture twice a day: when you dress it, wash off the spice with warm water, and roast it in paste, as we have ordered the haunch of venison: a haunch of mutton will take double the quantity of the preparation, and one day longer preparing.'*

SHETLAND VIVDA MUTTON

The word 'Vivda' is said to derive from the old Norse for 'leg meat'. Before salting was in general use, the islanders would simply dry mutton in order to preserve it.

The drying would be done in special square stone buildings called 'Skeos' which were developed with specialised ventilation systems allowing the wind to blow through, but inhibited predators from getting at the contents of the building, which would also have included fish. Being sited near the sea, the buildings would enable a salty sea breeze to be harnessed in the drying process, bringing with it an amount of salt. A draughty islander's house was also often disparagingly referred to as a skeo. Many of the original skeos survive to this day.

Once dried, the Vivda would hang for around 4-5 months before being consumed. However, the timing of the drying was critical. It had to be done when the flies were dormant, and the weather both cold and windy. If they got it wrong it could be dangerous. If too warm, or the air was not circulating sufficiently, the resultant bacteria could be fatal if eaten.

With the introduction of the salting process (*see page 148*), production of Vivda was dying out by the late 18th century and by the mid-19th production had virtually stopped.

14 A flitch is a complete side of bacon.

Indeed, when Samuel Hibbert visited Shetland in 1822, he wrote *'It is not long since it was customary, before using beef or mutton, not to salt it, but to hang it up in one of these places, until the wind, by which it was penetrated, should, at the necessary degree of temperature, have so completely dried the meat as to preserve it from putrefaction : it was also found, that any cave within which the tide flowed, named a helyer or hiallar, (the Iceland name at the present day for a skeo), had similar antiputrescent powers.'* Even by 1822, Hibbert notes that *'Vivda is no longer known.'*

Nevertheless, Vivda can still be found on the Faroe Islands, as can similar culinary delicacies across other parts of Scandinavia.

REESTIT MUTTON

The original Vivda dried mutton of Shetland was a slightly hit-and-miss process. Salting as well as drying provided a much more reliable option for preserving meat through the winter, when there was insufficient feed to keep animals alive through the worst of the winter weather. The Shetlanders put the cuts of mutton into a brine with salt and sugar for

Jack and Jessie Tattar at home on Shetland with reestit mutton hanging over the peat fire

10 to 21 days, after which it was hung to dry out high up in the rafters (reest) of the roof above the peat fire which was in the middle of the floor and lacked a chimney. Therefore it was partly smoked i.e. reestit, meaning 'scorched' in Gaelic. This helped the preserving and killed off flies and other pests in the crofter's home. The peat fire would also impart a special smoked flavour, and keep the meat dry, enabling it to be kept if necessary for years. The finished ham has pale creamy fat and deep red meat with a hard and dry texture, together with a salty and mature mutton flavour.

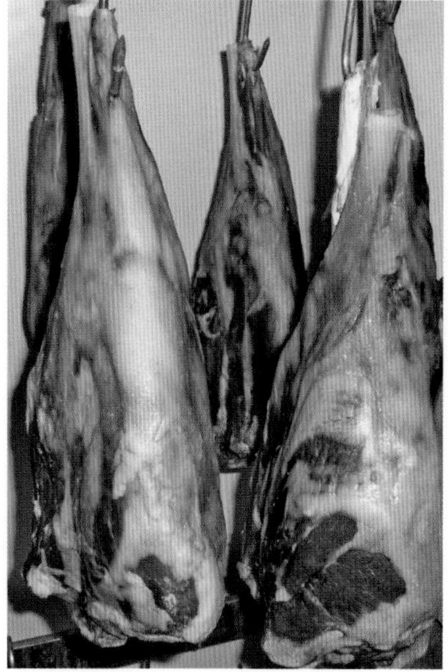

Reestit mutton hams

The best-known use for Reestit mutton is mutton soup, in which a small piece is added to a soup of cabbage, carrots, neeps (turnips) and tatties (potatoes). The meat was also used for cooking in a broth, after which the meat may be taken out and eaten separately with vegetables (*see page 165*).

An alternative use is to add it to a 'Shetland bannock' (a traditional unleavened bread). Today its main ingredient is wheat flour. Originally on Shetland it would have been 'bere meal'. Bere was an ancient and genetically pure variety of barley. Later this was replaced by oat meal, and now by imported wheat meal. Also in the bannock recipe, baking powder is included as the bere meal had little gluten to help it rise. Finally, salt, egg and milk were added.

The Reestit mutton could also be chopped finely and added to 'milgrew', which is a thin oat porridge.

Reestit mutton can probably be considered as Shetland's 'national' dish, and is mostly used at mid-winter around Yule tide, Christmas and New Year. It also forms an important feature of the festive fire celebrations on Shetland, on the last Tuesday of January, known as the 'Up-Helly-Aa'. This spectacle involves islander men dressed as Vikings, marching through the streets of Lerwick with flaming torches. The leader for the night, the 'Guizer Jarl' stands at the helm of his longship, which is dragged through the streets before being ceremonially burned (the galley, that is, not the Jarl!).

According to the book *Traditional Foods of Britain*, which in 1999 surveyed the current state of traditions such as Reestit mutton, there were three butchers in Lerwick still making and selling the Shetland delicacy. Many crofters still make their own Reestit to their own recipes – some saltier, some more sugary. Because

Thick slices of Reestit mutton ham

tastes have changed over the years, today the first one or two boilings of the water are normally poured away to suit the modern preference for lower levels of salt.

Globe Butchers in Lerwick still make traditional Reestit mutton. *'After legs are cut up they are soaked in a solution of water and salt for three weeks. You keep turning the legs every week in the salty solution. After three weeks they are taken out and hung up to dry for at least 2-3 weeks but can keep for months, as long as not packaged and just left to hang.'*

'My boy, our business is not to call hard names, but to take things as we find them, as the Highlandman said when he ate the braxy mutton.'

Madam How and Lady Why
Charles Kingsley (1819-1875)

BRAXY HAM

Braxy is an often fatal disease of young sheep and results from a rapid increase in naturally occurring flora in the sheep's gut when there is a sudden change of diet. Today this is easily treatable, but in the past it was a not unusual cause of sudden death in sheep. When times are tough, nothing is wasted, so as the particular bugs responsible do not affect humans, such sheep which have died of natural causes were used for meat by shepherds, and were known as 'sickness hogg' or 'Braxy mutton'. With a whole carcass of lamb or mutton available, it was often salted into ham in order not to waste it, and make it last as long as possible.

A folksong popular in the 1880s was called 'Killeman Braxy Ham', which tells the apparently true story of the theft of the skin of a braxy sheep. Suspicion falls on three young men who come to a farm late at night to see girls. A policeman comes to question the girls and they reluctantly give the names of the young men. A search ensues but the skin is not found.

Most references to the term 'braxy' are from northern England and Scotland.

'However, he gave me supper – braxy ham and oatcake, and I bought the remnants off him for use next day.'

John Buchan
Mr Standfast (1919)

Cooking Mutton Through the Ages

The first evidence of cooking mutton in the UK was from some 4,500 years ago. Neolithic farmers, around 2,500 BC, started to keep sheep, and were the first to cook by boiling, rather than simply roasting it over a fire. They used wooden or leather vessels into which hot stones were put to heat the water. Around the same time is the first evidence of ovens for baking meat, once it was boiled. Indeed, in 1952 Professor M. J. O'Kelly and his fellow archaeologists carried out an experiment at an ancient cooking site at Ballyvourney, County Cork.

At the very same place, sometime in the second millennium BC, someone had dug a trough into a boggy part of the peat, and had lined it with timber and stones. At either end they had made an arc-shaped hearth. Professor O'Kelly and his colleagues restored both the pit and hearths. Then, in the hearths they piled firewood and heated stones which they had broken from the local sandstone rocks. Once hot, the stones were transferred to the water trough, which brought the water to the boil in little over half an hour. It was kept simmering by dropping more red-hot stones into the trough every few minutes.

Finally, following descriptions from early Irish literature, a leg of mutton was wrapped in clean straw, tied with a twisted straw rope, and lowered into the boiling water. After nearly four hours, (allowing twenty minutes to the pound plus twenty minutes over) the meat was cooked through to the bone. It was quite uncontaminated by ash or mud. The archaeologists repeated the re-enactment of Neolithic cooking methods using the stone oven found on the site, again heated with hot stones. Within twenty minutes a crisp brown crust had sealed the meat, keeping in the juices. Three hours later the second leg of mutton was declared '*excellently cooked and most tasty*'.

By the time of the Celts around 100 BC, the favoured method of cooking mutton and meats in general was in a cauldron or on a spit, methods which survived in Britain well into the 16th century. Mealtimes for Celts were described by Posidonius, a Greek philosopher and writer, who travelled widely throughout the Roman world. He describes Celts in Gaul (where food would have been similar to that in Britain) eating a meal. Senior family members would sit on straw or hides, being waited on by their sons and daughters.

''We have but a shoulder of mutton with onion sauce,' said Mrs Crummles, in the same charnel-house voice; 'but such as our dinner is, we beg you to partake of it...' Mrs Crummles rang the bell. 'Let the mutton and onion sauce appear.''

Charles Dickens (1812-1870)
The Life and Adventures of Nicholas Nickleby

They ate with their fingers, in a *'cleanly but lion-like fashion, raising up whole limbs (of meat) in both hands, and biting off the meat, while any part which is hard to tear off, they cut through with a small dagger which hangs attached to their swords-sheath in its own scabbard. Beside them are hearths blazing with fire, with cauldrons and spits containing large pieces of meat. Brave warriors they honour with the finest portions of meat.'*

> *'..and on Monday, Tuesday, and Wednesday it consisted of beef, roast, hashed, and minced, and on Thursday, Friday, and Saturday of mutton.'*
>
> W. Somerset Maugham (1874-1965)
> *Of Human Bondage*

The Roman soldiers posted in Britain from all over the Empire ate some mutton, although from the bones found in the waste pits of Roman settlements and forts, not as much as beef or pork. Most preferred to eat the meat they were used to at home, whether that was Europe, the Middle East or even the Orient. The Roman methods of meat cooking were more sophisticated than had been seen it Britain before. Some meats were roasted over a low fire, and even double-walled portable ovens (*clibanus*) were used for dishes such as neck of mutton. As with the Celts, spits and cauldrons were also used.

The oldest collection of recipes to survive from antiquity, *De Re Coquinaria* ('The Art of Cooking') is attributed to Marcus Gavius Apicius, who is believed to have been a Roman gourmet and lover of luxury, who lived in the 1st century AD. Included in his book of recipes is 'Sauce for Mountain Sheep' (*Ius in ovifero fervens*). A later copy of the recipe describes it as being used with *'the meat of sheep from the woods, mountain sheep'*. The sauce consisted of pepper, lovage, cumin, dry mint, thyme, silphium (a plant used in classical antiquity as a seasoning and medicine, now thought to be extinct) moistened with wine, stewed Damascus prunes, honey, wine, broth, vinegar, raisin wine, and stirred with a whip of origany (a wild type of marjoram) and dry mint. Something of this type of sauce has remained with us today, albeit greatly simplified. We use three of the ingredients regularly when eating lamb – mint, vinegar and a sweetener, although today it is more often sugar rather than honey.

The Saxon invasions resulted, at least in eastern counties, in an increase in the use of sheep meat. In the Doomsday Book, Norfolk, Sussex and Essex record almost 130,000 sheep, but fewer than 9,000 cattle. As in previous cultures, the Saxons tended to roast the more tender cuts and stew the tougher ones.

In the late 16th century thick stews (pottages) of meats began to give way to fricassees or hashes. Hashes took their name from the French 'hacher' – to chop. One recipe of 1584 briefly describes making hash of cold mutton – *'Chop flesh small and fry it in sweet butter. Then put thereto a little white wine, salt, with ginger and serve it forth in fair dishes.'* By 1675, hashes had become slightly more sophisticated. Hannah Woolley in her *Gentlewoman's Companion* describes the French way of making hashed mutton *'Take a shoulder of mutton, and roast it three quarters and save the gravy; slice the one half and mince the other, and put it into a pipkin* [an earthenware cooking pot], *with the shoulder-blade, put to it some strong broth of mutton or beef gravy, large mace, some pepper, salt and a big onion or two, a faggot of sweet herbs, and a pint of white wine; Stew them all together close covered, then take away the fat, and put some oyster-liquor thereunto; add also three pints of great oysters parboiled in their own liquor; these materials being well stewed down, dish up your meat, pouring your liquor thereon, and uppermost lay your stewed oysters with sliced lemon and five carved sippets* [small pieces of toasted or fried bread used as a garnish, dipped in gravy]'.

'The supper was an excellent one too ... the tea service was extremely plain ... but the bread and the mutton chops, and the butter, and even the tea, were such as Mrs Powell's china was never privileged to bear.'

Welsh Mutton Chops
Susan Warner's description of a Welsh Farmhouse c. 1850

One Elizabethan recipe describes Carbonadoes of Mutton *'Cut a leg of mutton in thin fillets and to make it tender: chop it on both sides, with the back of a knife so that they be not chopped through. Then salt them well and lay them on a gridiron and broil them till they be enough, and with vinegar and minced onions serve them forth.'*

According to John Lawrence, writing in 1809, *'In England the working classes often prefer very fat mutton, which they cook with vegetables, particularly potatoes; but it is certainly not so wholesome and nutritious as meat somewhat leaner, and it is seldom or never brought to the tables of the affluent.'* One imagines that the working classes preferred fat mutton simply because it was cheaper. Indeed, Lawrence had done some research on this. *'From the widest inquiries I could ever make, and in the metropolis particularly, the labourers invariably reject over fatted mutton, when they have the choice, for there is this good reason, they must, from necessity, eat up all they buy, whereas the rich may admire, taste, and throw the remainder away.'*

By the Victorian age, cooking had become more varied, and for the rich, it offered many new flavours and ingredients. However, mutton remained a staple meat, with price, as ever, determined by quality.

The First Principles of Good Cookery was written by Lady Llanover in 1867. She lived through every decade of the 19th century and her reputation survives to this day. In her book, also published in Welsh, Lady Llanover includes a wide range of mutton recipes.

Using her character 'The Hermit' to voice her skills, she details mutton prepared in many ways including roast, hashed, haricot, and for pies, but of prime importance is the use of the Ffwrn Fach, the double boiler. Meat would be put in a tin pan with minimal water then the whole pan into another iron one in which water would simmer for hours. Akin to today's electric 'slow cooker', the 'double' produced wonderfully tender meat cooked in the succulence of its own juices. Using more water she describes 'The Hermit's Mutton Stew'. The pot would bubble for days. Once the main meat dish had been eaten the tasty broth would go on with different vegetables being added as appropriate. The 'double' would also be used for making a regular supply of tasty jelly stock from the bones.

William Kitchiner, in his 1871 book *Apicius Redivivus:* or, The Cook's Oracle, is still describing a hashed mutton dish, some three hundred years after the earliest reference. On roasting a leg of mutton he says that the cook should *'send up two sauce boats with it; one of the richest drawn gravy that can be made without spice or herbs; and the other of sweat sauce.'*

Several Victorian recipes likened a well-cooked piece of mutton to venison, without the bother of having to find venison.

Pies and stews were favourite ways of cooking mutton. McNeill in 1929 quotes a St Andrews professor describing the pies of his childhood which were made by the pie-wife: *'Delightful as were her pigeon and apple pies, her chef-d'oeuvre...was a certain kind of mutton-pie. The mutton was minced to the smallest consistency, and was made up in standing crust, which was strong enough to contain the most delicious gravy... There were no lumps of fat or grease in them at all... They always arrived piping hot... It makes my mouth water still when I think of those pies.'*

MUTTON IN THE ANTIPODEAN DIET

To some, eating mutton was a daily monotony. This was particularly true of the rural poor in New Zealand and Australia's sheep farming areas. 'Mutton, tea and damper' formed the basis of a sustaining, if unchanging, diet for many rural workers. Damper was a yeast-less substitute for bread, made of flour, salt, and water (sometimes milk) and cooked in the embers of the fire, which was damped down for the purpose – hence the name. Some used baking soda to leaven it. It developed as drovers and other itinerant stockmen, who travelled in remote areas for weeks or months at a time, were only able to carry a minimum range of dry food – normally flour, sugar and tea – supplemented by mutton from the sheep which accompanied them. Damper was cooked for ten minutes above the fire, then covered with ashes and cooked for another 20 to 30 minutes until it sounded hollow when tapped.

In 1843, Robert Dundas Murray, a Scots author having visited Australia wrote: '*You have mutton and damper today, – mutton and damper will appear tomorrow, and from that day till the end of the year, your dinner is mutton, boiled, roasted or stewed.*'

Australian poet and journalist C.J. Dennis (1876-1938) put it rather more vividly in his poem *Mutton*:

In the everlasting summer, when the town is limp with heat,
And the asphalt of the footpath curls your boots and burns your feet:
When you're creased and crabbed and sodden, and can hardly raise a crawl,
And the persperation's drippin' in a constant waterfall;
There's a penetratin' odor gets abroad and fairly roars;
It will creep in through the keyholes and it sneaks beneath the doors;
And it fills your happy home up from the cellar to the roof,
Until ev'ry other odour holds its breath and stands aloof.
That's Mutton! Mutton!
Everlastin' Mutton!
All-pervadin', never-fadin' smell of cookin' sheep.
Into ev'ry room 'twill roam, chasin' you from house and home,
Mutton flaunted, mutton-haunted, even in your sleep.

Butcher's shop, Australian outback, 19th century

Lady Mary Butler, the wife of a sheep farmer in the South Island of New Zealand wrote in her 1870 memoirs of the unique nature of Christmas *'It is a point of honour to have as little mutton as possible on these occasions, as the great treat is the complete change of fare. I only ventured to introduce it very much disguised as curry, or in pies.'*

Even in landowners' homesteads, mutton was an everyday affair. It was generally cooked as Murray described, but in both Australia and New Zealand at least one new dish became popular – Colonial Goose. With fond memories of the 'Old Country', settlers in Australia and New Zealand wanted reminders of Britain. So, with a dearth of geese and an abundance of sheep, they remodelled joints of mutton, both to imitate the taste of goose, and by

'But Mahbub Ali the kindly said,
'Better is speech when the belly is fed.'
So we plunged the hand to the mid-wrist deep
In a cinnamon stew of the fat-tailed sheep,
And he who never hath tasted the food,
By Allah! he knoweth not bad from good.

We cleansed our beards of the mutton-grease,
We lay on the mats and were filled with peace,
And the talk slid north, and the talk slid south,
With the sliding puffs from the hookah-mouth.'

Rudyard Kipling (1865-1936)
The Ballad of the King's Jest

some accounts, even the look of it. Most recipes consisted of boning out a leg or shoulder of mutton, and leaving the foot end of the bone in place to resemble the goose's head. The space where the bone had been was replaced with a traditional stuffing based on breadcrumbs, onion, parsley and thyme or sage, mixed with honey and dried apricots, and sometimes bound with milk or an egg. Once trussed up again to prevent leakage, the Colonial Goose was then marinated in a red wine mixture which was supposed to give it the appearance of goose when cooked. One recipe from Perth, Australia in 1910 suggested dredging the joint in flour, before roasting or braising, and serving with 'a good gravy'. Some served it with 'egg-shaped' potato croquettes or Scotch Eggs for the full goose effect.

A Welsh Mountain wether

Mutton ham canapés

Mutton for the Modern Cook

WHAT'S AVAILABLE?

Excellent quality mutton is still available in the UK, but only through specialist producers, who sell from the farm gate, farmers markets or on-line. Some butchers also offer mutton for sale *(see Directory of Suppliers page 183).*

WHAT TO LOOK FOR

Just as in Victorian Britain, it is still important to buy the right quality of mutton. Having some key information about the mutton you are considering buying will make life a lot easier. There are a number of criteria to look for and enquire about when you buy mutton:

Hanging

How long has the meat been hung before butchery? It is essential that the hanging has been done to the entire carcass before the butchers start cutting it up. Although some meat processors will pack large 'primal' cuts in vacuum packs to mature them, the traditional way is to hang the carcass in a cold room. Ideally hanging should be for at least 14 days, but mutton is often hung for a week to ten days.

'Now suppose, my pet, that we were married, and you were going to buy a shoulder of mutton for dinner, would you know how to buy it?'

Charles Dickens (1812-1870)
David Copperfield

Breed

As we have seen, the breed of animal will have an impact on the quality of the meat. If you are buying direct from the farmer this will be relatively easy to determine. One sign to look for is size of joints. Smaller animals (the mountain breeds, primitives and the Down breeds) tend to be tastier.

> *'And Jip must have a mutton-chop every day at twelve, or he'll die.'*
>
> Charles Dickens (1812-1870)
> *David Copperfield*

Fat

It is important to have some fat cover without too much, as the flavour and moistness will be enhanced by some fat. Much of this is personal taste, but it is as important to avoid meat with no fat as it is an over-fat piece of meat.

Butchering a loin of mutton

Origin

Where was the animal reared? If finished in a building where it was fed concentrate, then it is likely to be less tasty than if it came from the wild pastures of a hilltop. If it is said to be grass-fed, that is also good for taste, and in terms of fatty acid composition, good for you too.

Ewe or Wether?

The chances are that if you are lucky enough to find wether mutton (a few producers in our Suppliers' Directory offer it), and are keen on a mature but fairly mild flavour, then this is for you. A ewe, if properly finished, and properly hung, and cooked suitably slowly will be a real treat, and unlike anything you will have tasted before in terms of depth and complexity of flavour.

Age at Slaughter

The standard age defining mutton is 2 years old. Younger than this, and it is likely that the depth of flavour will not have developed into the full taste of mutton. As the Victorians discussed at great length, the age increases depth of flavour. However, it is unlikely that animals over eight years will be sold as mutton, and they are more likely to end up as pie meat or similar.

> *'Micawber came in from the bakehouse with the loin of mutton which was our joint-stock repast.'*
>
> Charles Dickens (1812-1870)
> *David Copperfield*

SEASONALITY

As modern mutton tends to be almost exclusively from ewes, so the availability tends to be seasonal, although there are some suppliers who have it available all year round *(see Directory of Suppliers page 183).* The periods of main availability follow the sheep farming calendar, as we have seen, in the autumn and after weaning lambs in early summer. For many producers this is October to April inclusive.

'There is a satisfaction in seeing an Englishman eat and drink, they do it so heartily, and on the whole so wisely, – trusting so entirely that there is no harm in good beef and mutton, and a reasonable quantity of good liquor.'

Nathaniel Hawthorne
The English Notebooks, 1870
(American Consul in Liverpool 1853-1858)

WHAT TO BUY?

Often the most cost-effective way to buy mutton is by the box – normally a half or a whole animal, butchered and individually packed. Alternatively, many outlets, particularly shops and farmers markets, offer individual cuts.

Mutton Cuts

Although up to the 19th century, (Stephens records in 1844) *'In almost every town there is a different way of cutting up a carcass of mutton,'* today it is very much more standardised. Mutton cuts are very similar to lamb. Depending on the breed of mutton, the sizes of cuts may be larger or, in the case of the Mountain and some Downland, smaller than the normal supermarket lamb sizes.

Once bought, mutton should either be stored, unwrapped, on a plate or container in the fridge for up to a few days, or frozen in a sealed plastic bag to prevent freezer burn.

Cuts of Mutton & Their Uses

The carcass of mutton can be roughly divided into three parts. The front legs (called shoulder), the ribs and back (the loin – chops or joint, and breast), and the back legs (just called the legs). Within these, joints can be bought with the bones in or out. The latter is referred to as 'boned and rolled', the advantage being that they are smaller to cook, and easier to carve. However, they may lack some flavour compared with cooking on the bone. Then there is diced and minced, which is often from the shoulder or trimmings. Steaks are normally from the back legs. The neck fillet, as with lamb, is arguably the most tender part of the animal. Neck, normally with the vertebra bones in, is inexpensive and used in the classic Lancashire Hotpot, or stews.

'The haunch is a joint of mutton frequently served up at large and elegant entertainments.'

John Chalmers Morton
A Cyclopedia of Agriculture
(1875)

MUTTON BUTCHERY

The Cuts of Mutton

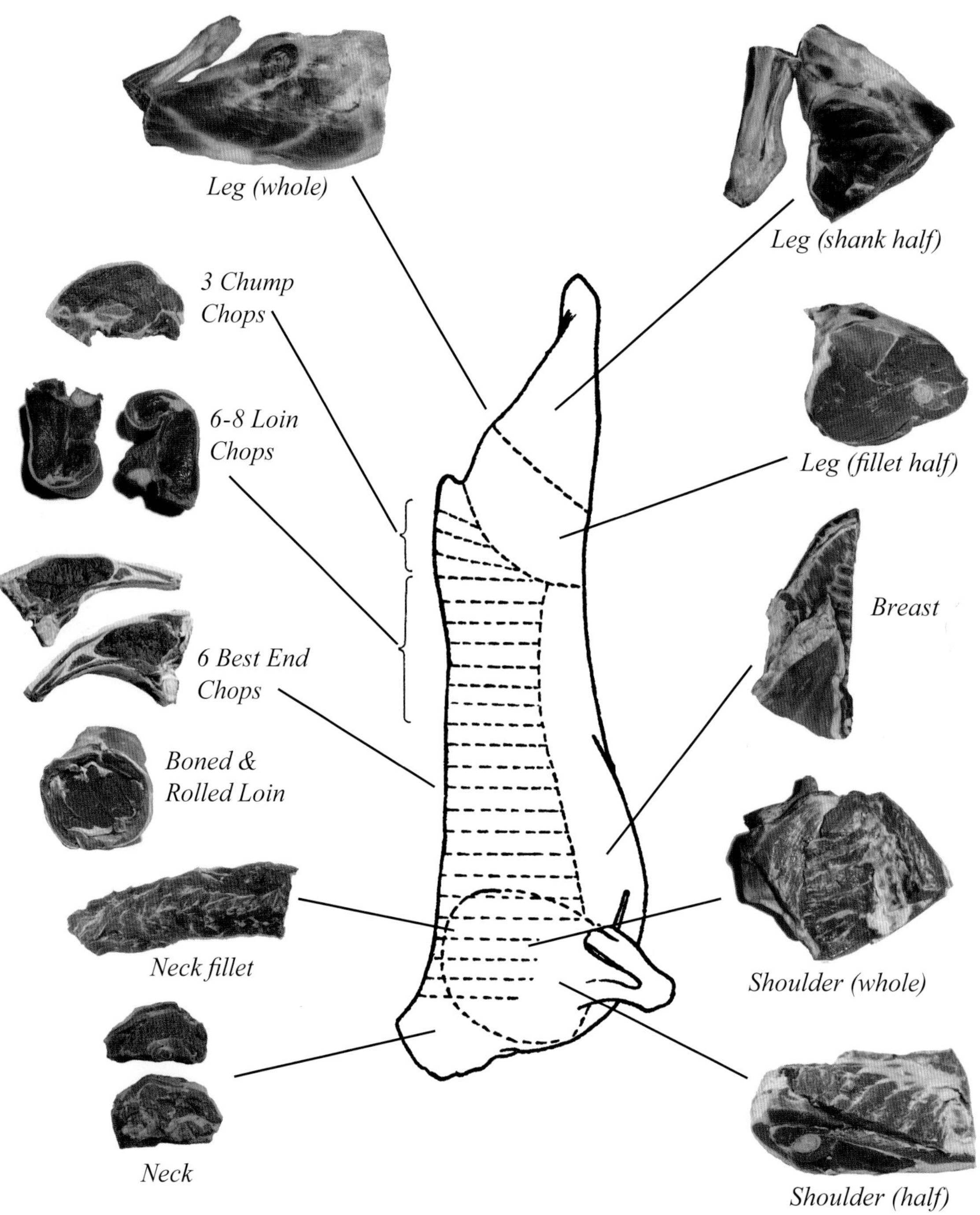

Joints

Legs

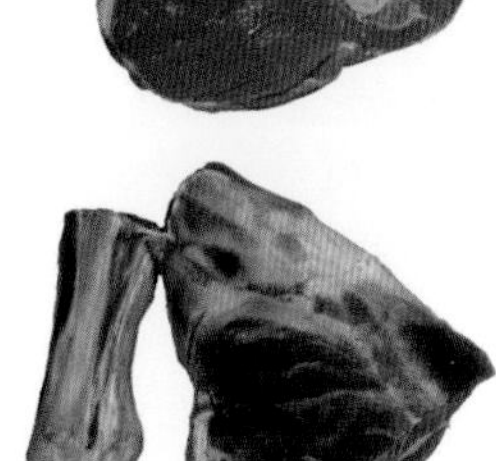

Otherwise known as the haunch or gigot, the classic Leg of Mutton joint is best roasted with the bone in. The Scottish Blackface mutton gigot contains a piece of fat known historically as the Pope's Eye, which was considered a real delicacy. The joint has generally little fat and excellent flavour. Even the potentially fatter Longwool breeds were rarely overloaded with fat on the legs. Sometimes sold as half legs, the shank end contains the knuckle, and is at the foot end. The fillet or chump half is more meaty than the shank, but some would say it has less flavour due to the reduced amount of bone. Either end of the leg can be roasted, braised, boiled or used in stews or pies. The Victorians preferred a Mountain breed leg for a small family, or a Southdown or Cheviot for a larger one.

Shoulders

With smaller blocks of muscles, the shoulder joint has a higher proportion of bone than the leg. However, in terms of flavour, it is considered by many to have that extra 'something'. Like the leg, it may be sold as a half shoulder, either as knuckle (foot end) or blade halves. May also be sold either with bone in or boned and rolled. Often it is boned out and diced.
In some authentic oriental and other cookery cultures, shoulder diced with the bone in is popular.

> *'This night Mrs Turner (who, poor woman, was removing her goods all this day, good goods into the garden, and knows not how to dispose of them), and her husband supped with my wife and I at night, in the office; upon a shoulder of mutton from the cook's, without any napkin or any thing, in a sad manner, but were merry.'*
>
> *Diary of Samuel Pepys*
> 4th September 1666

Saddle

This is the whole of the back and ribs, including the best end chops and the loin chops. Whilst there are many historic references to a saddle of mutton, we are no longer allowed to buy it, as all carcasses of mutton must be split down the back bone before butchery. Instead there are the two half-loins or racks which we can still enjoy.

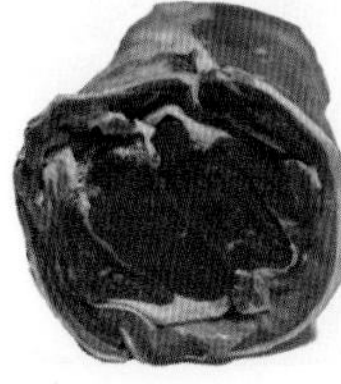

Loin or middle

The rack is one side of a saddle, split along the backbone. May be sold as boned and rolled loin, which makes a relatively thin, but easy to cook and

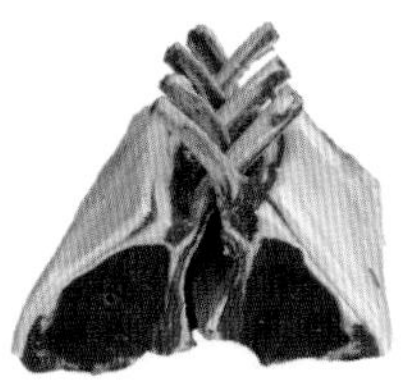

carve joint. Because of its 'Swiss Roll' shape, it will cook more evenly than a joint of varying shape.

With bones-in, a French Trim rack has the ribs partly exposed. This makes a small joint, relatively quick to cook, and very tender.

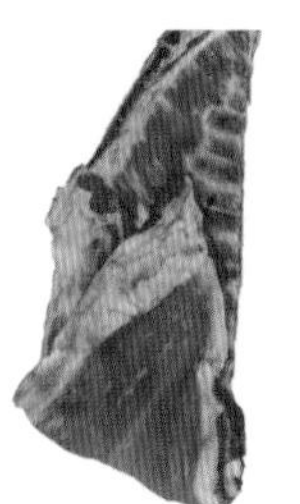

Breast

The cheapest cut of mutton, apart from neck, the breast can be slightly fatty, but has excellent flavour as a result. Can be bought on the bone, or boned and rolled. One breast suits one or two people, and can be pot-roasted, braised, boiled, on its own, or stuffed, or used in stews and casseroles.

Chops

As with lamb, there are three types of chops. Starting from the front of the carcass, next to the shoulder, and working backwards, they are:

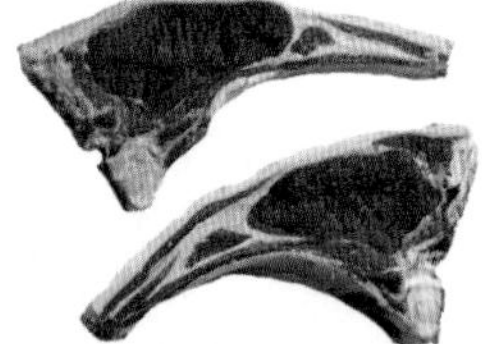

Best End chops or Cutlets

Containing a length of rib, these are the classic chop shape. Good for flavour, they have the lowest meat-to-bone ratio of the chops, and are consequently normally cheapest. A joint of all the best end chops is known as best end of neck.

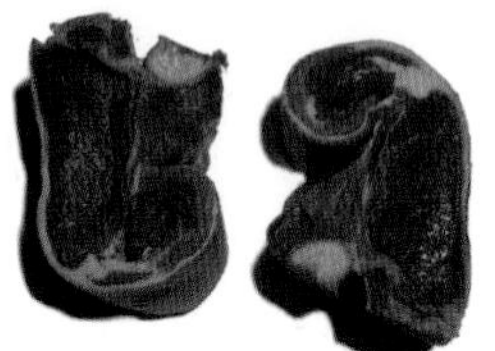

Loin Chops

No ribs, but a T-shaped piece of backbone mean that these are more meaty than best end. A double loin is a Barnsley chop.

> *'So, Twemlow goes home to Duke Street, St James's, to take a plate of mutton broth with a chop in it, and a look at the marriage-service, in order that he may cut in at the right place to-morrow;'*
>
> Charles Dickens (1812-1870)
> *Our Mutual Friend*

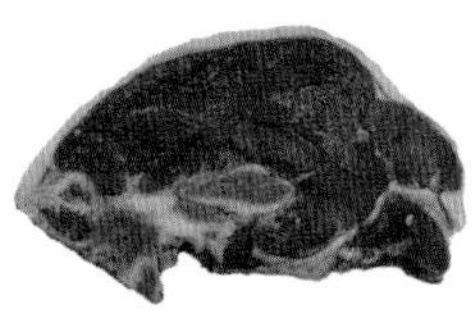

Chump chops

Nearest the leg, these are the leanest and largest of the chops, with the best ratio of meat to bone.

Steaks

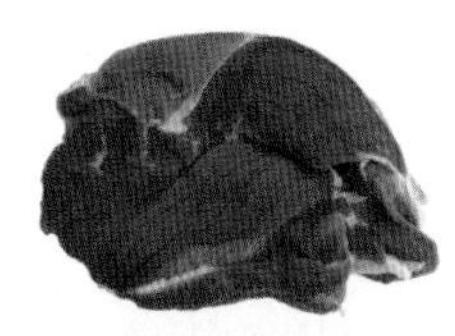

Cut normally from the leg. These can be used for a range of dishes.

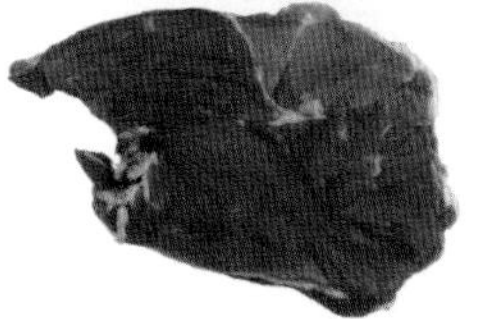

OTHER CUTS

Diced

Normally from the shoulder. A very useful cut, and handy for a range of uses, including stews, casseroles and kebabs.

Mince

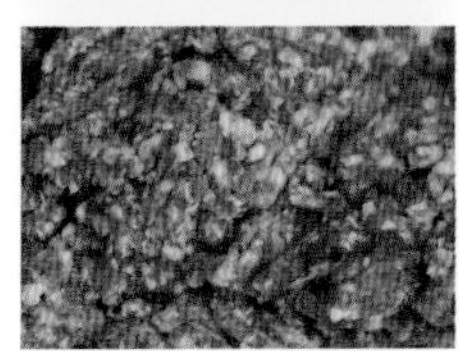

Also produced mostly from the shoulder and other trim, this is very versatile. Fat content may vary, and there is a happy medium – enough for maximum flavour without being over-fatty.

Neck Fillet

Basically the main muscle which moves the neck, this is a very popular, tender lean cut.

Neck

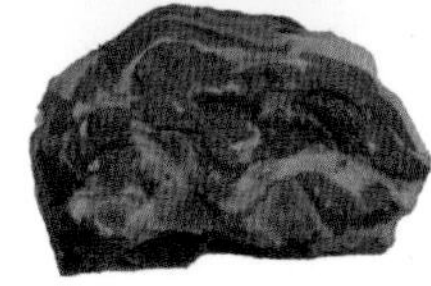

Also known as scrag end, it consists of rings of the neck, and despite the rather unattractive name, it is ideal for traditional slow-cooked hot-pots.

Offal

Liver, kidneys and heart make tasty but inexpensive meals.

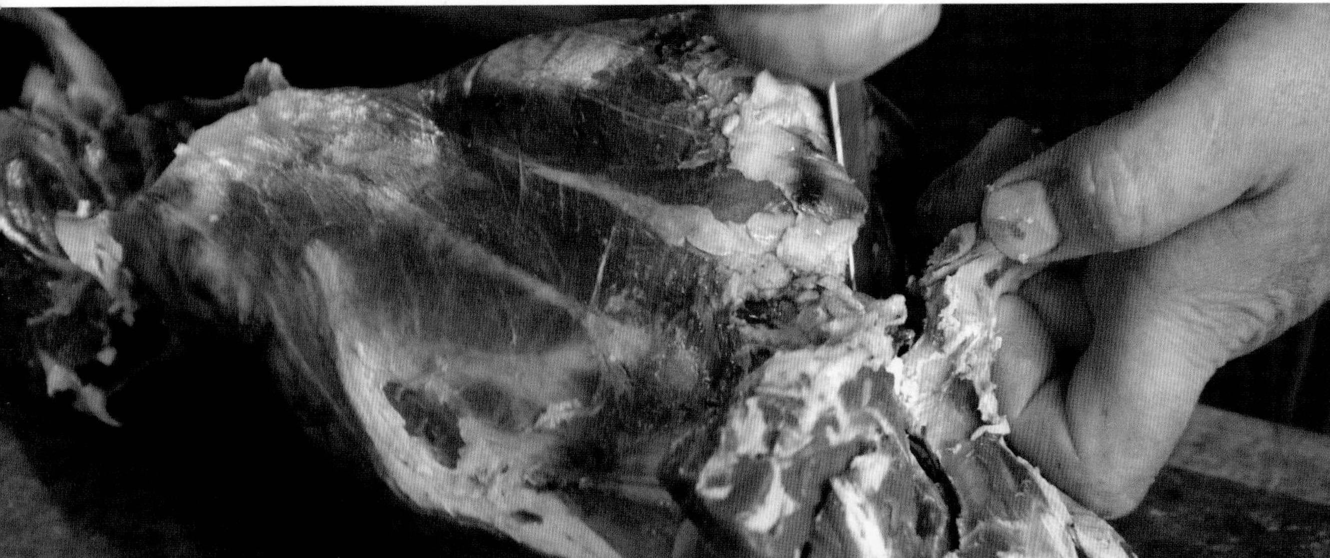

Cooking Mutton

As we have seen, in Victorian Wales, the Ffwrn Fach double boiler cooked meat long and slow, so its modern equivalent, the slow-cooker, is ideal for mutton, producing tender succulent meat every time. Whether you are cooking a roast or casserole, just prepare the ingredients, switch on and leave it until ready. Modern mutton cookery just couldn't be simpler!

Mutton is currently enjoying a revival of interest, with many cooks discovering its unique and complex flavour. There are exciting recipes from a number of different styles of mutton cookery. These include the traditional classic British style, the more spicy options from the Middle East, Africa and elsewhere, and the modern British which is coming up with some new takes on traditional ideas of our native mutton cookery.

The traditional British ways of cooking mutton are poaching, braising or stewing and this produces the classic British slow-cooked mutton, much-loved by previous generations. However, for just as long, if not longer, mutton has been used as a main ingredient in many other cultures; and other styles of cooking the meat have developed. Whether it is tagines from North Africa, hot curries from the Caribbean, or the great variety of dishes which have developed in the Far and Middle East, all these styles have shown how versatile mutton is.

Many of the world's cuisines involving mutton are based on long slow cooking as a stew with mutton, herbs and spices. With suitable accompaniments this opens up a great choice for the modern cook to produce a wide range of succulent and memorable meals.

Many modern lamb recipes are simply adaptations of older mutton dishes. However, this is not a two-way swap. Lamb recipes should not automatically be used for mutton, as they are quite different meats, and they need different handling and cooking to bring out the best in each. Lamb can produce beautifully succulent meals when cooked quickly (the 'Slam in the lamb' advertising slogan of a few years ago demonstrated that). However, mutton generally requires slow, unhurried cooking. Slow cooking of quality mutton that has been hanging for at least two weeks produces deliciously tender meat with a flavour completely different to that of lamb. Mutton's flavour is more intense and complex than that of lamb, and this means it will only improve and mature with long slow cooking. If the mutton is from a two-year-old animal, some people say that lean cuts will stand being cooked as lamb. This is best tried with extreme caution.

There are plenty of dishes which can be cooked with left-overs from joints or other dishes. With the greater depth of flavour, such mutton can be used in dishes like stir-fries, a warming winter broth or even a pizza.

Mutton casserole

MUTTON RECIPES

This section contains an eclectic cross-section of recipes chosen to illustrate the diversity of mutton in the kitchen, and the many varied ways it can be cooked and enjoyed. Mutton suppliers *(see Directory of Suppliers page 183)* are usually happy to give advice on cooking mutton, and often have recipes on their websites, or include them with their order.

SOUPS

Mutton Broth

From ancient times, 'broth' meant meat liquor, ie. the liquid produced from boiling meats – the most common method of cooking mutton. In historic recipe books, a broth could also mean a thick soup - the medieval 'pottage' - where vegetables and whatever meat could be found would be cooked in a large communal pot, and which often included barley grain: wheat is a relative newcomer to the British diet. This is one such recipe; as is typical of recipes before the mid-18th century, quantities are not given, but were left to the discretion of the cook. Such soups were served with oatcakes.

Ingredients

Scrag end of neck of mutton
shank bones
soup vegetables: onion, leek, carrot, celery, all coarsely chopped
bouquet garni (bay leaf/thyme/parsley)
extra chopped vegetables
barley grains (or pearl barley)
salt and pepper
chopped parsley/chives

Method

Put the meat and bones, soup vegetables and herbs into a large saucepan, cover with water, bring to the boil, take off any scum and simmer very gently for around 2 hours, or until the meat falls from the bone.

Strain the soup into a basin; pick out the best of the meat from the debris and reserve. Leave to cool so any fat rises to the top. Remove the fat, pour the broth into a clean saucepan, add a handful of pearl barley and extra chopped vegetables. Bring to the boil and simmer until the barley and vegetables are soft, around 40-50minutes, adding the reserved meat towards the end of the cooking time. Serve with a sprinkling of chopped parsley or chives.

Reestit Mutton Soup

This traditional Shetland soup uses Shetland's Reestit mutton ham – other mutton hams will work as well. The recipe was used by Globe butchers in Lerwick.

Ingredients

1kg Reestit mutton ham, potatoes, carrots, turnip, onion

Method

Place Reestit mutton ham in cold water. Bring to the boil and simmer for almost 2 hours or until tender. Remove meat from pan. The water will now be very salty, so remove some. Skim off the fat, add more water to dilute the saltiness to your own taste, then add chopped potatoes, carrots, turnip and onion in the quantities you would like. Boil until the vegetables are tender. Mash them into smaller pieces if required, and for the last 2 or 3 minutes add some of the chopped up cooked Reestit mutton.

Use any left-over cooked ham in other dishes or eat with potatoes and vegetables.

ROASTS

The Traditional British Roast Leg of Mutton

This is the traditional mutton dish, par excellence, which has remained virtually unchanged for centuries.

Ingredients

Mutton leg on the bone, butter or beef suet for rubbing the joint,
2 carrots, 2 onions, 2 celery sticks, bayleaf

Leg of mutton is a lean cut, and therefore benefits from a layer of fat rubbed over it to help keep it moist during cooking. In former times it was rubbed with mutton fat (and usually flour to form a crust); in the absence of mutton fat, these days butter or beef suet are both suitable. Ask your butcher to chop through the shank, and use this to make stock for gravy, simmering it with water to cover, together with a chopped carrot, onion, celery and bay leaf.

Method

Season the joint with salt and pepper, rub all over with butter or sprinkle with beef suet; and place in a roasting tin. Roast in a preheated oven, gas mark 2/300F/150C, allowing 40-45 minutes per 450g, until cooked through, basting once or twice.

Remove from the oven, cover loosely with foil and allow the meat to relax for half an hour or so in a warm place. Make the gravy in the usual way, using the meat juices and mutton stock if made.

Traditional Spiced Leg of Mutton

This recipe was a common way to prepare roast mutton in the UK for several hundred years until after WWII. Normally it would involve a leg, but shoulder or loin would do equally well.

Serves 6

Ingredients

Mutton leg (or shoulder)
butter for rubbing the joint
ground black pepper
powdered thyme
ground mace
fine oatmeal

Method

Lather the joint with the butter then sprinkle it well with black pepper, a little powdered thyme, a few pinches of mace and fine oatmeal - do not use salt. Cover the joint in foil and cook very slowly, Gas mark 2/300F/150C (until tender and cooked through, approximately 2½ to 3 hours). During the cooking, at least twice, remove the foil and baste the joint well, being careful to re-seal with the foil each time. When cooked, remove the joint from the oven, loosen the foil and let the meat rest for half an hour. For a delicious gravy, use the meat juices with a spoonful of capers added. The meat is equally good cut cold.

Caper Sauce

Caper sauce is a traditional accompaniment that compliments the flavours of mutton meat. Below, the recipe using the meat juices, is adapted from Jane Grigson's book *English Food*. Preparation time is about half an hour.

Ingredients

Serves 4-6

60g butter
60g plain flour
600ml cooking liquor (fat skimmed off)
2 egg yolks
90ml double cream
2 tbsp capers, drained and rinsed
1½ tbsp chopped parsley
juice of a lemon

Method

Melt the butter in a saucepan over a low heat and add the flour. Cook for a few moments before gradually whisking in the cooking liquor. Bring to the boil, stirring until it thickens then reduce the heat to let it simmer for about 15 minutes. In a bowl beat together the egg yolks with the cream and gradually add it to the sauce along with the parsley, stirring for a minute or two without letting it boil. Add the capers and the lemon juice, taste and adjust the seasoning.

'A select company of the Bath footmen presents their compliments to Mr Weller...a friendly soiree consisting of a boiled leg of mutton, with caper sauce, turnips and potatoes.'

Charles Dickens (1812-1870)
Pickwick Papers

Slow Baked Shoulder of Mutton

From: Jane Kallaway of Langley Chase Organic Farm, Wiltshire (*see page 191*).
Mutton shoulder has superb flavour and slow baking delivers meltingly tender meat that falls off the bone.

Serves 4-6

Ingredients

1 mutton shoulder
1 tsp salt
½ tsp black pepper
2 tbsp olive oil
4 onions, thickly sliced
1 head garlic, cloves separated and peeled
1 glass white wine
500ml stock
2 springs fresh rosemary

Method

Heat the oven to gas mark 7/425F/220C. Rub the mutton with salt and pepper. Put the oil in a high-sided roasting tin or heavy pot big enough to take the mutton. Add the onion and garlic and cook on the hob over a gentle heat until soft and golden, about 5-10 minutes. Remove the pot from the heat. Put the rosemary sprigs in the pot and place the mutton on top. Pour in the wine and stock. Cover the pot with a piece of foil and place in the oven. Immediately reduce the oven temperature to Gas mark 2/300F/150C and leave to bake for 3 hours.

Serve with creamy mashed potatoes and steamed, buttered carrots.

Stuffed Loin of Mutton

Serves 4-6

Ingredients

1 boned loin* of mutton with skin flaps
ground mace
salt and pepper
un-smoked ham to cover the joint
For the stuffing:
100g butter
125g chopped 'ready to eat' dried apricots
75g breadcrumbs
2 cloves of garlic, chopped
3 sprigs rosemary, chopped
zest & juice of 1 lemon

*The size of the loin can vary depending on whether it is from a small mountain or larger breed of sheep

Method

Spread out the boned loin and sprinkle with a little pounded mace, salt and pepper. Melt the butter and add the remaining stuffing ingredients. Mix well then spread a layer of stuffing over the meat, followed by a layer of ham. Roll up the prepared loin and tie it tightly with butcher's string, tucking in the flaps as you go to help secure the stuffing. Place the stuffed loin in a baking tray and roast at Gas mark 3 /325F/160C until tender, around 2 hours depending on the size of the loin. The skimmed juices make excellent fruity gravy and the meat is equally delicious served cold next day.

'Put on the joint!' And the waiters set a leg of mutton before Alice, who looked at it rather anxiously, as she had never had to carve a joint before... 'let me introduce you to that leg of mutton,' said the Red Queen.... 'Alice-Mutton;... Mutton-Alice.'... The leg of mutton got up in the dish and made a little bow to Alice.

Lewis Carroll (1832-1898)
Through the Looking Glass

Mutton Olives

This recipe has been adapted from a medieval recipe by Maggie Black in *Food and Cooking in Medieval Britain.*

Ingredients

4 thin slices of mutton leg
1 large onion
6 hard-boiled egg yolks
1 tbsp (15ml) shredded suet
2 tsp (10ml) finely chopped parsley
a pinch of ground ginger
a pinch of powdered saffron
salt
a little butter
cider vinegar for sprinkling
a little ground ginger, cinnamon and
black pepper, mixed, for sprinkling

Method

Beat the meat until thin and flat. Chop the onion finely with 4 egg yolks. Add the suet, parsley, ginger, saffron and salt to taste. Knead and squeeze until pasty. If necessary, add a few drops of water or a little extra parsley. Spread the stuffing on the meat slices and roll them up like small Swiss rolls. Secure with wooden toothpicks. Lay the mutton olives side by side in a greased baking tin, with the cut edges underneath. Dot them with butter. Bake, turning once, at gas mark 4/350F/180C, for 35-40 minutes. Baste once or twice while baking. Lay the mutton olives on a warm serving dish. Just before serving, sprinkle with vinegar and spices and garnish with the remaining egg yolks, crumbled.

'Sacrifice, if you please, three mutton cutlets for every one required. Tie them together, with the choicest and tenderest one in the middle. Grill them, turning them over often so that the juice of the two outer cutlets pervades the one between. When the outer ones are more than cooked, take all three off the fire with infinite precaution and serve only the middle one.'

King Louis XVIII of France (1755-1824)

CUTLETS

The following recipe is taken from a hand-written recipe book kept by the author's grandmother, Abi (pronounced Ayee-bye) Hall, who was a cook in service in north Devon between 1914 and 1922. Before her marriage she was Cook at Arlington Court, now a National Trust property. In the original recipes neither ingredients nor quantities are listed, Abi simply plunges into one glorious flowing account so that you almost sense the bustle of the meal preparation 'below stairs', feel the heat from the kitchen range and smell that mutton gently cooking.

Abi Hall

Abi's Mutton Cutlets

Serves 4

Ingredients

4 mutton cutlets (best end chops)
300ml good stock
two pickled walnuts
1 tbsp walnut vinegar (or other if not available)
30g butter
15g flour

Method

Fry the cutlets in fat until quite brown. Make a gravy with half a pint of good stock and 2 walnuts (pickled) minced, also a tablespoon of walnut vinegar. Thicken with butter and flour. Stew the cutlets gently in this for 1 hour.

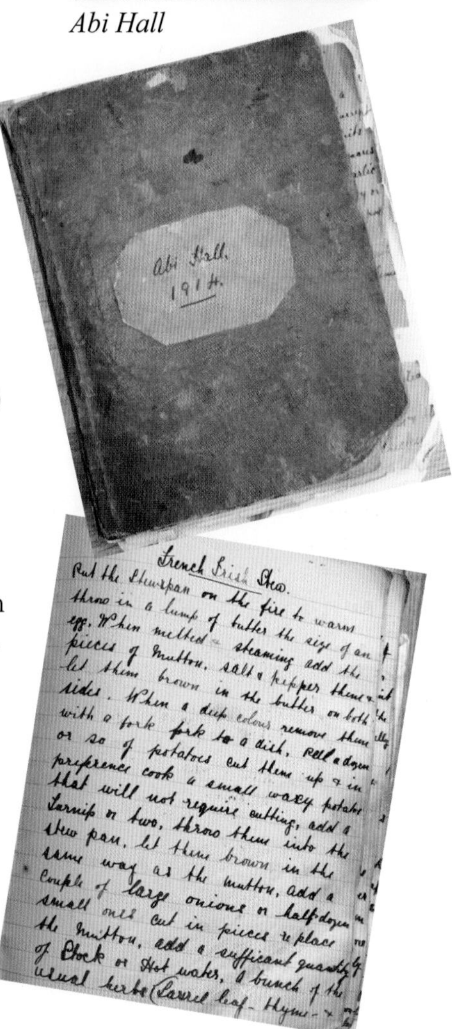

French Irish Stew.

Put the Stewpan on the fire to warm throw in a lump of butter the size of an egg. When melted & steaming add the pieces of Mutton. salt & pepper them & let them brown in the butter on both sides. When a deep colour remove them with a fork fork to a dish. Peel a dozen or so of potatoes cut them up & in preference cook a small waxy potato that will not require cutting, add a turnip or two, throw them into the stew pan. let them brown in the same way as the mutton, add a couple of large onions or half-dozen small ones cut in pieces & replace the mutton, add a sufficant quantity of Stock or Hot water, a bunch of the usual herbs (Laurel leaf - thyme - &

CASSEROLES

Mutton Casseroled in Ale with Prunes & Raisins

This is an adaptation from an English Elizabethan recipe which is familiar to us today through cooking styles from the Middle East, particularly the tagines. The cooking method is especially beneficial in bringing out the fine flavours of mutton and it also works well in a modern slow-cooker.

Serves 4

Ingredients

500g diced mutton
vegetable oil or butter for frying
1 onion, chopped finely
500ml bottle of real ale
½ tsp dried rosemary
½ tsp dried thyme
1 tsp dried parsley
½ tsp ground allspice
¼ tsp ground cloves
40g raisins
freshly ground black pepper
salt to taste
15g dried breadcrumbs
175g ready to eat, stoned prunes, halved

Method

Heat a little oil in a heavy casserole dish and quickly brown the meat. Remove the meat and set aside, leaving the juices to cook the onion until soft, adding a little oil or extra butter if necessary. Replace the meat in the dish and cover it with the ale. Add the herbs, spices and raisins then season to taste. Cover the dish tightly with a lid and place it in a moderate oven at gas mark 4/350F/180C, for 50 minutes. Remove the dish and add the breadcrumbs and the prunes, cover the dish and return it to the oven for a further 30-40 minutes or until the mutton is tender.

Abi's French Irish Stew

This is the second of Abi Hall's recipes from her time as cook at Arlington Court, north Devon, around the time of the First World War.

As the title suggests, the mutton stew is an international dish. In France, it is known as a Navarin Printanier. France even awarded an AOC (denomination certified origin) recognition for its Barèges-Gavarnie Mutton from the 19 Municipalities in the Hautes-Pyrénées, between Barèges and Gavarnie, Midi Pyrénées Region.

Ingredients

diced mutton
lump of butter (size of an egg)
a dozen or so potatoes
turnip or two
two large or six small onions
stock or hot water
bay leaf
thyme
parsley
salt and pepper

Method

Put the saucepan on the fire to warm, throw in a lump of butter the size of an egg. When melted and steaming add the pieces of mutton, salt and pepper them and let them brown in the butter on both sides. When a deep colour remove them with a fork to a dish. Peel a dozen or so potatoes, cut them up and in preference cook a small waxy potato that will not require cutting, add a turnip or two, throw them into the stew pan, let them brown in the same way as the mutton, add a couple of large onions or half dozen small ones, cut in pieces & replace the mutton, add a sufficient quantity of stock or hot water, a bunch of the usual herbs (laurel leaf*, thyme and parsley) cover the saucepan and let the contents simmer on a slow fire for two hours. If the sauce is not thick enough remove a small quantity just before serving, put it into a small bowl and add a teaspoonful of potato flour and pour it into the stew, skim the fat. Add salt and pepper to taste.

*bay leaf

OFFAL

Offal is a much-neglected group of cuts. Mutton liver, kidney and heart all lend themselves to tasty, inexpensive and nutritious meals even in a busy household. The following recipe is a family favourite.

Herby Mutton Hearts

Serves 2

Ingredients

2 sheep's hearts
3 tbsp butter
15g parsley
coriander sprig
2 tsp chopped thyme
1 tsp rosemary
50g breadcrumbs
2-3 rashers of fat bacon
2 tbsp finely chopped onion
2 tbsp flour
250ml boiling water
salt and pepper to taste

Method

Split and wash the hearts, removing any sinews. Soften the butter and add the herbs and the breadcrumbs. Stuff the hearts with the herb mixture and tie with butchers' string. Season the hearts with the salt and pepper and roll them in the flour. Chop the bacon and fry it gently, adding a little oil or butter if necessary, then add the onion. Cook this for 10 minutes then transfer it to a casserole dish. Next brown the hearts in the pan, turning them until sealed all over and add them to the dish. Rinse the pan with a little fresh water, scraping away at the residue then bring it to the boil and pour it over the hearts. Cover the casserole dish and cook gently at gas mark 2/300F/150C, until tender, about 3 hours. If the gravy is still too thin, reduce it down.

'Mutton Haricot: Boil a sheep's head in the normal way...'

From a Gloucestershire recipe book

LEFTOVERS

There is a strong tradition in Britain of using-up cooked mutton. In these days when so much food is wasted, yet budgets are tight, what better way of making the most out of a roasted joint, than by making quick and easy meals out of the unused portion? Leftover cooked mutton lends itself well to tasty stir fries or even pizza toppings.

Abi Hall's hand mincer

Shepherd's Pie

This is probably the most familiar use of cold cooked mutton (or lamb). The history of meat pies in Britain goes back many centuries, but the Shepherd's Pie style which uses cooked potato topping instead of pastry is a relatively recent dish, as potatoes were only widely available in the UK from the mid-18th century. Whilst Cottage Pie, a beef dish with a potato topping, appeared in recipes from the late 18th century, the first use of the term 'Shepherd's Pie' is thought to be in 1870. This is why, in 1861, in her book of Household Management, Mrs Beeton calls her Shepherd's Pie recipe 'Baked Minced Mutton'. Indeed many Victorian recipes include a layer of potato in the bottom of the dish, in order to keep the contents moist.

Mrs Beeton's Baked Minced Mutton

Ingredients

The remains of any joint of cold roast mutton
1 or 2 onions
1 bunch of savoury herbs
pepper and salt to taste
2 blades of pounded mace or nutmeg
2 tbsp of gravy
mashed potatoes

Method

Mince an onion rather fine, and fry it a light-brown colour; add the herbs and mutton, both of which should be also finely minced and well mixed; season with pepper and salt, and a little pounded mace or nutmeg, and moisten with the above proportion of gravy. Put a layer of mashed potatoes at the bottom of a dish, then the mutton, and then another layer of potatoes, and bake for about ½ hour.

Mutton Croquettes

Another family favourite.

Serves 6

Ingredients

500g cooked mutton, minced
Oil for frying
2 small onions finely chopped
1 clove garlic, crushed
½ tsp ground turmeric
½ tsp chilli powder
2 tbsp lemon juice
1 medium par-boiled potato, grated
½ tsp garam masala
2 eggs
50g breadcrumbs
Salt

Method

Heat 4 tablespoons of oil in a pan and gently fry the onions, add the crushed garlic, chilli powder and turmeric and cook gently for a few minutes. Remove the pan from the heat and combine the onion mixture with the grated potato, garam masala powder and one of the beaten eggs, adding salt to taste and mixing well. On a floured board shape the mixture into a dozen or so croquettes. In turn dip each croquette in the remaining beaten egg then roll it in the breadcrumbs. Set the croquettes aside to chill until firm. Deep fry until golden brown, then drain and serve with Caper Sauce (*see recipe on page 167*).

'Maimed Hepburn from the croft-
gate cries
'Come, buy my hot and tottling pies!
Fine mutton pies, fat, piping hot,
One for a penny, four a groat.''

Charles Spense (1779-1869)

'He said 'I look for butterflies
That sleep among the wheat:
I make them into mutton-pies,
And sell them in the street.''

Lewis Carroll (1832-1898)
Through the Looking Glass

MUTTON PIES

Kerry Mutton Pies

From Darina Allen; a great supporter of mutton, Ireland's best-known cook, best-selling author and television cookery presenter. Darina explains that Mutton pies, made in Kerry, were served at the famous Puck Fair in Killorglin in August and taken up the hills when men were herding all day. The original hot water crust pastry was made with mutton fat but we have substituted butter for a really delicious crust.

Serves 6

Ingredients

450g boneless mutton (from shoulder or leg - keep bones for stock)
275g chopped onions
275g chopped carrots
1 tbsp parsley
2 tsp thyme leaves
300ml mutton or lamb stock
2 tbsp flour
salt and freshly ground pepper
Pastry
350g white flour
175g butter
110ml water
pinch of salt
1 egg beaten with a pinch of salt to glaze

Equipment:
2 tins, 15cm in diameter, (4cm high) or 1 x 23cm tin

Method

Cut all surplus fat away, then cut the meat into small neat pieces about the size of a small sugar lump. Render down the scraps of fat in a hot, wide saucepan until the fat runs. Discard any pieces. Cut the vegetables into slightly smaller dice and toss them in the fat, leaving them to cook for 3-4 minutes. Remove the vegetables and toss the meat in the remaining fat over a high heat until the colour turns. Stir the flour into the meat. Cook gently for 2 minutes and blend in the stock gradually. Bring to the boil, stirring occasionally.

Return the vegetables to the pan with the parsley and thyme leaves, season with salt and freshly ground pepper and leave to simmer, covered, until meat is tender. This may take up to 1 hour.

Meanwhile make the pastry. Sieve the flour and salt into a mixing bowl and make a well in the centre. Dice the butter, put it into a saucepan with the water and bring to the boil. Pour the liquid all at once into the flour and mix together quickly; beat until smooth. At first the pastry will be too soft to handle but as it cools it will become more workable. Roll out to 0.6cm thick, to fit the tin or tins. (The pastry may be made into individual pies or one large pie.)

Fill the pastry-lined tins with the slightly cooled meat mixture. Make lids from the remaining pastry, brush the edges of the base with water and egg wash and put on the pastry lids, pinching them tightly together. Roll out the trimmings to make pastry leaves or twirls to decorate the tops of the pies, make a hole in the centre and egg wash carefully. Bake the pie or pies at Gas Mark 6/400F/200C for 40 minutes approx. Serve hot or cold.

RECIPES AROUND THE WORLD

Simple Mutton Curry

In Asia and elsewhere, the term mutton includes both older sheep and goat. Mutton and spices are a marriage made in heaven! Curry pastes are the modern cook's short cut to a quick and easy balance of flavoursome spices. Balti paste works well with mutton to bring out the depth of flavour of the meat but why not experiment with different ready-made curry pastes. The method is straightforward but check the instructions on the jar for any variations if using a different type of paste.

Serves 4

Ingredients

500g diced mutton shoulder
60g butter
1 large onion finely diced
½ 283g jar of Balti Curry Paste
1 x 400g can of chopped tomatoes
200ml water

Method

Melt the butter in a heavy pan then fry the onion until golden. Stir in the curry paste and fry for three minutes. Add the mutton pieces to the pan and toss until sealed. Add the chopped tomatoes and cook for 5 minutes. Add the water, stir well and cover. Simmer until the meat is tender, at least 45 minutes, stirring from time to time. Check the consistency during cooking, adding more water if the mixture becomes too dry.

Bobotie (pronounced Bo-boor-tee)

One of the greatest contributions to South African food culture has been made by the Malay community. In the 17th century, these were slaves transported by the Dutch East India Company from the Dutch colonies in Indonesia, particularly Java. Later these were joined by dissidents to Dutch rule who were exiled to South Africa by the Dutch authorities in the Far East. They brought with them their knowledge and a combination of sweet and sour as well as spicy sauces, curries, chutneys, and blatjangs (pronounced blud-youngs), which is a condiment traditionally served with bobotie and other meat dishes. It is a cross between fruit chutney and jam. These spice combinations and flavours create very tasty yet mild dishes that have become part of South African cookery, and which work well with mutton.

The author's student daughter and her friends are particularly fond of this traditional recipe which has been a family favourite for many years.

Serves 4

Ingredients

500g minced mutton
1 slice white bread
200ml milk
1 medium onion
60gm seedless raisins
60gm blanched almonds
2 tsp apricot jam
2 tsp fruit chutney
1 tsp curry powder
½ tsp turmeric
1 tbsp lemon juice
1 tsp salt
2 tsp butter or oil
2 eggs
1 bay leaf

Method

Soak the bread in half the milk, squeeze to remove the milk and mix the bread with the minced mutton. Mix all the other ingredients, except the butter/oil, eggs, milk and bay leaf. Melt the butter/oil in a frying pan and brown the meat mixture lightly. Turn out into a casserole. Beat the eggs and the rest of the milk together and pour over the meat. Garnish with the bay leaf. Bake in the oven at gas mark 4/350F/180C until set, about 50 minutes.

THE MODERN BRITISH STYLE

This selection of recipes reflects the modern take on cooking delicious mutton meals.

Mutton with Sumac and Butterbeans

Mutton and dry beans are a classic combination. This recipe was sent to us by the late Clarissa Dickson Wright, celebrity chef and staunch advocate of mutton.

Serves 4-6

Ingredients

1.4-1.8kg loin mutton, boned and rolled
3 tbsp rapeseed oil
500g shallots, chopped
1 tablespoon sumac or the peel of 1 lemon
2 wine glasses white wine
3 tbsp brandy
pinch cayenne pepper
pinch paprika
1½ tbsp runny honey
2 cloves of garlic, peeled and roughly chopped
salt
180g butter beans or haricot beans, soaked overnight
white wine vinegar (optional – to taste)

Method

Heat the oil in a heavy casserole and brown the shallots. Remove the shallots with a slotted spoon and set aside. Rub the mutton with sumac or, alternatively, pierce the meat and put slivers of lemon peel in each of the slots. Put the mutton into the casserole and brown all over.

Add the wine, brandy, cayenne pepper, paprika, honey, garlic and 1-2 teaspoons of salt. Stir and simmer uncovered for 1½ hours.

Alternatively, place in the oven at gas mark 3/325F/170°C. Add the beans, cover the casserole and cook for a further 1 hour, or until the meat is tender. If necessary, you can add a little water at this point and then taste. If light, add another tablespoon of runny honey and a little white wine vinegar.

Tagine of Mutton and Chickpeas

This recipe was developed for the organic meat company which was founded, and owned until 2009, by the author and his wife. It was a customer favourite. Like many mutton dishes this is especially suitable for cooking in a slow-cooker.

Serves 6-8

Ingredients

1kg diced mutton
4 tbsp olive oil
2 onions, finely chopped
6 garlic cloves, crushed
1 tsp ground coriander
1 tsp ground cumin
1 tsp ground paprika
½ tsp ground ginger
½ tsp ground cinnamon
¼ tsp chilli powder
1 tbsp plain flour
2 x 400g tins chopped tomatoes
250ml water
400g tin chickpeas, drained
90g raisins
salt & black pepper
mint or coriander to garnish

Method

Heat the oil in a large, heavy casserole over medium heat. Add the onions and cook until softened, about 5 minutes. Add the garlic, coriander, cumin, paprika, ginger, cinnamon and chilli and cook, stirring, until spicily fragrant, about a minute. Add the mutton, sprinkle the flour over it, stirring until thoroughly coated with the spiced mixture, then cook gently until lightly browned all over, 10-15 minutes. Add the tomatoes and water, mix well and bring to a simmer.

Cover the casserole dish and transfer it to the oven. Bake for about 1¾ hours at gas mark 3/325F/170C.

Take out the dish and stir in the chick peas and raisins and cook for a further 30 minutes or until the meat is tender. Add salt and pepper to taste.

Serve hot, garnished with herbs and with hot buttered couscous or mashed potato.

Spiced Mutton Kebabs

This recipe is from Jo Budden of award winning Higher Hacknell Farm in Devon (*see Directory of Suppliers page 190*). Jo has long experience of producing and cooking mutton. This recipe works well by using the most tender cuts and by marinating overnight. Be sure to choose a two-year-old mutton, well-hung.

Serves 4

Ingredients

700g diced mutton from the loin or neck fillet
150ml olive oil
2 tbsp lemon juice
2 garlic cloves, crushed
2 tsp crushed coriander seeds
1 tsp ground ginger
1 tsp ground cumin
2 bay leaves, crumbled
salt, black pepper
2 limes, cut in wedges
pitta bread

Method

Put the diced mutton in a shallow dish. Mix together the olive oil, lemon juice, garlic, spices, bay leaves and seasoning, then pour this marinade over the meat and mix well. Cover the meat and chill for around 12 hours. Thread the meat and wedges of lime onto kebab skewers, then brush with the marinade. Barbecue or grill for approximately 10 minutes, turning to ensure the meat is cooked. Serve with pitta bread.

'...but, madam,' said she,
'I can get any kind of mutton in
an instant from the butcher's.'

Henry Fielding (1707-1754)
The History of Tom Jones,
a Foundling

Directory of Suppliers

There is a good selection of traditional mutton suppliers in the UK. Just as wine drinkers have a choice of grape varieties and terroirs which add to the pleasures of tasting different wines, so with mutton. There is much interest and enjoyment to be had from comparing the differences in flavour and texture of the meat reared in different environments, the breeds of sheep, and the periods of hanging.

This directory is as accurate as possible at the time of writing, and is based on information given by the individual suppliers. Despite many enquiries, it has not been possible to identify any mutton suppliers based in Northern Ireland, although most mainland producers will deliver there.

It does not attempt to be a comprehensive list of all producers, and many other local suppliers and independent butchers offer mutton.

Divided geographically, the directory gives information about the main aspects of producing mutton, giving you the tools to select.

THE FARMING

Environment Most suppliers sell animals from their own farm. The others will know where the mutton was reared. How much does location of rearing affect the taste? You can try for yourself.

Organic The Organic system of farming uses minimal routine drugs and other chemicals and operates to very high animal welfare standards. There is good evidence that the effect of Organic farming on the environment and wildlife is better than an intensive farming system. Each Organic farm is thoroughly inspected at least annually to ensure it maintains the legally defined Organic standards. Importantly in Organic sheep farming, some chemicals are not allowed for routine dipping, and all drug use at least doubles the legal period between dosing and slaughtering. All Organic food is certified by a number of UK bodies, including the Soil Association, Organic Farmers and Growers, Scottish Organic Producers Association and Quality Welsh Food Certification. It must also display the EU organic logo (pictured).

Breeds Use the information given by the supplier together with the general advice in the previous 'Buying Mutton Today' chapter and the List of UK Breeds which follows this section.

Ewes or Wethers As we have seen, most mutton available today is from ewes. However, there are a few producers who can supply wether mutton. Another interesting point of comparison.

THE BUTCHERY

Age at slaughter The accepted minimum age for mutton is two years. Below this it is strictly speaking known as hogget or shearling, which produces meat with a flavour less complex than that of mutton.

Hanging The suppliers were asked how long they hang their mutton. This varies between 7 and over 21 days. Some will hang to order. By trying different hanging periods, you should be able to establish the period which you find the most delicious.

Awards The list includes a number who have won recognised awards for the quality of their mutton.

THE SELLING

Seasonality Some producers have mutton only at certain times of the year, others have year-round availability.

Buying The outlets listed vary from village shops, to butchers, farm shops, farmers markets and mail order.

Cuts or Boxes There are two ways to buy mutton, either by individual cuts (leg, mince, etc.) or by selection boxes, which usually represent a half or whole animal. Many of the suppliers listed can butcher to your specific requirements.

SCOTLAND

A Taste of Galloway

Mail Order & from Farm or Shops
www.atasteofgalloway.co.uk 01848 330622
sales@atasteofgalloway.co.uk
Laughtmuirside Farm, Thornhill, Dumfries & Galloway DG3 5DH
Contact: Chirstie and Callum Baird
Home produced beef, lamb and mutton from a family farm in the Scottish Borders.
Breed: Scottish Blackface
Ewes or Wethers: ewes Age: 5 years +
Hanging period: 7 days+
Season available: June-July, November
Cuts or Boxes: either
Other Outlets: Glasgow & Edinburgh farmers markets

Aberfoyle Butchers

Mail Order & from Farm or Shops
www.aberfoylebutcher.co.uk 01877 382473
contact@aberfoylebutcher.co.uk
Mayfield, 206 Main St, Aberfoyle, Stirling FK8 3UQ
Contact: Jonathan Honeyman
Independent butcher in the heart of the Trossachs, offering a variety of mutton breeds, each with its own unique qualities and specific characteristics. Supply trade and retail consumers.
Breed: Various including Blackface and Mule
Ewes or Wethers: both Age: 2-7 years
Hanging period: 7-14 days
Season available: all year if suitable quality
Cuts or Boxes: cuts
Other Outlets: Call for outlets supplied

Blackface Meat Company

Mail Order & Collection by appointment
Best Seasonal Product in Britain - Taste of Britain 2005
www.blackface.co.uk 01387 730326
ben@blackface.co.uk
Crochmore House, Irongray, Dumfries DG2 9SF
Heather-bred Scottish Blackface mutton and other meats from the wilds of Scotland. Mutton featured on the TV programme The Hairy Bikers.
Breed: Scottish Blackface
Ewes or Wethers: both Age: 2-5 years
Hanging period: 7-14 days
Season available: all year-round
Cuts or Boxes: both

Cruinn Foods

Mail Order & from Farm
01546 850241/239
caroline@jeronsons.freeserve.co.uk
Creag a Mhadaidh, Achnamara, Lochgilphead, Argyll PA31 8PT
Contact: Nancy Tuthill
Home-produced lamb and mutton, grazed on heather moorland and natural pasture, locally butchered.
Breed: Scottish Blackface
Ewes or Wethers: ewes Age: 2 years +
Hanging period: 14 day
Season available: April to December
Cuts or Boxes: cuts

Hebridean Mutton

Mail Order
www.hebrideanmutton.co.uk 01851 621722
07876 504463 sandy@hebrideanmutton.co.uk
10 Tolsta Chaolais, Isle of Lewis, HS2 9DW
Contact: Ali and Sandy Granville
Hebridean Mutton believes in producing food slowly, and to minimise stress on animals by minimising their transport. The mutton is slaughtered on the island in the autumn and delivered throughout the UK in time for Christmas.
Breed: Hebridean Blackface
Ewes or Wethers: wethers Age: 2.5 years +
Hanging period: 7 days
Season available: September to December
Cuts or Boxes: box

J.K. Mainland

Butchers Shop & Mail Order
www.jkmainlandbutchersfarmshop.com
01595 692355 jkmainland@mail.com
177 Commercial St, Lerwick, Shetland ZE1 0HX
Contact: Ronnie Obern
Shetland's last traditional butcher, selling quality local produce from their own farm and other local farmers to supply Shetland beef, lamb, mutton and pork and a 130-year-old haggis recipe. Speciality is traditional Shetland Reestit mutton.
Breeds: Shetland & Shetland cross Texel
Ewes or Wethers: ewes Age: 2 years +
Hanging Period: 14-21 days
Season available: year-round
Cuts or box: either

Liddesdale Free Range

Mail Order & Farm or Shop
www.liddesdalefreerange.co.uk 01387 376210
farm@liddesdalefreerange.co.uk
Boghall, Kirndean Farm, Newcastleton, Roxburghshire TD9 0SG
Contact: Mary Howlett & Paul Bell
A family farm producing naturally-reared mutton, lamb and hoggets, free-range French label rouge breed chickens, Gloucester Old Spot pigs, and Shorthorn beef cattle.
Breed: Blackface crossbred
Ewes or Wethers: ewes Age: 3-4 years
Hanging period: 14 days
Season available: October to early summer
Cuts or Boxes: both
Other Outlets: Edinburgh; Stockbridge's French-themed market; Kelso Farmers' Market, Rosehill Farmers' Market at Carlisle livestock auction; also butchers/farmshop in Hawick, Scottish Borders selling home-reared meats, plus local breed beef.

Macbeth's

Mail Order & from Butchers Shop
Noisettes – Gold Star in Great Taste Awards
www.macbeths.com 01309 672254 info@macbeths.com
11 Tolbooth Street, Forres, Moray IV36 1PH
Contact: Jock Gibson
On-line butcher supplying mutton and a range of other meats from its own farm.
Breed: Suffolk x Cheviot; Rare breeds inc Hebridean
Ewes or Wethers: both
Age: 2-5 years Hanging period: 7 days
Season available: September to December
Cuts or Boxes: cuts

Newmiln Farm Organic

Mail Order & Farm or Shop
Mutton described as "exceptional" by AA Gill (2012)
www.the-organic-farm.co.uk 01738 730201
sascha@hughgrierson.co.uk
Hugh Grierson Organic, Tibbermore, Perth PH1 1QN
Contact: Hugh and Sascha Grierson
Seasonal Scottish mutton farm-reared, together with beef, lamb, chicken and rare breed pork. Butchery done on site, and deliver nationwide to households, shops and restaurants.
Breed: Easycare x Texel
Ewes or Wethers: ewes Age: 5 years +
Hanging period: 7 days
Season available: July to November
Cuts or Boxes: both
Other Outlets: Edinburgh Farmers' market

Peelham Farm Produce Organic

Mail Order & Farm Shop
www.peelham.co.uk 01890 781328
info@peelham.co.uk
Peelham Farm, Foulden, Berwick upon Tweed, Berwickshire TD15 1UG
Contact: Denise and Chris Walton
Organically-reared slowly-grown mutton and other meats. Mutton specialities include dry-cured mutton ham (smoked & unsmoked), cooked sliced mutton ham (smoked or unsmoked) mutton ham and caper pie, and air-dried juniper mutton prosciutto.
Breed: Lleyn and Lleyn x Texel
Ewes or Wethers: ewes Age: 3-5 years
Hanging period: 14 days
Season available: October to May
Cuts or Boxes: both
Other Outlets: in Edinburgh, Glasgow and Northumberland

The Well-Hung Lamb Company

Mail Order & Collection by appointment
www.wellhunglamb.co.uk 01408 641451 / 07747 865871 robin@rogartcroft.co.uk
Reidchalmai Croft, Rogart, Sutherland, IV28 3XE
Contact: R.J. and P.R. Calvert
Reidchalmai Croft is a small family-run business in the Highlands, dedicated to high-welfare animal production. Specialities: mutton pies and hams
Breed: North Country Cheviot, with Texel and Mule crosses
Ewes or Wethers: both
Age: 3½ years + Hanging period: 21 days +
Season available: most of the year
Cuts or Boxes: both
Other Outlets: Farmers' markets, shows and events and craft markets

Windsheil Organic

Mail Order & Farm
www.windshiel.co.uk 01361 883863
seb@windshiel.demon.co.uk
Duns, Berwickshire TD11 3TU
Contact: Sharon or Joe Baker
Home-grown organic mutton, lamb, beef and pork from the family farm in the Lammermuir Hills.

Breed: Lleyn
Ewes or Wethers: ewes
Age: Normally 3 years +
Hanging period: 7-10 days
Season available: most of the year
Cuts or Boxes: cuts
Other Outlet: Local shops and caterers

NORTHERN ENGLAND

Askerton Castle Estate Organic

Mail Order & Farm or Shops
www.askertoncastle.co.uk 01697 73332
info@askertoncastle.co.uk
Brampton, Cumbria, CA8 2BD
Contact: Chris Evans
An organic farm specialising in hardy native breeds in the beautiful wild countryside near Hadrian's Wall in North East Cumbria.
Breed: Scottish Blackface & Kerry Hill
Ewes or Wethers: ewes Age: 3 years +
Hanging period: 7 days
Season available: all year round
Cuts or Boxes: cuts
Other Outlets: local farmers' markets

Broom House Farm Organic

Mail Order & Farm Shop
www.broomhousedurham.co.uk 0191 3718839
broomhousedurham@btinternet.com
near Witton Gilbert, Durham DH7 6TR
Contacts: Mark and Jane Grey
On-farm butchery for home-grown beef, sheep and pork, café and other on-farm activities
Breed: Lleyn
Ewes or Wethers: ewes Age: 2 years +
Hanging period: min. 10 days
Season available: all year round
Cuts or Boxes: both
Other Outlets: Durham farmers' market, Sedgefield farmers' market, Durham Saturday market

Edge & Son Butchers

Mail Order & Farm or Butchers Shops
www.traditionalmeats.com 0151 645 3044
mail@traditionalmeat.com
61 New Chester Road, New Ferry, Wirral CH62 1AB
Contact: Callum
Award-winning traditional butcher selling range of rare native breed meats, including Hebridean mutton from Cheshire Wildlife reserves. Sold from two shops.
Breed: Hebridean, Swaledale
Ewes or Wethers: both Age: 2-4 years
Hanging period: 7 to 21 days
Season available: all year round
Cuts or Boxes: both
Other Outlets: Farm shop at Church Farm, Church Lane, Thurstaston, Wirral CH61 0HW. Various farm shops around Wirral/Cheshire. Call for details.

Hallsford Farm Produce

Mail Order
www.hallsford.co.uk 01228 577329
thefarm@hallsford.co.uk
Haggbeck, Heathersgill, Carlisle CA6 6JD
Contact: Andrew & Helen Tomkins
Family farm and online/mail order shop, using own livestock (shorthorn beef and saddleback pork).
Breed: Llanwenog & crosses
Ewes or Wethers: mostly ewes Age: 4 years +
Hanging period: 14 days
Season available: September to May
Cuts or Boxes: cuts
Other Outlets: Hallsford catering street food

Heritage Foods

Mail Order
www.heritagefoods.co.uk 07732 757043
info@heritagefoods.co.uk
Yew Tree Farm, Coniston, Cumbria, LA21 8DP
Contact: Caroline Watson
Herdwick hogget and mutton available online; Farm Assured
Breed: Herdwick
Ewes or Wethers: both Age: 2–5 years
Hanging period: 7–21 days
Season available: year-round
Cuts or Boxes: both

J W Mettrick & Son

Mail Order & from Butchers Shops
Best Lamb/Mutton Product at the North West Fine Foods with Mutton Cutlets
www.mettricksbutchers.co.uk 01457 852239
john@mettricksbutchers.co.uk
20 High Street, Glossop, High Peak, Derbyshire SK13 8BH

Contact: John Mettrick
The mutton sold in this renowned butchers shop comes from a very small number of farms in the Peak District, within ten miles of the shop, and has been enjoyed by the local community for decades.
Breeds: Whiteface Woodland, Derbyshire Gritstone and Texels
Ewes or Wethers: ewes Age: 2 years +
Hanging period: 14 days
Season available: all year round
Cuts or Boxes: cuts
Other Outlets: 2nd butcher's shop at 86-88 Station Road, Hadfield, Glossop, Derbyshire SK13 1AJ 01457 852129 and 63 Melbourne Street, Stalybridge SK15 2JJ 0161 3047896

J. Brindon Addy

Butchers Shop
www.jbrindonaddy.co.uk 01484 682897
info@jbrindonaddy.co.uk
Penistone Road, Hade Edge, W. Yorks HD9 2JG
Contact: Brindon Addy
Traditional family butchers, and members of Q Guild. Supply full range of local meats and seasonal mutton.
Breed: Mainly Texel cross
Ewes or Wethers: both, mainly ewes
Age: various
Hanging period: 14 days
Cuts or Boxes: cuts

Keer Falls Forest Farm

Mail Order & Farm Shop
www.keerfalls.co.uk 015242 21019
philip@keerfalls.co.uk
Keer Falls Forest Farm, Arkholme, Carnforth, Lancs LA6 1AP Contact: Philip Onions
Mutton reared on herb-rich pastures in north Lancashire and on the edge of the Lake District, and fed only home-grown hay and the finest feeds.
Breeds: Whitefaced Woodland, Ryland & Wensleydale
Ewes or Wethers: both Age: 2 years +
Hanging period: as requested by customers
Season available: all year round
Cuts or Boxes: boxes

Mansergh Hall Farm

Mail Order & farm by appointment
www.manserghhall.co.uk 015242 71397
shop@manserghhall.co.uk
Kirkby Lonsdale, via Carnforth, Lancs LA6 2EN
Contact: Amanda or Simon Gorton
Mutton and other meats from own and local farms, available by mail order, local markets and on-farm butchery by appointment.
Breeds: North Country Cheviot and Texel cross
Ewes or Wethers: ewes Age: 3-6 years
Hanging period: 14 days +
Season available: spring, autumn and winter
Cuts or Boxes: cuts
Other Outlets: Low Sizergh Barn, nr Kendal; also local charter markets: Carnforth, Lancaster, Kirkby Lonsdale, Lancaster University Farmers' Market (term time only).

Northumbrian Quality Meats

Mail Order
www.northumbrianqualitymeats.co.uk 01434 270320
steve@northumbrianqualitymeats.co.uk
Monkridge Hill Farm, West Woodburn, Hexham, Northumberland NE48 2TU
Contact: Steve Ramshaw
Award-winning meats produced on their own farm includes mutton, lamb and Wagyu and Angus beef.
Breed: Blackface
Ewes or Wethers: both Age: 2 years +
Hanging period: 14 days
Season available: August to April
Cuts or Boxes: cuts

Paganum Produce

Mail Order & Shop
www.paganum.co.uk 01729 830902
info@paganum.co.uk
Church End Farm, Kirkby Malham, North Yorkshire, BD23 4BU Contact: Chris Wildman
Meat from individual farms in the Yorkshire Dales, including Dales Mutton. Also produce some Mutton charcuterie including Mutton Ham, Mutton Bacon and Mutton Pancetta. All grass fed.
Breed: Blueface Leicester, Swaledale, Mules and Suffolk
Ewes or Wethers: both Age: 3 years+
Hanging period: 7 days
Season available: October to April
Cuts or Boxes: both
Other Outlets: Town End Farm shop, Airton, Skipton N. Yorks BD23 4BE www.townendfarmshop.co.uk

Pepperfield Farm

Mail Order & Farm Shop
Gold and Silver from Great Yorkshire Show for mutton sausages
www.pepperfieldfarm.co.uk 01325 720575 / 07849026561 pepperfieldfarm@hotmail.co.uk
Dalton-on-Tees, Nr Darlington, North Yorkshire DL2 2NS Contact: Terry & Joanne Laheney
Home grown mutton from rare Wiltshire Horn sheep, together with a range of other meats from the farm.
Breed: Wiltshire Horn
Ewes or Wethers: both Age: 18-30 months
Hanging period: 14 days +
Season available: year-round Cuts or Boxes: both

Swillington Organic Farm Organic

Mail Order & Farm or Shops
www.swillingtonorganicfarm.co.uk
07974 826876; Shop: 0113 2869129
info@swillingtonorganicfarm.co.uk
Garden Cottage, Coach Road, Swillington, Leeds LS26 8QA Contact: Jo Cartwright
Produces own organically certified mutton. The farm has a diverse range of habitats including woodland, marsh, pasture and ponds, providing a haven for wildlife and the perfect place for our organic rare breed pigs and native breed cattle and sheep as well as free range organic poultry.
Breed: Texel x Lleyn
Ewes or Wethers: ewes Age: various
Hanging period: 14–21 days
Season available: autumn and winter
Cuts or Boxes: both
Other Outlets: Local farmers' markets

Westmorland Farm Shops

M6 Tebay Motorway Services Cumbria
www.tebayservices.com 01539 711338
info@tebayservices.com
M6 northbound J38-39 north & south
Contact: David Morland
A farm shop in the M6 Westmorland motorway services. Officially opened by HRH Prince of Wales in 2004, with the butchery supplied from the owners' family farm nearby. A first for the British motorway network, driven by the Dunning family's passion for local produce. All produce sold is locally produced within 30 miles. Produce can be ordered ahead for later collection.
Breed: Texel & Mule Ewes or Wethers: ewes
Age: 2-3 years
Hanging period: Variable in on-site maturing room
Season available: year round Cuts or Boxes: cuts
Other Outlets: M5 Gloucester Motorway Services (J12-11a) northbound.

Yew Tree Farm

Farm shop
015394 41433 info@yewtree-farm.co.uk
Yew Tree Farm, Coniston Cumbria LA21 8DP
Contact: John Watson
Herdwick mutton, lamb and hogget, together with Belted Galloway beef available from Yew Tree Farm, once owned by Beatrix Potter.
Breed: Herdwick
Ewes or Wethers: both Age: 2-5 years
Hanging period: 7-21 days
Season available: year-round
Cuts or Boxes: both

MIDLANDS

A. J. Pugh Butchers

Mail Order & Butchers Shops
www.ajpughbutchers.co.uk 01588 638584
ajpughbutchers@yahoo.co.uk
46 Church St, Bishops' Castle, Shropshire SY9 5AE
Contact: Tom Pugh
Traditional Butchers offering locally-sourced quality meat from two shops in Welsh Borders and online, including mutton and home-made sausages.
Breed: Purebred Shropshire
Ewes or Wethers: ewes Age: 3 years
Hanging period: 10+ days
Season available: all year round
Cuts or boxes: both
Other outlets: Butchery at Harry Tuffins, Whitehall Supermarket, Knighton, Powys LD7 1DA
01547 520786

Alternative Meats Ltd

Mail Order & Farm or Shops
www.alternativemeats.co.uk 01948 871200
info@alternativemeats.co.uk
The Butchery, Home Farm, Combermere, Whitchurch, Shropshire SY13 4AL
As the name suggests, a mail order company which sells a range of less-common meats. Sources Herdwick mutton from Millbeck Farm, Langdale, Cumbria (The Lake District).
Breed: Herdwick

Ewes or Wethers: ewes Age: 2 years +
Hanging period: 7-10 days
Season available: all year round
Cuts or Boxes: both
Other Outlets: supplies independent retailers

Huntsham Farm

Mail Order
www.huntsham.com 01600 890296
richard@huntsham.com
Ross-on-Wye, Herefordshire HR9 6JN
Contact: Richard Vaughan
Home produced rare breed mutton available from time to time
Breed: Ryeland
Ewes or Wethers: ewes Age: 2 years +
Hanging period: 10 days
Season available: seasonal
Cuts or Boxes: box

Ludlow Food Centre

Farm Shop
www.ludlowfoodcentre.co.uk 01584 856000
john@ludlowfoodcentre.co.uk
Bromfield, Ludlow, Shropshire SY8 2JR
Contact: John Brereton
The Centre offers a wide range of food, 80% sourced locally, and is part of the Earl of Plymouth's Oakly Park Estate which covers some 8,000 acres. Mutton sourced from local flocks of Shetland sheep and estate flock. All beef, lamb and pork also from the estate along with a selection of game and vegetables.
Breed: Shetland, Lleyn and Welsh Mule Cross
Ewes or Wethers: both Age: 3-4 years
Hanging period: 14 days
Season available: October to May
Cuts or Boxes: both

Pentre Farm Organic

Farm or Shops
01547 520332 jcatherineh@hotmail.com
Pentre, Bucknell, Shropshire SY7 0BU
Contact: Catherine Humphreys
Organic smallholding specialising in mutton and lamb, selling locally and wholesale.
Breed: Soay and Texel cross
Ewes or Wethers: ewes
Age: 2-3 years Texel, 3-4 years Soay
Hanging period: 14 days +
Season available: year-round
Cuts or Boxes: cuts to order
Other Outlets: Local delivery, Bishop's Castle and Ludlow farmers' markets

Weobley Ash

Mail Order & Farm or Shops
www.weobleyash.co.uk 01544 267684
helen@weobleyash.co.uk
Stansbatch, Leominster, Herefordshire HR6 9LW
Contacts: Helen and David Pickersgill
A family farm creating high quality produce including mutton, lamb and hogget. Apple juice & cider from their orchards and home-produced eggs.
Breed: Lleyn
Ewes or Wethers: ewes Age: 4 -5 years
Hanging period: 10-14 days
Season available: all year round
Cuts or Boxes: both
Other Outlets: Kington Country Market and Presteigne, Kington and Knighton Farmers' Markets

WALES

A. J. Pugh Butchers

Mail Order & Butchers Shop
www.ajpughbutchers.co.uk 01547 520786
ajpughbutchers@yahoo.co.uk
Harry Tuffins, Whitehall Supermarket, Knighton, Powys. LD7 1DA Contact: Tom Pugh
(*see* main A.J.Pugh entry on page 188 for more details)
Traditional Butchers offering locally sourced quality meat from two shops in Welsh Borders and online, including mutton and home-made sausages.

Aran Lamb

Mail Order & Farm or Shops
Wales True Taste Awards
www.aran-lamb.co.uk 01678 540603/07799 576031
sales@aran-lamb.co.uk
Cwmonnen Farm, Llanuwchllyn, Nr Bala, Gwynedd LL23 7UG
Contacts: Maldwyn and Margaret Thomas.
Award-winning farm in north Wales producing Welsh Mountain lamb and mutton.
Breed: Welsh Mountain
Ewes or Wethers: ewes Age: 3 years +
Hanging period: 14 days
Season available: year-round
Cuts or Boxes: boxes

Other Outlets: Farmers' markets, food fairs and food events, with mobile catering, selling cooked produce from the farm.

Daphne's Original Welsh Lamb

Mail Order
www.daphnesoriginalwelshlamb.co.uk 01745 813552
lamb@daphneswelshlamb.com
Rose Hill Cottage, Henllan, Denbigh LL16 5BA
Contact: Daphne Tilley
Family-run farm, locally slaughtered, delivered straight from the Welsh Hills
Breed: Beulah Mules; Beltex Texel Mules
Ewes or Wethers: ewes Age: 2 years +
Hanging period: 21 days
Season available: winter to late-spring
Cuts or Boxes: cuts
Other Outlets: orders by telephone, some areas of London delivered by own transport, otherwise courier.

Penrhiw Farm Organic

Mail Order & Farm or Shops
Highly Commended, Wales True Taste Awards
01449 412949 penrhiw.farm@virgin.net
Penrhiw Farm, Trelewis, Treharris CF46 6TA
Contact: Celia Thomas
This family-run organic hill farm above the Taf Bargoed Valley, rears its own mutton, lamb and Aberdeen Angus beef.
Breed: South Wales Mountain (Nelson)
Ewes or Wethers: ewes Age: 2-8 years
Hanging period: 14 days
Season available: September to June
Cuts or Boxes: cuts
Other Outlets: Available from farmers' markets at Usk, Riverside and Rhiwbina in Cardiff, and from the butcher's shop in Treharris "Cig Mynydd Cymru".

Rhug Estate Organic

Mail Order & Farm Shop
www.rhug.co.uk 01490 413000 contact@rhug.co.uk
Rhug Estate, Corwen, Denbighshire LL21 0EH
Contacts: Mr Jon Edwards, Rhug Estate (Retail Manager)/ Charlotte (sales)
Large farm shop and comprehensive mail order range from estate in North Wales; also supply wholesale.
Breed: various breeds
Ewes or Wethers: ewes Age: 2 years +
Hanging period: 7 days
Season available: Sept, Oct, Feb & March
Cuts or Boxes: both
Other Outlets: wholesale

Slade Farm Organics Organic

Mail Order, Local Delivery & Farm Shop
Great Taste Awards 2012 for leg of mutton
www.sladefarmorganics.com 01656 880048
info@sladefarmorganics.com
Pitcot Farm, Wick Road, St Bride's Major, Bridgend CF32 0TF
Contact: Polly Davies
All meat is from home-grown animals. Wide range including mutton.
Breed: Romney & Romney cross
Ewes or Wethers: mostly ewes Age: 18 months +
Hanging period: 14 days +
Season available: year-round
Cuts or Boxes: cuts

Treberfedd Organic

Mail Order & Farm or Shops
www.treberfedd.co.uk 01570 470 672
info@treberfedd.co.uk
Dihewyd, Lampeter, Ceredigion SA48 7NW
Contact: Jack Cockburn (Farm Manager)
Sells mutton from own Llanwenog breed sheep.
Breed: Llanwenog
Ewes or Wethers: both Age: 2-3½ years
Hanging period: 14 days
Season available: October to May
Cuts or Boxes: both; boxes delivered locally
Other Outlets: Organic Fresh Food Company, Lampeter

SOUTH-WEST ENGLAND

Higher Hacknell Farm Organic

Mail Order & collection by appointment
www.higherhacknell.co.uk 01769 560909
info@higherhacknell.co.uk
Burrington, Umberleigh, Devon EX37 9LX
Contacts: Tim and Jo Budden
From their Devon farm, the Buddens supply a range of award-winning meats including mutton from their own flock. Also ready-made meals from their own beef and lamb and local organic chicken and pork.
Breed: Lleyn Ewes or Wethers: Ewes
Age: 2 years + Hanging period: 14 days +

Season available: all year round
Cuts or Boxes: both
Other Outlets: Marshford Organic Shop, Northam; River Cottage Axminster and Plymouth.

Jon Thorner's Bridge Farm Shop

Farm or Shops
www.jonthorners.co.uk 01749 830138
info@jonthorners.co.uk
Pylle, Shepton Mallet, Somerset BA4 6TA
Contact: Jon Thorner
Farm shop, butchery and coffee shop supplying locally-sourced meats and other products.
Breed: various
Ewes or Wethers: both Age: 2-3 years
Hanging period: 10 days +
Season available: all year (may be frozen)
Cuts or Boxes: cuts
Other Outlets: Farrington's Farm Shop, Home Farm, Farrington, Gurney, Bristol BS39 6U; Hare Hatch Sheeplands, London Road, Twyford, Berkshire RG10 7HW; Street Co-Operative Store, 84-86 West End, Street, Somerset BA16 0LP; Whiterow Farm Shop, Beckington, Frome, Somerset BA11 6TN; plus other independent retailers.

Langley Chase Organic Farm Organic

Mail Order & Farm Shop
18 Organic Food Awards; 2 Star Great Taste Award; Gold Taste of the West Awards
www.langleychase.co.uk 01249 750095
post@langleychase.co.uk
The Farm Office, Langley Chase Organic Farm, Kington Langley, Wiltshire, SN15 5PW
Contact: Jane Kallaway
Award-winning organic rare-breed Manx Loaghtan mutton and lamb that has been hung for 14 days.
Breed: Manx Loaghtan
Ewes or Wethers: ewes Age: 4-5 years
Hanging period: 14 days
Season available: all year round
Cuts or Boxes: Whole or half mutton, prepared to individual specification.

Laverstoke Park Organic

Mail Order & Farm or Shops
www.laverstokepark.co.uk 0800 334 5505
customer.services@laverstokepark.co.uk
Overton Road, Overton, Nr Basingstoke, Hampshire RG25 3DR Contact: Caroline Smith
Wide range of organic meats, including mutton from their own farm, together with other produce.
Breed: Lleyn Ewes or Wethers: ewes
Age: approx 4 years Hanging period: 7 days
Season available: year-round
Cuts or Boxes: cuts
Other Outlets: Butchers Shop, 35 King Street Parade, Twickenham TW1 3SG (Tel 020 8744 1112).

Pipers Farm

Mail Order or Shops
www.pipersfarm.com 01392 881380
support@pipersfarm.co.uk
Cullompton, Devon EX15 1SD
Contacts: Peter & Henri Greig
Multi-award-winning farmers and butchers. Retailing online and through two local farm shops.
Breed: Swaledale Ewes or Wethers: ewes
Age: 5-6 years Hanging period: 21 days
Season available: October to May
Cuts or Boxes: both
Other Outlets: Pipers Farm Butchers Shop, 57 Magdalen Road, Exeter EX2 4TA; Powderham Castle Food Hall, Kenton, Exeter EX6 8JE

Sheepdrove Organic Farm Organic

Butchers Shop
(see main Sheepdrove entry, page 193)
www.sheepdrove.com 0117 973 4643
Bristol.shop@sheepdrove.com
3 Lower Redland Road (just off Whiteladies Road) Bristol BS6 6TB

Steeptonbill Farm

Mail Order & Farm Shop
www.justgoodstuff.net 07824 702398 or 07891 079615 tess-steeptonbill@live.co.uk
Steeptonbill Farm, Catherine's Well, Milton Abbas, Blandford Forum, Dorset DT11 0AT
Contacts: Steve Gould and Tess Evans
Suppliers of the local rare breed Portland mutton, part of the Slow Food Movement's Ark of Taste. The sheep are grazed on chalk downland, rich in wild plant species, including Dorset Wildlife Trust's nature reserve. Speciality: mutton ham. Rare Breeds Survival Trust's finishing unit for Portland sheep.
Breed: Portland Ewes or Wethers: both
Age: 2 years + Hanging period: 7 to 10 days
Season available: all year round
Cuts or Boxes: both
Other Outlets: Local restaurants

The Thoroughly Wild Meat Co. Ltd

Mail Order
www.thoroughlywildmeat.co.uk 07770 392041 or 01963 824788 twm@btinternet.com
The Royal Bath & West Showground, Shepton Mallet, Somerset BA4 6QN
Contacts: Andrew & Lavinia Moore
Suppliers of rare breed and speciality meat. Seasonally available salt marsh mutton and salt marsh and rare breed lamb, as well as beef and pork.
Breed: Mainly South Wales Mountain cross or Suffolk cross Ewes or Wethers: mainly ewes
Age: 3 years + Hanging period: 10-14 days
Season available: Spring and Autumn
Cuts or Boxes: both
Other Outlets: Shows & markets – *see* website.

Tregullas Farm

Mail Order & Collection by appointment
www.tregullasfarm.co.uk 01326 290122
info@tregullasfarm.co.uk
The Lizard, Nr Helston, Cornwall TR12 7NL
Contacts: Rona & Nevil Amiss
Grass-fed mutton, lamb and goat produced on this National Trust farm on the Lizard in Cornwall.
Breed: Hebridean cross Ewes or Wethers: both
Age: 2½-4 years

Westmorland Farm Shops

M5 Gloucester Motorway Services
www.gloucesterservices.com 01452 528202
info@gloucesterservices.com
M5 Northbound (J12-11a)
Contact: David Morland
A farm shop in Gloucester Services on the M5 (northbound). Southbound due to open May 2015. All produce sold is locally-produced within 30 miles, with the animals slaughtered just a few miles away. Produce can be ordered ahead for later collection.
Breed: various Ewes or Wethers: ewes
Age: 2-3 years Hanging period: Variable in on-site maturing room
Season available: year round Cuts or Boxes: cuts
Other Outlets: M6 Motorway Services (J38-39) north and southbound.
Hanging period: 7-10 days
Season available: August to January
Cuts or Boxes: both
Other Outlets: Local farmers' markets

Well Hung Meat Organic

Mail Order
www.wellhungmeat.com 0845 230 3131
hello@wellhungmeat.com
The Well Hung Meat Company, Tordean Farm, Dean Prior, Buckfastleigh, Devon TQ11 0LY
Contacts: Paul Williams & Harriet Hoare
Good range of award-winning organic mutton, lamb and beef amongst others. All meat is from local animals which have been grass-fed, and can be butchered to requirements.
Breed: Scottish Blackface
Ewes or Wethers: ewes Age: 2 years +
Hanging period: 7 days
Season available: all year round
Cuts or Boxes: cuts

SOUTH-EAST ENGLAND

Back to Nature Farm Produce

Farm Shop
www.shabdenparkfarm.co.uk 01737 552744
enquiries@shabdenparkfarm.co.uk
Shabden Park Farm, High Road, Chipstead, Surrey CR5 3SF Contact: Kirstie Banham
Native breed mutton, lamb, beef and pork reared using traditional farming methods. Traditionally hung, butchered and hand-prepared.
Breed: Suffolk crossed Mules
Ewes or Wethers: both Age: 2-7 years
Hanging period: 14-21 days Cuts or Boxes: both
Season available: approx October to April

Burscombe Cliff Farm Organic

Mail Order, Farm or Shops
www.kfma.org.uk/BurscombeCliffOrganicFarm
01233 756468 llinos@phonecoop.coop
Burscombe Cliff Organic Farm, Egerton, Ashford, Kent TN27 9BB
Contacts: Hilary Jones and Ben Garratt
The farm produces organic mutton and other meats, all slaughtered locally. Sustainability and animal welfare are essential to the way they work.
Breed: Lleyn, some Wensleydale X and Badgerface
Ewes or Wethers: Ewes Age: variable
Hanging period: 10 days
Season available: Mainly spring or autumn
Cuts or Boxes: both
Other Outlets: Peckham, Eltham, Whitstable and Wye Farmers' Markets.

Drovers Hill Farm Organic

Mail Order & Collection by appointment
www.drovershillfarm.co.uk 07729 823644
hello@drovershillfarm.co.uk
Drovers Hill Farm, Saunderton, Nr Princes Risborough, Bucks HP27 9NJ
Contact: Nicola Knop
The farm has a flock of pedigree, organic Lleyn sheep, chosen as they make good mothers and are hardy enough for our exposed farm in the Chiltern Hills.
Breed: Lleyn
Ewes or Wethers: ewes Age: 2 years+
Hanging period: 14 days
Season available: Aug to Dec Cuts or Boxes: cuts

Green Farm Lamb

Collection by appointment or Shops
www.greenfarmlamb.co.uk 01263 577441
jo@greenfarmlamb.co.uk
Green Farm, Little Barningham, Norwich, Norfolk NR11 7LW Contact: Jo Daniels
Home-grown lamb and mutton available through Norfolk Farmers Markets.
Breed: North Country Mules cross Suffolk, Texel and Charollais
Ewes or Wethers: ewes Age: 2 years +
Hanging period: 12–14 days Season available: all year round
Cuts or Boxes: both
Other Outlets: Farmers' markets at Aylsham, Aldborough, Caverham Garden Centre, Fakenham and various regional shows.

Lee House Farm Organic

Collection by appointment or Farmers Markets
www.leehousefarm.co.uk 01403 753311
info@leehousefarm.co.uk
Plaistow, Billingshurst, West Sussex RH14 0PB
Contact: Grant Roffey
Organic farm selling its own produce from the farm or from local Farmers Markets.
Breed: various Ewes or Wethers: ewes
Age: 2 years + Hanging period: 14 days +
Season available: Sept to May
Cuts or Boxes: cuts
Other Outlets: Twickenham & Cranleigh Farmers' Markets

Romshed Farm Organic

From Farm
www.romshedfarm.co.uk 01732 463372
romshed@weald.co.uk
Underriver, Sevenoaks, Kent TN15 0SD
Contact: Fidelity Weston
Organic mutton and other home-produced meats available from the farm and locally.
Breed: Mainly Lleyn Ewes or Wethers: ewes
Age: 2 years + Hanging period: 14 days
Season available: variable Cuts or Boxes: both

Sheepdrove Organic Farm Organic

Mail Order
www.sheepdrove.com 01488 674747
sales@sheepdrove.com
Sheepdrove Road, Lambourn, Berkshire RG17 7UU
Contact: Ashley Taylor
Home-produced meats including mutton from their own organic farm in Berkshire. Pastures planted with herbs for mutton flavour.
Breed: Shetland cross, pure Shetland, Lleyn and Herdwicks. Ewes or Wethers: both
Age:2 years + Hanging period: 14 days
Season available: mainly September to May, but can be all year. Cuts or Boxes: cuts
Other Outlets: Bristol and Maida Vale, London

Stansted Park Farm Shop Organic

Mail Order & Collection by appointment
www.stanstedfarmshop.com
Shop: 02392 413576; Office: 02392 631851
info@stanstedfarmshop.com
Maze Courtyard, Stansted Park, Rowlands Castle, Hants PO9 6DX
Contact: Fred Duncannon
Farm shop and mail order service for mutton and a wide range of organic foods many produced on the Goodwood Estate
Breed: Southdown x Mule
Ewes or Wethers: ewes Age: 3 years +
Hanging period: 14 days +
Season available: August to March
Cuts or Boxes: boxes

Wick Farm Meats

Mail Order & Shop
www.wickfarmmeats.co.uk 01206 738656
christine.faircloth@virgin.net
Wick Farm Wholesale Meats, Church Road, Layer-

De-La-Haye, Essex CO2 0EW
This family-run retail and wholesale butchery company raises sheep and cattle on their farm, supplying meat both directly to the public and also on a wholesale basis to restaurants, pubs, schools and takeaways.
Breed: Suffolk and Texel
Ewes or Wethers: both Age: various
Hanging period: 7 days
Season available: all year round
Cuts or Boxes: cuts

LONDON

Burscombe Cliff Farm Organic
Farmers markets
(*see* main Burscombe entry under South East England for more details)
01233 756468 llinos@phonecoop.coop
Dulwich, Peckham & Eltham Farmers Markets.

The Ginger Pig
Six Butchers shops in London *(see below)*
www.thegingerpig.co.uk 01751 460 091
enquiries@thegingerpig.co.uk
Grange Farm, Levisham, North Yorkshire, YO18 7NL
A London butchery business of six shops, supplied by its own farms in North Yorkshire, plus a few collaborative partner farms. All mutton comes from Ginger Pig farmland. Also supplies hogget. Best to order ahead by phone to ensure availability of cuts required.
Breed: Blackface, Scotch Mule & Dorset Down
Ewes or Wethers: ewes Age: 3-8 years
Hanging period: 7 days Season available: all year
Cuts or Boxes: cuts
Six shops: Borough Market, London Bridge, SE1 1TL; Moxon Street, Marylebone, W1U 4EW; 137-139 Askew Road, Shepherd's Bush, W12 9AU; Lauriston Road, Hackney, E9 7HJ; Greensmiths Market, Lower Marsh, Waterloo, SE1 7RG; 55 Abbeville Road, Clapham, SW4 9JW

Laverstoke Park Farm Organic
Butchers Shop
(*see* main Laverstoke entry, page 191, under South West England for more details)
www.laverstoke park.co.uk 020 8744 1112
twickenhamshop@laverstokepark.co.uk
35 King Street Parade, Twickenham TW1 3SG

Lee House Farm Organic
Farmers Market
(*see* main Lee House Farm entry, page 193, under South East England for more details)
www.leehousefarm.co.uk 01403 753311
info@leehousefarm.co.uk
Twickenham Farmers Markets

Lidgates Butchers
Mail Order & from Shop
www.lidgates.com 0207 727 8243
info@lidgates.com
110 Holland Park Avenue, London W11 4UA
Well-respected London butcher, and Q Guild member. Sells from West London shop or by mail order delivery.
Breed: various Ewes or Wethers: either
Age: 2 years Hanging period: 7 days
Season available: year-round Cuts or Boxes: cuts

Sheepdrove Organic Farm Organic
Family Butcher
(see main Sheepdrove entry, page 193)
www.sheepdrove.co.uk 0207 266 3838
maidavale.shop@sheepdrove.com
5 Clifton Road, Maida Vale, London W9 1SZ

Turner and George
Mail Order & Butchers Shop
www.turnerandgeorge.co.uk 020 7837 1781
info@turnerandgeorge.co.uk
399 St John Street London EC1V 4LD
Contact name: James George
Traditional quality butcher supplying Yorkshire mutton, as well as other meats, produced by a group of five farmers in the uplands of north Yorkshire. All the animals are entirely grass fed.
Breed: Herdwick and Blackface
Ewes or Wethers: wethers Age: 2 years
Hanging period: 10-14 days
Season available: all year, but mainly in the colder months
Cuts or boxes: cuts

for background and links see
www.muchadoaboutmutton.com

UK Sheep Breeds

As we have seen, Britain has been blessed with some far-sighted agriculturalists who have formalised sheep breeds for all ecological niches and systems of production.

Part of the joy of buying mutton direct from suppliers is to compare various breeds and production systems. Do the mountain breeds taste sweeter than the lowland? Are the primitive breeds lean and tasty? Need the longwool breeds be fat, and can they actually be rather tasty if managed for the purpose of producing tasty mutton?

What is important is that you know what you are buying. On the following pages is a table showing more details of the breeds' histories and uses.

Far right column: currently on Rare Breeds Survival Trusts' 2014 Watchlist of most endangered breeds

Photo	Breed & Establishment	Origin	Type	Rare Breed
	Badger Face Welsh Mountain	Dating from the 1st Century, coloured wool type of Welsh Mountain sheep. Good quality mutton.	Mountain	
	Balwen Welsh Mountain	This tough hardy breed is from the Upper Tywi Valley in south west Wales since 19th century. Ideal smallholders sheep, as it can survive with little or no concentrate feed, and requires little attention. Good mutton quality.	Mountain	Rare Breed
	Beltex	Belgium (UK 1989) to increase meat quantity. Their double-muscle traits brought a new dimension to British lamb production. Originally developed as the Belgian Texel, from double-muscle traits.	Imported for lamb production	
	Berrichon Du Cher	France 1780s (UK 1980s) to produce lean lambs	Imported for lamb production	
	Beulah Speckled Face	Locally bred in mid-Wales since mid-19th century. Traditionally good mutton quality.	Hill	
	Blackface	Ancient roots in North England/ Scotland, from before 12th century. Produces a smaller carcass, but of excellent mutton quality.	Mountain	
	Black Welsh Mountain	Prized for black wool & mutton, from Middle Ages; Improved in late 19th century, black sheep re-selected. Good quality mutton.	Mountain	
	Bluefaced Leicester	Descendants of Robert Bakewells' improved Dishley Leicester, they evolved near Hexham in Northumberland at the beginning of the 1900's. Used to breed to produce crossbred ewes from the Blackface and Swaledale ewes.	Lowland	

Bleu de Maine	Originated in the 19th century in western France in the Maine-et-Loire, Mayenne and Sarthe regions, from crossing of Leicester Longwool and Wensleydale from 1855 to 1880 with the now extinct Choletais breed.	Imported for lamb production	
Borderdale	New Zealand crossing since 1969 of Border Leicester with local Corriedale breed. Dual purpose breed for meat and wool, and used for further cross breeding.	New Zealand Dual purpose breed	
Border Leicester	Descendents of Bakewell's Dishley Leicesters late 18th century. Improved around 1850 in Northumberland.	Lowland	Rare Breed
Boreray	Cross between Scottish Blackface and Hebridean late 19th century.	Primitive	Rare Breed
Brecknock Hill Cheviot	Descendants of 17th century Cheviots in Brecon Beacons area. Further developed in mid-19th century.	Mountain	
British Milksheep	20th century breed, developed for milk production and cross breeding for high lambing % .	Milk	
British Rouge	Rouge denotes the skin colour of the Face. Originates from Loire area, and is renowned for its rich thick milk. Originally a dairy sheep producing Camembert cheeses. Now kept for its milk production and quality of lambs.	Imported for lamb production	
Cambridge	Breed founded in 1964 at Cambridge University from variety of UK native breeds to produce crossbred lambs for meat.	New meat breed	
Castlemilk Moorit	Developed in early 1900s in Dumfriesshire to produce attractive-looking sheep for parklands, and for wool.	Parkland	Rare Breed
Charmoise	Bred in early 19th century in France from Kent sheep to produce small hardy lambs for French hill areas.	Imported for lamb production	

Charollais	Developed in Loire, France in 19th century from local breeds crossed with Bakewell's Dishley Leicesters	Imported for lamb production	
Cheviot	14th century breed from uplands of northern England. Often used to produce cross-bred Mules with Border Leicester or Blueface Leicester	Hill	
Clun Forest	Developed in 19th century in high grasslands of the Welsh borders from now extinct local breeds. Previously well known for producing 2 year old wether mutton.	Hill	
Coopworth	A dual-purpose New Zealand cross between the Romney and Border Leicester, suited to good grass conditions. Also popular in Australia and USA.	New Zealand Dual purpose breed	
Corriedale	A breed developed in late 19th century for the ecological needs of New Zealand by crossing a Romney with Merino. Used for both wool and meat.	New Zealand Dual purpose breed	
Cotswold	Descended from sheep grazing the Cotswolds since Roman times. Major wool breed in Middle Ages.	Longwool	Rare Breed
Dalesbred	Only formalised as a breed in 1930 from hardy native sheep found in upper areas of Yorkshire Dales, and West Yorkshire, north Lancashire and Cumbria.	Mountain	
Dartmoor (Greyface)	Improved in 19th century from original moorland sheep by crossing with Leicester and Notts Longwool. Hardy.	Longwool	Rare Breed
Derbyshire Gritstone	One of the oldest breeds in UK, developed in 1750's from hills around Vale of Goyt in Derbyshire. Hardy breed able to survive in harsh conditions.	Mountain	
Devon Closewool	Developed in 19th century in Exmoor and north Devon. Well adapted to native upland areas. Survives well on poor quality grassland. Produces good yield of high quality fleece.	Hill	
Devon and Cornwall Longwool	Combination in 1977 of South Devon and Devon Longwool flocks. Produces good lambs and good yield of long staple high quality wool.	Longwool	Rare Breed

	Breed	Description	Type	Status
	Dorset Down	Produced by two breeders in late 19th century by improving indigenous Down sheep with Hampshire and Wiltshire blood lines. Ewe is fertile every month of year, produces excellent quality lamb carcass.	Downland	Rare Breed
	Dorset Horn & Poll Dorset	Dorset Horn is one of Britain's oldest breeds, producing lambs throughout the year if required. Many exported to New World where Polled (hornless) version was developed and brought back to UK. Prolific breeders and adaptable to varied climatic conditions.	Downland	Rare Breed
	Exmoor Horn	Direct descendants of horned sheep which have roamed Exmoor for centuries. Hardy and used in crossing with other breeds such as Border Leicester.	Hill	
	Friesland	Dairy sheep from Holland imported first into UK in 1953. Very prolific and good milk yield.	Dairy	
	Galway	Ireland's only surviving native breed thought to be closely related to old Roscommon breed. Numbers declined dramatically in the late 20th century, now reviving. Said to be known for good quality mutton.	Longwool	Rare Breed
	Hampshire Down	Developed around 1820, from crossing Wiltshire Horn with the Berkshire Knot and the Southdown. Used for increasing fertility in the light downland soils of Wiltshire, Hampshire and Berkshire. Excellent meat carcasses.	Downland	
	Hebridean	Ancient breed of native sheep, thought to be of Viking origin. Brought from the brink of extinction in the 20th century, and used for parkland sheep.	Primitive	
	Herdwick	Origins unknown, but could be Norse in origin. Recorded from 12th century in Lake District. One of the hardiest of breeds. Excellent quality mutton, with dark, fine-grained and well-flavoured meat. The breed was protected by Beatrix Potter who bequeathed much of her land to the National Trust, on the condition that Herdwicks grazed on it.	Mountain	
	Hill Radnor	A native of mid Wales, the Hill Radnor is able to survive on poor pasture and is hardy. Although traditionally much sought after for its mutton, the breed is now rare.	Hill	Rare Breed

	Ile De France	The result of a cross between the Dishley Leicester and Merino this French breed is a good meat producer.	Imported for lamb production	
	Jacob	Quoted in the Book of Genesis, the Jacob was a well-known Park sheep by the 18th century. Now used for its coloured wool and excellent quality meat.	Primitive	
	Kerry Hill	The distinctive colouring of the face is recorded in mid-Wales from 1809. Widely used for crossing for good carcass.	Hill	
	Leicester Longwool	A descendent of Robert Bakewell's Dishley Leicester breed, it is now one of the rarest Longwool breeds. When crossed with mountain breeds produces good quality carcass.	Longwool	Rare Breed
	Lincoln Longwool	The backbone of the wool industry in Lincolnshire in the Middle Ages, and the basis of Bakewell's Dishley Leicester breed.	Longwool	
	Llanwenog	Bred in west Wales in the late 19th century, from a cross between the Shropshire and local sheep. Used for early lamb for towns of south Wales.	Lowland	
	Lleyn	Said to be descended from a white Irish breed brought across to the north Wales Lleyn Peninsula and crossed with the local breed. Good milker, and now widely used for lamb production.	Lowland	
	Lonk	An ancient breed from the Lancashire and Yorkshire Pennines. Hardy and prolific, they produce good carcasses.	Hill	
	Manx Loaghtan	An ancient breed, associated with the Soay and others, from the Isle of Man. Unusual in having four horns. The Manx name describes the dark colour of the wool.	Primitive	Rare Breed
	Masham	An established half-bred cross in the 19th century, they are the progeny of Teeswater and either Dalesbred or Swaledale. Very hardy.	Half-bred	
	Meatlinc	Developed in the 1960s from two British and three French breeds for meat production.	New meat breed	

Norfolk Horn	One of the oldest UK breeds, associated with the Saxon Black-faced sheep. Like many ancient breeds, the flavour of its mutton and lamb is very good.	Lowland	Rare Breed
North Country Cheviot	Developed in the north of Scotland in the late 18th century form sheep on the Cheviot Hills of the Scottish Borders.	Hill	
North of England Mule	The result of crossing Bluefaced Leicester and Swaledale or Northumberland Blackface. Hardy, thrifty and long-lived.	Half-bred	
North Ronaldsay	Native of the Orkneys, and one of the oldest breeds in the UK. Live almost entirely on seaweed on Orkney. Very hardy and prolific. High quality meat and wool.	Primitive	Rare Breed
Oxford Down	Formed in the 1830's the breed was developed for mutton and wool. Large numbers exported to New World, especially USA.	Downland	Rare Breed
Perendale	A New Zealand bred cross between the Romney and Cheviot. A good breed for meat production, and versatile for different environments.	New Zealand meat breed	
Portland	An old breed from Dorset, predating the Romans. Good milkers and high quality mutton and wool. King George III insisted on Portland mutton when visiting the region.	Primitive	Rare Breed
Romney Marsh	Originating from the Kent marshes, successfully improved and exported widely. Important in the historical development of New Zealand sheep industry.	Longwool	
Rough Fell	Originated in native heath sheep found in northern Britain in Middle Ages, but subsequently crossed with other breeds. Very hardy upland sheep.	Mountain	
Ryeland	Developed by the monks of Leominster around 1200, this is the original "golden hoof" of the Medieval wool trade. The House of Lords Woolsack is thought to be stuffed with Ryeland wool. Later breeding improved meat quality.	Lowland	
Scotch Halfbred	The cross-bred originated in the mid-19th century by crossing Border Leicester and North Country Cheviot. Mostly bred in Scotland and Northumberland.	Half-bred	

Scotch Mule	A half-bred cross between Blueface Leicester and Scottish Blackface ewe.	Half-bred	
Scottish Greyface	A half-bred cross between Border Leicester and Blackface ewe. Predominantly found in Scotland and Northern England.	Half-bred	
Shetland	Believed to have been brought to Shetlands by the Vikings. Developed by islanders to produce fine, soft multi-coloured wool.	Primitive	
Shropshire	Developed in mid-1800's from local breeds in West Midlands and Welsh Marches to become one of the predominant breeds of the late 19th century. Formed in 1882, it has the oldest breed society in the world. Excellent mutton and lamb.	Downland	
Soay	The most primitive breed in Britain, and has unique characteristic of scattering not flocking when alarmed. Good for grazing in low fertility areas. Good eating quality mutton.	Primitive	Rare Breed
Southdown	The native breed of the Sussex downs, improved by Ellman and others into one of the most popular breeds worldwide in the late 19th century. Said by many to offer the best mutton.	Downland	
South Wales Mountain	Native to the hills of South Wales, also known as the Nelson. Good mothering qualities, and hardy. Like all mountain breeds, good for mutton.	Mountain	
Suffolk	First appeared in 1810 as a cross of the Norfolk Horn and Southdown. Now spread throughout the sheep meat producing world.	Downland	
Swaledale	A late developer in UK breed terms, being first registered in 1919. Produced by local farmers through selected breeding of local sheep in north Yorkshire and Cumbria	Mountain	
Teeswater	Now a rare breed, developed 200 years ago in north east England. Used for cross-breeding with other hill breeds to produce the Masham.	Hill	Rare Breed
Texel	Developed since Roman times on the Dutch island of Texel. Improved in late 19th century with infusion of blood from British breeds. In UK since 1970s now one of the commonest meat breeds and crosses, producing very lean meat.	Imported for lamb production	

	Welsh Halfbred	Half-bred cross between a Border Leicester and a Welsh ewe	Half-bred	
	Welsh Hill Speckled Face	Believed to be a cross between the Kerry Hills breed and the Welsh Mountain, the breed only became formally established in 1969. Hardy. Very good mutton.	Mountain	
	Welsh Mountain	The Welsh Mountain sheep have survived for centuries in the harsh and unforgiving environment of the Welsh hills and mountains. Good mothers. Produce excellent mutton, and are the basis for the reputation of Welsh mutton & lamb.	Mountain	
	Welsh Mule	A half-bred cross between a Blueface Leicester and a Welsh ewe - Welsh Mountain, Speckleface or Beulah.	Half-bred	
	Wensleydale	Originated in north Yorkshire in the 19th century. Has distinctive blue head and ears.	Longwool	Rare Breed
	White Face Dartmoor	An ancient breed which has long inhabited both Dartmoor and Exmoor. Hardy and producing meat of high quality.	Mountain	Rare Breed
	White Faced Woodland	From the Pennines, was called Penistone in the 17th century. Related to Swaledale and Lonk, with fine wool maybe from Merino imported by King George III. A popular mutton breed.	Mountain	Rare Breed
	Wiltshire Horn	Ancient breed with obscure origins, possibly Roman. Related to the Down breeds of southern England. Naturally sheds its hairy wool, so does not need shearing	Downland	
	Zwartbles	Developed in Friesland, Holland in early 20th century, to graze dairy farms.	Imported for lamb production	

Origins of the main UK sheep breeds

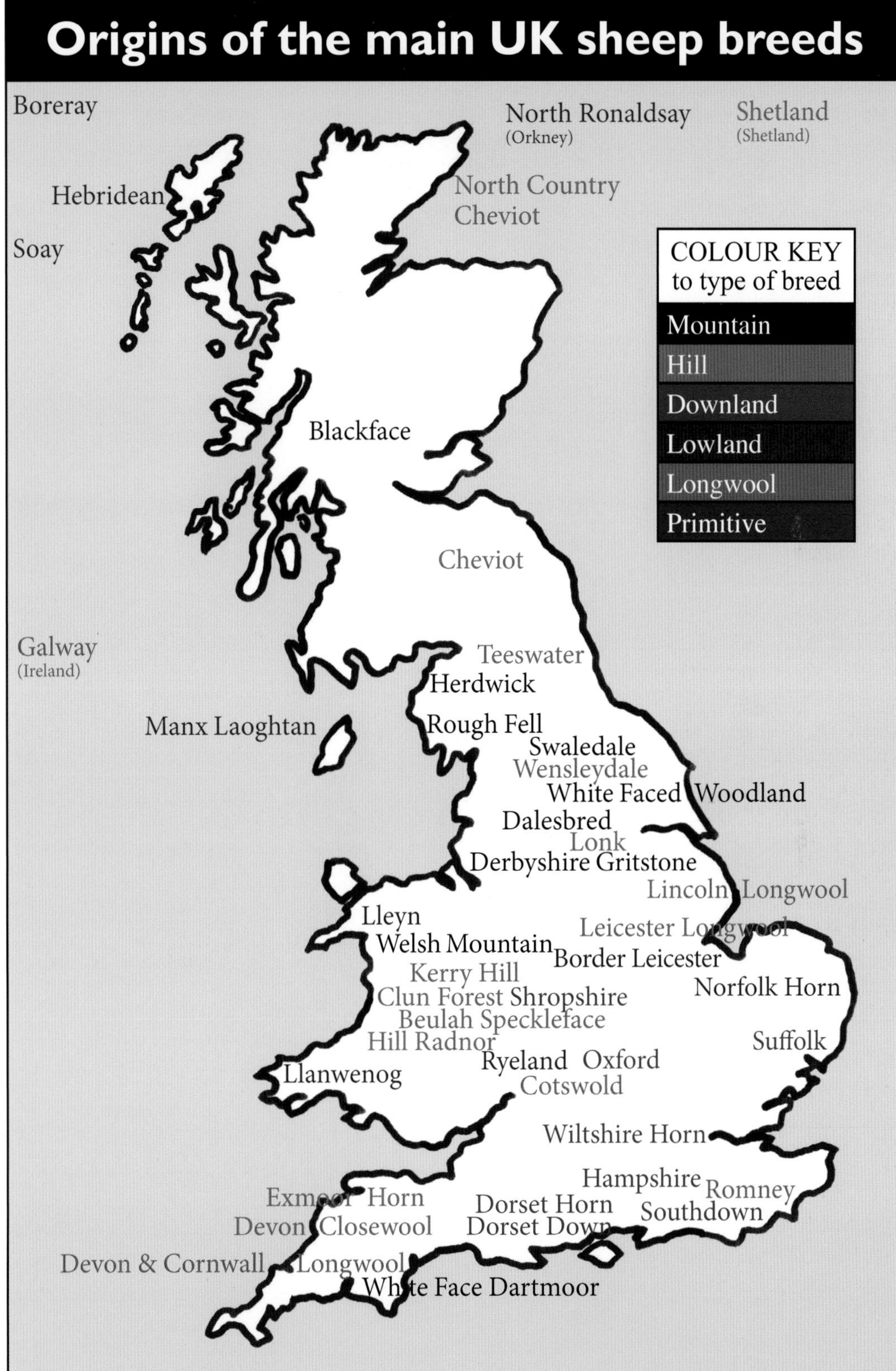

National mutton organisations

English Beef & Lamb Executive (Eblex) The organisation for the English beef and sheep industry.
Telephone 01480 482980; www.eblex.org.uk

FARMA a co-operative of farmers, producers selling on a local scale, and farmers' markets organisers. Telephone: 0845 45 88 420; www.farma.org.uk
12 Southgate Street, Winchester, SO23 9EF

Hybu Cig Cymru Meat Promotion Wales (HCC) Organisation responsible for the development, promotion and marketing of Welsh red meat. Telephone 01970 625050; www.hccmpw.org.uk

Mutton Renaissance The Mutton Renaissance campaign was launched in 2004 by the Prince of Wales to support British sheep farmers who were struggling to sell their older animals, and to get this delicious meat back on the nation's plates. Telephone: 01684 893661, The Sheep Centre, Malvern, Worcs. WR13 6PH

National Sheep Association A specialist organisation dedicated to safeguarding the interests and future of sheep farmers throughout the UK.
Telephone 01684 892661; www.nationalsheep.org.uk; joanne@nationalsheep.org.uk
Sheep Centre, Malvern, Worcs. WR13 6PH

Q-Guild Butchers Represents the highest quality butchers and independent meat retailers in the UK. Telephone 01738 633 160; www.qguild.co.uk; info@qguild.co.uk
8-10 Needless Road, Perth, PH2 0JW

Quality Meat Scotland QMS's core function is to work with the Scottish red meat industry to improve its efficiency and profitability. Telephone: 0131 472 4040; www.qmscotland.co.uk
email: info@qmscotland.co.uk
Rural Centre, West Mains, Ingliston, Newbridge EH28 8NZ

Rare Breeds Survival Trust
The leading national charity working to conserve and protect the UK's rare native breeds of farm animals.
Telephone: 024 7669 6551;
Email: enquiries@rbst.org.uk;
www.rbst.org.uk;
Stoneleigh Park, Nr Kenilworth, Warwickshire CV8 2LG

Royal Academy of Culinary Arts (RACA) Britain's leading professional association of Head Chefs, Pastry Chefs, Restuarant Managers and suppliers, and a long-standing advocate of mutton. Telephone: 0208 673 6300; www.royalacademyofculinaryarts.org.uk; info@academyofculinaryarts.org.uk. 53 Cavendish Rd, London SW121 0BL.

The Slow Food Movement (UK) In the fast modern junk food environment, Slow Food is the voice of calm, reason and quality. They work to promote the greater enjoyment of food through a better understanding of its taste, quality and production.
Telephone: 020 7099 1132 ; www.slowfood.org.uk; info@slowfood.org.uk
4 Blenheim Crescent, Notting Hill, London, W11 1NN

Traditional Breeds Meat Marketing Company Committed to organising the supply and promotion of the highest quality meat from pedigree British rare and traditional breeds
Telephone/Fax: 01285 869666; E-mail: info@tbmm.co.uk; www.tbmm.co.uk
FREEPOST (GL442), Cirencester, Gloucestershire GL7 5BR

Glossary of sheep terms

As we have seen, the world of sheep is filled with a lexicon of its own, with its own wonderful words and phrases such as raddle, thrunter or yow. Listed below are some commonly-used words or phrases.

This listing does not attempt to be comprehensive, especially as many words involved in sheep farming are regional and even contradictory in their meaning when used in different parts of the country.

* denotes dialect or old usage word

Backed, Cast or Farwelted A sheep on its back, unable to rise.

Belting, Dagging Removing with shears wool at rear-end of sheep, to prevent flies laying eggs.

Barren Ewe A female sheep unable to breed (*see also* 'gimmer').

Bields* Shelters (northern Britain).

Bing Feed passage.

Bolting* Bundle of straw (Herefordshire).

Boost* Instrument for marking sheep (usually with hot tar), often bearing the owner's initials.

Bottle, Cade, Pet or Poddy lamb Orphaned lamb, hand-reared on a bottle.

Bound Stock (*see* 'Hefted') Sheep so familiar with their hillside (heft) they don't need fencing in.

Batting* Jacketing sheep, usually hoggs, to protect them from cold in winter.

Breeding-in-and-in In-breeding to exaggerate positive traits in offspring.

Broken-mouthed Older sheep (normally 6+ years old) with brokern or missing incisor teeth. May still be used for breeding at lower altitudes.

Buchts* Sheepfolds or gathering pens (Border District and Scotland)).

Buisted Marked (with tar) after shearing.

Cade Hand-reared (bottle-fed) lamb.

Caroirich Big* ('Little Sheep') Four-horned sheep indigenous to the Highlands.

Cast Ewes Old breeding ewes which are sold off hill farms to lower-ground farmers who take one last crop of lambs from them. Typically crossed to produce breeding ewes for lowland.

Claris, clags (*see* 'Dags').

Clatting Removing wool from inside of thighs and around udder prior to lambing.

Couples Pairs of ewes and lambs, as sold together at markets.

Crones Old ewes.

Crossing Sire A broad term for rams used to cross-breed sheep.

Crues* Sheep folds.

Cuckoo lambs Late lambs born after mid-April.

Crutching Shearing parts of a sheep (especially the hind end of some woollier breeds), to prevent fly-strike. See 'dagging'.

Cull ewe A ewe no longer suitable for breeding, and sold for meat.

Dags, Claris Dung attached to sheep's wool, normally at tail end. Should be removed to prevent flies laying eggs.

Dagging Cutting off dags/claris from wool. *See also* 'crutching'.

Dal-o'-Goyt* Early name for Derbyshire Gritstone.

Diamond, Dinmont Ram, Dinmont Tup Ram 1-2 years old, after first shearing.

Dipping Completely immersing sheep in chemical bath or shower to control external parasites. Now replaced by safer 'pour-on' insecticides.

Dipping crook Tool for immersing or

retrieving sheep from dip bath.

Dishley Breed now known as Leicester.

Downs Short-wooled sheep breeds originating on chalk downlands

Draft ewe Ewe too old for rigours of high altitude rough grazing and moved (drafted) to lower, gentler grazing, often on another farm.

To draw lambs To select lambs which are ready for selling.

To Dock To cut the tail or clean out the rear parts of sheep to avoid fly-strike.

Double, Couples Twins.

Droving, Driving Walking sheep away from the farm to market or other farm.

Drover Person who moves sheep a long distance, often to market.

Ear tag Plastic, metal or electronic tag clipped to sheep's ear with identification number.

To Ean, to Yean To give birth to a lamb.

Eild, Yel, Yale or Yeld Ewes* Barren ewes (northern Britain).

Ewe Female sheep of breeding age. See also 'Yow'.

Ewe Lamb Female lamb

Ewe Hogg (or Gimmer, Theave, Theif or Chilver)* Breeding lamb from weaning until first shearing.

Fanks* Gathering pens (mid-west Scotland).

Farwelted A sheep stuck on its back.

Flushing Improving the nutrition of a ewe prior to mating, to improve fertility.

Fold (or **Sheepfold**) A holding pen for sheep, or fenced area around root-crop grazed by sheep.

Forester* Type of black-faced mountain sheep found in Wales and West.

Gimmer (or **Ewe Hogg**) A female sheep in its first year, between weaning and shearing. One that has not bred. *See also* 'theave'.

Glat* Gap in hedge.

Glatting* Repairing gaps (Welsh Borders).

Gleamy, Dagley Weather suitable for flies to lay eggs on sheep.

Haggerill Heeder* Ram lamb.

Half Long Cheviot ram x Blackface ewe.

Hammel Small shed.

Heft Large open hill where sheep stay put. About 5 hefts make up a hirsel, which was traditionally the territory of one shepherd.

Hefting The ability, passed down from ewe to lambs, to keep to a particular part of unfenced upland grazing areas, enabling neighbouring farmers to graze their animals on the open hills without the need for fences.

Hindering weather Damp.

Hirsel Piece of ground (about 5 hefts) and flock traditionally looked after by one shepherd.

Hog, Hogg, Hoggerel, Tup-Hog, Hogget, Shearling, Teg A male or female sheep between being weaned and first shearing, roughly 9–18 months of age (until it cuts two teeth).

Hoof-shears Tool for trimming hooves, similar to garden secateurs.

Hovel* Building for housing livestock.

Inbye, Intake Improved pasture taken in and fenced from hillside, normally on lower altitudes. Often used for harvesting hay or silage.

In-lamb Pregnant ewe.

Intake see 'Inbye'

Jobbers* Sheep dealers.

Kemp Short, hollow, hairy fibre usually found about the head and legs of sheep, particularly mountain breeds.

Kindly Bred* Describes superior Shetland Island sheep.

Lachan Light brown colour of sheep in the Highlands.

Lamb Bed, Wither, Wether Terms for ewe's uterus.

Lambing The process of giving birth in sheep. Also the work of tending lambing ewes (shepherds are said to lamb their flocks).

Lambing pen Area within a lambing building where a ewe and her lamb(s) are kept confined, to encourage bonding, and ensure ewe's milk is available.

Lambing percentage The average number of lambs reared per ewe mated, expressed as a percentage. In harsh upland areas, this can be as low as 80% to over 150% in milder lowland areas.

Lamb fries Cooked lamb's testicles.

Lamb's fry Lamb's liver (as food).

Laughton, Loghtan* Term used to describe colour of Isle of Man sheep (brown colour).

Linton* Alternative name for Heath sheep.

Lugmark* Local term in northern England for identifying cut in lamb's ear.

Lunky A hole in a wall large enough to admit one sheep at a time.

Maid A ewe in its second year (teg) that has been to the ram but has proved barren.

Marden layers Recently-planted sheep pastures.

Mardy Stupid, off-colour, sickly.

Milk-clipping Shearing the milking ewes.

Mob A group of sheep treated in a particular way within a flock.

Mule A cross-bred sheep, hardy and suitable for meat. Progeny of a mountain or upland ewe crossed with a Bluefaced Leicester ram. Regional types include Welsh Mule (from a Bluefaced Leicester ram and a Welsh Mountain ewe).

Mugg, Mugs* Breed of Northumberland sheep, early name for Wensleydales.

Old-season lamb Lamb born last year and sold for slaughter after this year's lamb crop becomes available (new season lamb), in UK around May.

Parrot-Mouthed Malformation of the mouth.

Pirls Small knots of wool as seen in a Wensleydale.

Pug, Teg A sheep in its second year.

Pinds Sheepfolds.

Raett* Sheepfold.

Raddle Coloured pigment, often mixed with oils, used for marking sheep on their wool for various purposes. Raddle block attached to chest of rams to mark ewes they mate, with different colours denoting each ram or period of mating.

Ram, Tup An un-castrated adult male sheep.

Ringing Shearing the wool from around the pizzle (penis) of a ram.

Rooing Removing the fleece by hand-plucking, particularly on primitive breeds such as Shetlands or Soay. Carried out in late spring, when natural moulting begins.

Rounds Circular walls built to protect sheep from snow drifts.

Ruddy* Local Cumbrian term for raddle.

Salving, Smearing* Treating sheep with a mixture usually tar and butter, to protect against cold (or parasites). Now obsolete.

Set-to An orphan lamb given to a foster mother.

Shearing, Clipping Removing the fleece by use of shears. Mechanical shears have now replaced hand-shearing. Carried out by farmers, or specialist professional shearers.

Shearling A yearling sheep 1-2 years

old before its first shearing. Also hogget, old-season lamb, teg.

Sheeder* Female lamb.

Shots* Culls or small lambs.

Sheepdog or **Shepherd dog** Highly trained working dog (often Collie), used to move or control sheep in conjunction with shepherd.

Sheepwalk Word used particularly in Wales for area of rough grazing in upland areas.

Shepherd Person who looks after sheep on a farm. Maybe farmer or employed person.

Shepherding The act and skill of looking after sheep by a shepherd.

Shepherd's crook A staff with a hook at one end, used to catch sheep by the neck or leg.

Smout Hole in a wall large enough to admit one sheep at a time (*see* 'Lunky').

Speaning* Weaning (Northern term)

Spiv Ewe A ewe in low condition that will not fatten.

Stells* Circular stone wall, roofless shelter (Northumberland).

Store A sheep not yet ready for slaughter usually sold to be fattened at lower altitude.

Sucker An un-weaned lamb.

Swaddles* Swaledale sheep.

Teg (*see* 'Hog')

Terminal Sire A ram of good meat breed, used to sire prime lambs for slaughter.

Theave or theaf* (plural: theaves) Regional term for a young ewe before her first lambing. In some areas can also mean a castrated male sheep between first and second shearing. See also 'gimmer'.

Thrunter Three-year-old ewe.

Tup Ram.

Tup lamb Uncastrated male until weaned.

Tup Hogg; Wether Hogg; Hogget, or **Teg** Castrated male, post-weaning.

Tupping Mating in sheep, or the mating season (autumn, for a spring-lambing flock).

Twinter Two-year-old ewe.

Two-shear Ram Uncastrated male sheep between 2nd and 3rd shearing.

Two-shear Wether Castrated male sheep between 2nd and 3rd shearing.

Weaner A young lamb, now on solid food, until it is about a year old.

Wether, Wedder A castrated adult male sheep.

Wrees* Gathering pens (SW Scotland).

Yel or **Yale Ewe*** Scottish Borders term for a barren ewe. (also Eild or Yeld ewe).

Yoke A piece or pieces of wood attached to the neck of sheep which regularly break through hedges or fences, to prevent them doing so.

Yow Regional term for a ewe.

> *"What will your honour be pleased to have for supper? I have mutton of all kinds, and some nice chicken."*
>
> Henry Fielding (1707-1754)
>
> *The History of Tom Jones, a Foundling*

Acknowledgements

Firstly, a big thank you to my family for their encouragement and support in the writing of *Much Ado*. I am also indebted to many people for their help in its production. In particular I must thank Lynda Brown, award-winning food writer, specialising in organic food and farming, for her tireless mentoring and advice. In addition, I am also very grateful to the following for their special areas of expertise: Basil & Jean Baldwin, New South Wales, Australia; Dr Siam Bhayro, Senior Lecturer in Early Jewish Studies, University of Exeter; Jo Budden, Higher Hacknell Farm, Devon; Nigel Elgar, agricultural advisor and former livestock farmer; Ronnie Eunson, QMS Board member, Shetland; Tara Garnett, Food Climate Research Network, Centre for Environmental Strategy, University of Surrey; Ed Goff, farmer, Shropshire; Prof Tim Gorringe, St Luke's Professor of Theology, Exeter University; Bill Grayson; Ali and Sandy Granville, Isle of Lewis; Doug Griffiths & butchery staff, Shropshire; Herefordshire Heritage Services; Hybu Cig Cymru/ Meat Promotion Wales; Norman Jones, Portland Breed; Jane Kellaway, Langley Chase Organic Farm; Kington Museum, Herefordshire; Mark Measures & Joy Greenall, farmers; Philip Onions, farmer; The Q-Guild of Butchers; Di and Athol Saunders, KwaZulu Natal, South Africa; Judith Sheen, Chief Executive, International Sheepdog Society; Prof. Liam A. Sinclair, Dept. Animal Production, Welfare & Vet Sciences, Harper Adams University; Sara Jane Stanes OBE, Chief Executive, Royal Academy of Culinary Arts; Margaret Stewart, Quality Meat Scotland; Phil Stocker, Chief Executive, National Sheep Association; John and Richard Thomas, livestock farmers, mid-Wales; John Thorley OBE, FRAgS; Liz and Derek Turner, The Thomas Shop, Penybont, Powys; Prof Jeff Wood, Professor Emeritus, Bristol Veterinary School, University of Bristol. Finally, I'd like to thank my publishers Merlin Unwin Books for all their support and encouragement throughout this project. If I have omitted anyone who has helped me along the way, my apologies.

Scots Pines were traditionally planted to mark ancient drovers' routes

Photographic Credits

Page	
vii	National Library of Wales
4	Scott Polar Research Institute, University of Cambridge
16, 116, 135	Ali and Sandy Granville, Isle of Lewis
22	Claire Blake
22	www.colonialsense.com
28, 156	Carolyn & Rosa Kennard
29	British Wool Marketing Board
31	High Weald Dairy
39	The British Library
48	Museum of London
55	Dixon Galleries, State Library of NSW, Australia
70	Rural Museums Network
70	Somerset Heritage Service
71, 129	Kington Museum, Herefordshire
72	Classic Canes
76	EBLEX (English Beef and Lamb Executive)
81	International Sheepdog Society
91, 93	Josephine Clarke, Knill Farm, Herefordshire Classic Canes Ltd
97	National Portrait Gallery
98	Leicester Longwool Breed Society
99	Sussex Past
111	Thomas Shop
121, 138	National Library of Wales
126	Te Ara, the Encyclopedia of New Zealaand, The Ministry of Culture and Heritage, NZ.
127	Bendigo Art Gallery, Victoria 3550 Australia
129	Royal Mail
132	HCC (Hybu Cig Cymru/Meat Promotion Wales)
148	Shetland Museum & Archives
149	Globe Butchers, Shetland
155	State Library of Victoria, Australia
170	Mutton Olive recipe: permission English Heritage © Maggie Black and English Heritage 1985
202	Wiltshire Horn Breed Society

Particular thanks are due to the British Wool Marketing Board for supplying many of the breeds photos featured on pages 195-202. All other photographs in the book are the author's own.

References

FARMING & SOCIAL HISTORY

The Complete Farmer; or General Dictionary of Agriculture and Husbandry, Anon., 1807
The Farmer and His Market Report by the Land and Nation League on the Marketing of Home-Grown Food, 1927
The Distant Scene, Fred Archer, 1967
British Agriculture the Principles of Future Policy, Viscount Waldorf Astor & Benjamin Seebohm Rowntree, 1938
Akenfield: Portrait of an English Village, Ronald Blythe, 1969
The English Village, Victor Bonham-Carter, 1952
Wild Wales, George Borrow, 1862
Modern Farming, S. Graham Brade-Birks, 1950
A Perspective of Wages and Prices, Henry Phelps Brown & Shelia V. Hopkins, 1981
Cottage Economy, William Cobbett, 1822
The Complete Grazier and Farmers' and Cattlebreeders' Assistant (re-written), William Fream, 1908
Farming Techniques from Prehistoric to Modern Times, G.E. Fussell, 1965
Shepherds of Britain, Adelaide Gosset, 1911
A Farmer's Year: Being his Commonplace Book for 1898, H. Rider Haggard, 1899
The Village Labourer 1760-1832, J. L. Hammond & Barbara Hammond, 1911
A Description of the Shetland Islands, Samuel Hibbert, 1822
Practical Farming and Grazing, Clark Hillyard, 1840
Shepherd's Life, W. H. Hudson, 1910
England's Thousand Best Churches, Simon Jenkins, 1999
Country Voices, Charles Kightly, 1984
A General Treatise on Cattle, the Ox, the Sheep, and the Swine, John Lawrence, 1809
Agricultural Notebook, Primrose McConnell, 1910
Report on the Marketing of sheep, Mutton and Lamb in England and Wales, Ministry of Agriculture and Fisheries, 1931
A Cyclopedia of Agriculture, John Chalmers Morton, 1855
A History of English Farming, C.S.Orwin, 1949
Sheep Production, John B. Owen, 1976
The Folklore of Radnorshire, Roy Palmer, 2001
The Shepheardes Calender, Edmund Spenser, 1579
The Land: Now and Tomorrow, Sir Reginald George Stapleton, 1935
The Book of the Farm, Henry Stephens, 1844
Wold Shep, A. G. Street, 1946
A History of British Livestock Husbandry 1700-1900, Robert Trow-Smith, 1959
A Short History of Farming in Britain, Ralph Whitlock, 1966
The Rural Cyclopedia, Rev. John M. Wilson, 1849
Wiltshire Folklore, Kathleen Wiltshire, 1975

DROVING

The Drovers, K. J. Bonser, 1970
The Drovers' Roads of Wales, Shirley Toulson & Fay Godwin, 1977
The Drove Roads of Scotland, A.R.B. Haldane, 1952
Wales and the Drovers, Philip Gwyn Hughes, 1988
The Drovers, Shirley Toulson, 1980

References

SHEEP FARMING & BREEDS

British Sheep and Wool, British Wool Marketing Board, 2010
Sheep, Alan Butler, 2006
Two Hundred Years of British Farm Livestock, Stephen Hall & Juliet Clutton-Brock, 1989
Profitable Sheep Farming, M.McG Cooper & R.J. Thomas, 1965
An Agricultural Geography of Great Britain, J.T. Coppock, 1971
Sheep Husbandry, Allan Fraser, 1949
Live Stock of the Farm, Prof C. Bryner Jones, 1913
A Shepherd's Watch: Through the Seasons with One Man and His Dogs, David Kennard, 2005
Agriculture, James A.S. Watson & James A.More &, 1945
British Sheep (ninth Edition), National Sheep Association, 1998
Fream's Elements of Agriculture, D.H. Robinson, 1972
Sheep and Man, M.L. Ryder, 1983
The Farming Year, J.A. Scott Watson, 1938
The Grazing Animal, J.F.H. Thomas, 1947

NEW ZEALAND & SOUTH AFRICA

Station Life in New Zealand, Lady Mary Anne Barker, 1870
In Search of South Africa, H. V. Morton, 1948

COOKING & FOOD

The Book of Household Management, Mrs Isabella Beeton, 1861
Food and Cookery in Medieval Britain, Maggie Black, 1985
The Englishman's Food: A History of Five Centuries of English Diet, J.C. Drummond & Anne Wilbraham, 1957
The Country Housewife's Family Companion, William Ellis, 1750
Food in England, Dorothy Hartley, 1954
The Complete Cook, Nell Heaton, 1947
The Housekeeper's Oracle, William Kitchener, 1817
The First Principles of Good Cookery, Lady Llanover, 1867
Traditional Foods of Britain, Laura Mason and Catherine Brown, 1999
An Encyclopædia of Domestic Economy, Thomas Webber & Mrs Parkes, 1855
Food and Drink in Britain, C. Anne Wilson, 1973

Index

Abattoirs 133-134
Age at slaughter 158
Australia 12-14, 48, 51, 54-6, 93, 95, 102, 126-127, 154
Badger Face Welsh Mountain 96, 192
Bakewell Robert 47, 97-100
Beeton, Mrs 11, 32, 45, 137, 139, 143, 175
Bible 24, 36
Bibliography 210
Black Death 60
Black pudding 30
Blackface 16, 17, 37, 100-101, 105, 137, 161, 184
Bluefaced Leicester 84, 96, 102, 104, 106, 187
Bobotie 179
Bone 30
Border Leicester *(see Bluefaced)* 84
Branding iron 61
Braxy ham 145, 150
Breeding evolution 107
Breeds, table of UK sheep 195-203
Broth, mutton 165, 166
Butchery 160-163
Candles 30, 34, 35
Caper sauce 167
Carcass, ideal mutton 143
Casserole mutton 172, 173
Castrating 91
Cheviot 43, 96, 100, 101, 103, 105 161
Choosing mutton 135-144
Christ the Good Shepherd 78
Clearances, Highland 29, 42, 49, 82
Cliver 75
Cloth, mutton 27
Clun Forest sheep 59, 97, 102, 114, 197
Concentrate feed 87
Cooking mutton (historic) 151-154
Cooking mutton (modern) 157-182
Counting sheep 45, 73
Crofters 17, 43, 149
Crook, shepherds' 77
Croquettes, mutton 176
Culls 84
Cured mutton 145, 146, 185
Curried mutton 178
Cutlets 171
Cuts of mutton 159
Cynefin 59
Darina Allen 177
Derbyshire Gritstone 96, 187
Dipping 86
Dishley Leicester 97-99
Dixon Wright, Clarissa 180
Domesday Book 37, 139
Downland breeds 62, 102
Drafts 84
Drover's paths 122
Drovers 121-131
Drovers inns 123, 124
Dunedin, SS 51
Ellman, John 97
Empire 49
Enclosures 39, 40, 44
Ewe mutton 4
Family farms 117-119
Faroe Islands 148
Fat, mutton 32
Fertiliser, chemical 112
Finishing mutton 121, 132
Fleeces 31, 95
Flock Books 101
Foot and Mouth disease 60
Four-course rotation 62
Gaiters, Shepherds' 80
Gimmers 75, 205, 206
Glossary of sheep terms 205-209
Gordon, Robert Jacob, Colonel 52, 53
Halfbreds 103
Hanging a carcass 6, 7, 8, 136, 157
Heart, mutton, with herbs 174
Hefts 59, 61, 207
Herb pasture 8
Herdwick 37, 84, 96-7, 101, 105, 137, 146
Hill Radnor 96, 102
Hill sheep 102, 106
Hirsels 59, 60
Hogs 75
Hogget 2, 75, 183
Horn, sheep's 31
Housed sheep 38
Hut, Shepherd's 70
Insulation (wool) 117
Islam 24
Jacobs sheep 96, 103
Jones, David 123, 124
Kebabs, spiced mutton 182
Kerry mutton pies 177
Lambing 88-90
Lambing percentage 89
Lancers, Mutton 27
Lanolin 32, 92
Leicester Longwool 98
Leys 115
Liberties 59
Lleyns 102, 112, 185, 199
Loin of mutton (stuffed) 169
Longwool sheep 103
Lonk 96
Lowland breeds 62, 102, 106
Macarthur, John 55
Mackenzie, James 126
Manure 36, 39
Manx Loaghtan 103, 107, 191, 199
Map of UK breeds 203
Marking sheep 61

Index

Medicine horn 69
Merino 41, 50, 52-6, 116
Middle Ages 37
Milk, ewes 30
Modern breeds 112
Monasteries 38, 39, 42
Mouflon 36
Mountain sheep105
Mules 103
Mutton ham 145, 146, 166, 185, 187
National Mutton Organisations 204
Navajo Churro 56
New Leicester 97
New Zealand 48, 49-52, 92-5, 102, 126, 154-5, 196
Nursery rhymes 25
Olives, mutton (recipe) 170
Omega 3 & 6 12-14
Origin of word 'mutton' 20
Parchment 31
Parkland sheep 103
Pellets 87
Permanent pasture 115
Place-names 22
Portland 139
Prices, mutton 47
Primitive sheep 103
Pub names 23, 123, 124
Raddle 85
Railways 128-130
Rare Breeds Survival Trust 108
Rationing 19
Reestit mutton147-150, 166, 184
Refrigeration 49
Roast leg of mutton 166
Romans 37
Rushes (candles) 34, 35
Ryeland 40-41, 100, 102, 104, 201
Salt marsh mutton 142
Salt pie lane 140
Saltpetre 145
Scotch Mule 96, 103, 193
Scots pines 121, 122
Shakespeare and mutton 23, 65, 137
Shearing 93-95
Shearling rams 75, 208
Sheep dogs 81
Sheep populations 45
Shepherd's pie 175
Shepherds 65-72, 78, 79, 80
Shetland Vivda mutton 147
Shoulder of mutton 168
Shropshire breed 100
Silage 110-111
Slang 26
Slow-cookers 19
Smithfield market 125
Smock, shepherds' 78, 79, 80
Soap 30, 33
Soay 36, 82, 97, 103, 107, 189, 208
South Africa 48, 50, 52-54, 93, 102
Southdown 57, 62, 96, 99, 100, 102, 107, 135, 139-141
Spiced leg of mutton 167
Straw-cooked mutton 151
Sumac and butterbean mutton 180
Super-meat 12
Suppliers Directory 183-194
Swaledale 37, 96, 101, 105
Tagine of mutton 181
Tailing 91
Tallow 15, 32-35, 50
Teeth 76
Tegs 75
Texel 107, 112, 113
Theaves 75
Ticks 62
Tinned mutton 57
Traceability 109
Travelling stock routes 128
Triplets 89
Tup 75, 85
Upland landscape 116
Upland sheep farms 60
Urial sheep 36
USA 48, 56-57, 128
Vikings 37
Vivda mutton 147, 148
Wartime 18
Washing sheep 91
Weaning 91
Wedder lamb 75
Welsh mutton 137-139
Wensleydale 103, 113, 208
Wether 3, 16, 141
Wild plants 20
Wool 30, 46, 117
Wool churches 40
Wool price 16
Woolsack 37
Yearling 2, 4, 75, 208

Above: Sheep at Gladestry, Welsh Borders